TAKHOMA

TAKHOMA

Ethnography of Mount Rainier National Park

ALLAN H. SMITH

Washington State University Press
Pullman, Washington

Washington State University Press
PO Box 645910
Pullman, Washington 99164-5910
Phone: 800-354-7360
Fax: 509-335-8568
E-mail: wsupress@wsu.edu
Web site: wsupress.wsu.edu

First printing 2006

Library of Congress Cataloging-in-Publication Data

Smith, Allan H. (Allan Hathorn), 1913-
Takhoma : ethnography of Mount Rainier National Park / Allan H. Smith.
p. cm.
Includes bibliographical references.
ISBN 0-87422-284-2 (alk. paper)
1. Indians of North America--Washington (State)--Mount Rainier National Park--Antiquities. 2. Archaeological surveying--Washington (State)--Mount Rainier National Park. 3. Mount Rainier National Park (Wash.)--Antiquities. I. Title.
E78.W3S65 2005
979.7'78201--dc22 2005032230

WSU Press gratefully acknowledges the support received from Washington's National Park Fund, the Northwest Interpretive Association, and Mount Rainier National Park.

Front cover: Painting of Indian Henrys Hunting Ground.

Contents

Acknowledgments

Greg C. Burtchard
Mount Rainier National Park

I first encountered Allan H. Smith's remarkable ethnographic study in 1995 when I was working for a nonprofit consulting firm. At that time, I was awarded a contract to complete what I believed to be Mount Rainier National Park's first archaeological overview. While conducting background research in the park archives, however, I found several typed, mimeographed copies of Dr. Smith's work under the title "Ethnographic Guide to the Archaeology of Mt. Rainier National Park." His report was part of a combined ethnographic and archaeological research project awarded to Washington State University's Department of Anthropology over 30 years prior to my study.

The WSU project called for Dr. Smith to review regional ethnographies, study park records, and interview Indian tribal elders who were familiar with the Mount Rainier vicinity. To fit the unique constraints of this ethnographic-archaeological effort, he had been obliged to complete these tasks in an extremely short period of time in the spring and early summer of 1963, prior to the archaeological survey work scheduled to begin later that summer. The intent was to employ these sources for the following goals:

(A) Develop a better understanding of the ways in which Native American people used the Mount Rainier area within the living memory of informants.

(B) Extend those use patterns as far into the more distant past as possible with a study of archival and ethnographic records.

(C) Use combined sources to predict the environmental circumstances conditioning places at which most of those activities would have taken place.

Smith hoped that this information would be useful in guiding the subsequent archaeological survey, led by Dr. Richard H. Daugherty, to the most probable places where prehistoric and early historic-period activities occurred. In developing and conducting this study, Smith and Daugherty proved to be well ahead of their time—both in the use of a combined ethnographic and archaeological approach, and in their conviction that Indian people routinely used rugged and seemingly remote interior landscapes, such as those of the Mount Rainier area.

It was clear from the outset, however, that Dr. Smith's report was much more than simply an archaeological guidebook. Indeed, judging from the number of sites actually found during the subsequent survey (only two in 1963), the ethnography was of little benefit at that time in pinpointing the location of archaeological resources. Environmental variables affecting the type, location, and visibility of archaeological remains in the mountains were simply more complex than anticipated in the early 1960s.

Rather, the value of Smith's work lay in the rich picture it painted of long-standing Native American use of the Mount Rainier area. Despite the project's limited time-frame, Smith produced a manuscript replete with valuable information on the role the locality played in the lives of Indian people living in its vicinity during the late 19th and early 20th centuries. Topics included in his study address such issues as tribal identities and boundaries, intertribal relations, resources used, the mountain's spiritual significance, travel and trade routes, and much more.

Valuable though it was, this ethnography and the combined informant and archival information it contained languished in virtual obscurity in a few mimeographed and photocopied versions for more than 30 years. After discovering the report, I began bringing it to the attention of other professionals in hopes of stimulating its publication for wider distribution. By this time, Allan was quite elderly and in failing health. It was clear that our time was limited if the book was to be released within his lifetime.

I soon found that the park service's Pacific West Regional Anthropologist, Dr. Fredrick F. York, had similar ideas, and already had begun faithfully transcribing the original text, page by page, into a digital format. Unfortunately, Allan passed away before publication could become a reality, but not before his work had become well known and respected among those most closely involved with Mount Rainier's pre-contact human past. My acceptance of the position as park archaeologist and cultural anthropologist in 2000 finally provided a foundation to pursue publication more effectively. This book—*Takhoma*, the Sahaptin term for what is now more widely known as Mount Rainier—is the culmination of this effort.

A number of individuals and organizations deserve credit for bringing *Takhoma* to light. Among the many who offered insights and contributions in the preparation of this volume, special attention should be given to the work of Fred York, who completed the original transcriptions and made them available for this publication; to Dr. Wayne Suttles, who reviewed Allan's linguistic transcriptions; to Darin Swinney, who converted barely legible mimeographed maps into publishable images; to Dr. Barbara Lane, who reviewed Allan's work and evaluates its place within the greater body of Pacific Northwest ethnographic literature in the Foreword; and to Dr. Richard Daugherty, who partnered in the original WSU project, and who took the time to comment on Allan's personal character and on the archaeological survey that followed his ethnographic work so many years ago.

Glen Lindeman, WSU Press editor-in-chief and a former Allan Smith student, advanced the cause of publication and edited this book at the Press. I was pleased to assist Glen in the editing effort. Our added informational updates in *Takhoma* are included in brackets. Also, the preferred modern-day tribal designation "Yakama" has been substituted for "Yakima," a spelling formerly in use at the time of Allan's research.

The National Park Service and Mount Rainier National Park provided primary organizational support for the publication of *Takhoma*. Assistance also came from Washington's National Park Fund, a nonprofit association dedicated to restoring and preserving Mount Rainier, North Cascades, and Olympic national parks; and by the Northwest Interpretive Association, a foundation that promotes appreciation of the natural and cultural history of the Pacific Northwest through the publication of interpretative materials and books. I know that Allan also would have appreciated the support of Washington State University, as expressed by WSU Press and its editorial staff, in the final production and distribution of his work.

The valuable assistance of the above named individuals and institutions notwithstanding, greatest recognition should be given to Allan Smith and to his Indian informants, whose appreciation for Mount Rainier and its long-term human past shines through in the pages of this book; and, of course, to Takhoma itself—a mountain that, for thousands of years, has sustained, challenged, and inspired human beings living in its shadow.

Foreword

Dr. Barbara Lane
Victoria, British Columbia

Allan Smith's report originally was submitted to the National Park Service in 1964 as a typed manuscript entitled "Ethnographic Guide to the Archaeology of Mt. Rainier National Park." Unpublished until now, Allan's work has been known only to a relatively small number of anthropologists—mainly archaeologists who have copied and distributed it among themselves over the years.

This pioneering report was designed to test certain general premises about Indian use of mountainous territory and, in particular, to serve as an informant-based guide to archaeological research at Mount Rainier National Park. Its initial use was to assist a fellow member of Washington State University's Anthropology Department, Richard H. Daugherty, in conducting the Mount Rainier area's first formal archaeological survey. Since that time, it has continued to stimulate archaeologists to explore high altitude locales in Mount Rainier National Park and elsewhere in the Cascade and Olympic ranges.

It is interesting to note that renewed archaeological studies in Mount Rainier National Park since the mid 1990s have demonstrated a substantial precontact Native American presence in that area, much of which took place in settings presaged by the Smith ethnography. The archaeological record, limited to just two prehistoric sites in 1963, burgeoned to more than 90 in 2005, and promises to grow larger as studies continue. Among the most exciting of the recent results is the examination of prehistoric rockshelter sites, one of which was first recorded during the original Washington State University project. Archaeological material recovered from this site documents use of an array of edible plants and animals, including wild hazelnut, elderberry, mountain goat, marmot, and mountain beaver.

Interesting as these archaeological findings are, it is Smith's ethnographic work that attracts most of my attention here. As a cultural anthropologist and contemporary of Allan Smith, I was delighted to have the opportunity to write the Foreword to this long-overdue publication. I was familiar with some of his later work, such as the *Ethnography of the North Cascades* (1987), and was impressed by the thoroughness and level of scholarship evident in that work. I also was particularly interested in his Mount Rainier ethnography because he interviewed several Indian informants known to me—Muckleshoot tribal members Louis Starr and Matilda Barr, and Nisqually member Bill Franks Sr.—all persons that I found to be highly knowledgeable and reliable sources.

The present publication makes Allan Smith's work accessible to a wider range of readers—cultural anthropologists, ethnohistorians, archaeologists, and anyone with a general interest in Mount Rainier National Park. Anthropologists and ethnohistorians in particular will be challenged to re-examine and discover untapped possibilities in the source materials that have served them in the past. In particular, researchers concerned with tribal collecting and hunting locales within the park (and in other mountainous areas) will need to consult this report.

It is important to recognize that, prior to 1963, no formal archaeological work had been undertaken in Mount Rainier National Park, and little to none at higher elevations elsewhere in the Cascade Range or in the Olympic Mountains. Anthropologists assumed that mountain landscapes had been little used, and as a result, contained scant evidence of prehistoric human presence, especially in upper elevation sub-alpine and alpine zones. It was recognized that Indians transited the mountain passes en-route to localities east and west of the Cascades, but most ethnologists and archaeologists believed that prehistoric people focused their lives on lower elevation coastal and river valley settings. Mountains were considered to be places admired at a distance, or obstacles encountered or avoided on the way to more important lowland areas elsewhere. Such beliefs persisted well into the 20th century, despite historical accounts and limited ethnographic data indicating that Mount Rainier was visited in late summer to early fall by parties of Indians on berry collecting and hunting expeditions.

In my opinion, the major contribution of the present work lies in Smith's description and analysis of physical and natural aspects of the park relevant to aboriginal access to, and use of, high-elevation mountain resources. He provides thorough lists of mountain passes and trails, stream systems and lakes, parks and meadows, and other physical and environmental features, while carefully noting their respective elevations, plant and animal assemblages, and potential importance to indigenous people. Smith assessed the botanical and zoological data to discover the times and places at which berries, mammals, and birds would have been available, and discusses their value as collectable resources.

For this data, Smith relied largely on the *Mount Rainier Nature Notes* (*MRNN*) compiled by the park staff during the 1920s and 1930s. These reports provided firsthand observations by park naturalists, which allowed Smith to note variations in the timing of berry harvests from year to year and at different elevations, and changes in mammal fur quality from summer to winter, as well as in bird plumage according to the season. Changes of coat or plumage may be significant, of course, if these animals were taken for fur or feathers in the past.

Working with *MRNN* reports, Indian informants, and other sources, Smith concluded that the primary purpose of Indian trips to Mount Rainier, at least in early historic times, was to harvest huckleberries (wild mountain blueberries). Smith states that hunting was a secondary and less important activity carried out by men in the general vicinity of women and children, who took primary responsibility for collecting and drying the berries. Smith also concludes that these trips were of short duration, lasting a matter of one or two weeks. While his conclusion that hunting was secondary to berry gathering may be correct, at least for the historic period known to his sources, I believe that his estimate of the time spent, and perhaps the complexity of activities conducted, is almost certainly under calculated.

I suggest that Smith's estimates, while being most informative, tend to understate a more elaborate past reality. This is due, I think, to the limited time-frame available for the original study, which was obliged to be completed prior to Richard Daugherty's subsequent archaeological survey in the summer of 1963. I believe that in the rush to complete his work, Smith was compelled to spend less time with his Indian informants than would otherwise be desirable, and overlooked some tangentially related, but useful, ethnographic sources.

For example, historical and ethnographic records document that mountain beaver was used for food and fur by Indian people in the Mount Rainier vicinity (Lewis and Clark, [1806] 1959; Gibbs, [1855] 1877; Cooper, 1860; Suckley, 1860; Suckley and Gibbs, 1860; Taylor, 1918; Elmendorf, 1960). The fur was considered particularly desirable for robes, the manufacture of which required a substantial number of animals. Over twenty pelts were sewn together to form a single robe, necessitating the acquisition of large numbers of mountain beaver, and, arguably, an extended stay in the mountains. While not mentioned by Smith, it is quite likely that these animals were taken at Mount Rainier, a notion made all the more certain by their documented presence in the archaeological context.

It is important to note, too, that mammals such as mountain beaver shared habitats with a variety of other economically useful plant and animal species, the number and importance of which tend to be understated in the present report. Indeed, ecological and archaeological studies now suggest that upper forest, sub-alpine, and alpine landscapes at Mount Rainier and in other Northwest mountain regions provided a wide variety of resources useful to hunting and gathering people; resources most effectively collected in aggregate.

Smith is almost certainly correct in placing primary use in the late summer to autumn. This was, and remains, the time when fur is at its pre-winter best, body-fat is greatest, and plants are generally most productive in the mountains. In short, references to gathered plants and hunted animals in this volume should be taken in a wider context in which multiple resources were sought, arguably over a longer seasonal span, than implied by informant interviews and sources consulted by Smith in 1963. The references cited above provide tantalizing clues to a richer pre-contact past.

As I have already noted, researchers and general readers alike with an interest in Indian collecting and hunting in the Pacific Northwest's mountains will have a particular interest in this book. Undoubtedly, part of this attention will focus on the issue of Indian use areas, or tribal boundaries, around Mount Rainier. Smith recognized this concern and attempted to identify specific tribal groups in regard to their utilization of particular lands in what is now Mount Rainer National Park.

I applaud his effort, but feel that I should draw attention to Smith's own cautions in regard to designating tribal entities and tribal territories. First, he made it clear that the term "tribe" as used in his report was intended simply to identify named groups specified in the literature that was reviewed, and was based upon how they were referred to by themselves, by other Indians, and by contemporary non-Indians. Smith warned that his use of the term was not intended to connote a technical meaning in a professional anthropological sense (that is, a "tribe" as a particular level of political organization). He also cautioned that his tribal boundary designations within the park were intended only to suggest areas that were more intensively used by one group than another. The landforms set off by these "tribal boundaries" are more properly viewed as traditional use areas that shifted through time as dictated by needs and pragmatic concerns of different groups using the Mount Rainier area in the past. The boundaries are not intended to convey a sense of inflexible legal limits as conceived in the modern sense.

Overall, Smith's willingness to venture into unknown territory, and to suggest strategies to find answers to questions that anthropologists in general had not heretofore addressed, mark this report as a milestone in Northwest anthropology. Its publication is long overdue and I recommend it highly. Please be aware, however, that as an ethnographic account, the short study period resulted in certain shortcomings in the report. Foremost among these is the fact that the time devoted to the ethnographic field inquiry clearly was exceedingly brief, and heavily weighted toward Yakama informants in contrast to other tribes on the southern, western, and northern margins of Mount Rainier. Furthermore, the literature search did not include several important sources. Absent, for example, are late 1700s and early 1800s logs and journals, mid-1800s scientific reports, and George Gibbs' 1855 (published 1877) ethnological account of the Indians of Washington Territory.

Smith's time-caused omissions pertaining to the full range of published documents and the unpublished anthropological field data collected prior to the 1960s impacts the depth of his report in regard to certain tribal groups and land-use practices. Understated, or missing altogether, for example, are important details about Muckleshoot collecting and hunting activities on the flanks of Mount Rainier and elsewhere within the park area. My attention was drawn to the missing Muckleshoot material in particular because of my familiarity with it. Please recognize, too, that unpublished field data also exists for other tribes affiliated with the national park area. However, the published sources not consulted by Smith, as well as the unpublished records to which he did not refer, actually provide further support for Smith's theories and propositions regarding Indian use of Mount Rainier's resources.

In closing, we should recognize that, in the four decades that have passed since Allan Smith conducted his research, a great deal more has been learned about Indian occupation and utilization of mountainous regions. At a time when very little was known of long-term Indian use of mountain landscapes, Smith was a pioneer in suggesting that the Indian use of these areas made sense and had been an integral part of subsistence activities for a very long time. I have mentioned that recently identified archaeological evidence supports many of Allan Smith's predictions. Continuing search into the documentary records, and the on-going exploration of rockshelters and other sites in mountainous environments, undoubtedly will produce additional information about the human history of these landscapes.

But for now, I suggest that readers settle back, read, and enjoy Smith's work for its many insights; and in the process, come to appreciate more fully the long-standing relationship between Indian people and such high elevation places as Mount Rainier National Park.

References Cited

Cooper, J.G.
1860 Report upon the Mammals Collected on the Survey, Chapter I: Report by J.G. Cooper, M.D. In *Reports of Explorations and Surveys, to Ascertain the Most Practicable and Economical Route for a Railroad from the Mississippi River to the Pacific Ocean*, Vol. XII, Book II. Thomas H. Ford: Washington, D.C.

Elmendorf, W.W. (with A.L. Kroeber)
1960 [1992] The Structure of Twana Culture: With Comparative Notes on the Structure of Yurok Culture, *Research Studies*. Monographic Supplement No. 2. Vol. XXVIII, No. 3, Washington State University, Pullman. Reprinted with same title by WSU Press, 1992.

Gibbs, George
[1855] 1877 Tribes of Western Washington and Northwestern Oregon, Part II. Department of the Interior, U.S. Geographical and Geological Survey of the Rocky Mountain Region. In *Contributions to North American Ethnology*, Vol. I.

Lewis, Meriwether, and William Clark
[1806] 1959 *Original Journals of the Lewis and Clark Expedition, 1804–1806*, Vol. 4. Reuben Gold Thwaites (editor). Antiquarian Press: New York..

Smith, Allan H.
1987 *Ethnography of the North Cascades.* Report to the North Cascades National Park Service Complex and Cultural Resource Division, Pacific Northwest Region, Seattle. Center for Northwest Anthropology, Washington State University Project Report Number 7, Pullman, Washington.

Suckley, George
1860 Report upon the Mammals Collected on the Survey, Chapter II: Report by Dr. Geo. Suckley, U.S.A. In *Reports of Explorations and Surveys, to Ascertain the Most Practicable and Economical Route for a Railroad from the Mississippi River to the Pacific Ocean,* Vol. XII, Book II. Thomas H. Ford: Washington, D.C.

________, and George Gibbs
1860 Report upon the Mammals Collected on the Survey, Chapter III: Report of Dr. Geo. Suckley, U.S.A., and Geo. Gibbs, Esq. In *Reports of Explorations and Surveys, to Ascertain the Most Practicable and Economical Route for a Railroad from the Mississippi River to the Pacific Ocean,* Vol. XII, Book II. Thomas H. Ford: Washington, D.C.

Taylor, Walter P.
1918 Revision of the Rodent Genus *Aplodontia*, *University of California Publications in Zoology* 17 (16): 435–504.

Mount Rainier Archaeological Survey, 1963

Dr. Richard H. Daugherty
Lacey, Washington

Allan H. Smith (1913–1999), a graduate of Yale, was the quintessential scholar. He was accomplished in all aspects of anthropology and also was meticulous and exceptionally capable as a Washington State University administrator, as Director of Anthropology for the National Science Foundation, and during the Korean War as an anthropologist in the Ryuku Islands Trust Territories, where he served as a civilian, but with a rank equivalent to a brigadier general.

Our acquaintance began in 1950 when he hired me to join in developing WSU's anthropology program. He concentrated on ethnography, I on archaeology. At the time, the two of us constituted the entire faculty for the department. He could type so fast it was quicker to turn out finished copy himself than to dictate, a matter of some dismay to his secretaries. As a lecturer, he was so enthusiastic that he practically bounced as he talked, and students flocked to his courses. Yet he was self-deprecating. On one occasion, a frazzled graduate student came into the office saying he was having trouble translating something from German. Although Allan said he was not sure he remembered the language well, he took the paper and instantly read it aloud in English. His brilliance was that kind, and he shared it.

Actually, Allan had many languages at his command. Such linguistic skill is of great advantage for an ethnographer because it takes a keen ear to accurately hear and phonetically write out the distinctive sounds of words that informants use to describe objects, practices, and beliefs within their culture. Allan was excellent at this. His field notes were voluminous; his handwriting a fine, neat script. His files were superbly organized, his library admirably extensive—and also superbly organized; his wife Trudy was a librarian at the university. In short, Allan Smith was remarkable in many ways.

In the early 1960s, Mount Rainier park superintendent John Rutter arranged with WSU for a two-pronged investigation—an ethnographic field and historical study regarding aboriginal use of the park area by neighboring Native American groups, and an archaeological survey that entailed checking the entire mountain for sites. The timeframe was so short, however, that Allan was given only a few spring and summer weeks for doing the preliminary work. Allan did the ethnography and prepared the excellent report presented in this volume. For the archaeological survey, there were six of us—myself as principal investigator plus graduate students Barbara Grater, Winston Moore, Roger Nance, Charles Nelson, and David Rice.

Two particular considerations regarding archaeology in Washington at the time of the survey are relevant in understanding the background of our Mount Rainier investigation. One is that the state had very few professionally trained archaeologists in the early 1960s. Furthermore, almost all of us were occupied surveying and excavating along the Snake and Columbia rivers where dams were being built, and where immense areas, long used by humans, were due for imminent inundation. This concentration on river-basin studies meant that other areas within the state were neglected, including the coasts and the uplands. The cause of this neglect was not disinterest, but rather the simple lack of field archaeologists and sufficient time to study the region more broadly.

The second consideration, a matter of continuing relevance, is that the history of a people many generations back in the prehistoric past cannot be completely or precisely inferred from the memories and traditions of living people. The ethnographic record can inform, and to some extent guide, archaeological studies, but the two approaches differ. Archaeology requires physical evidence in the form of artifacts and features left on and under the surface of the ground. Ethnographically, we knew that Indian people regularly met trading partners in the high country, and that they came to mountain meadows to pick berries, gather medicinal plants, and hunt, but we did not know all the locations utilized, or how far back their presence dated.

Now much more of that information is available. Legislation, largely dating from the 1970s and 1980s, requires government agencies to survey and document cultural resources on federal and state lands. This has permitted these agencies to appoint staff archaeologists and contract with other professionals to investigate cultural resource issues. As a result, hundreds of high-country archaeological sites are known today, due largely to the fact that federal agencies are the stewards of most of the foothills and mountains within the state, and have made the investments necessary to support these studies. We now know that Native American uses of the Pacific Northwest's mountains were multi-faceted and extended far into the prehistoric past. These archaeological sites range from quarries, where stone for implements was acquired, to berry camps, hunting sites, base camps, and more. In some cases, antiquity extends to at least 8,000 years ago and to elevations as high as 7,500 feet (and probably higher).

But none of this was known in 1963. Our survey, paired with Allan Smith's ethnographic study, was a bare beginning. For the archaeological survey, we divided into three teams of two each, hiking up river corridors leading to the sub-alpine areas and following known and likely aboriginal travel routes and today's Wonderland Trail. Once at treeline, we checked ridgelines and meadows. Eager to demonstrate that Indian people had long used these places as Allan's informants had indicated, we searched for artifacts such as projectile points and scattered flakes left from their manufacture, and for hearths or other signs of habitation.

While we underestimated the difficulties in finding sites in heavily vegetated mountain terrain, and did not fully understand the site-obscuring effects of Mount Rainier's volcanic past, our project was not without success. Our team was able to document the park's first known prehistoric archaeological site—a shallow cave-like rock overhang. The rockshelter evidently had been used at some unknown time in the past; for tucked into a niche at the back we found a small, crude, conical stone pipe someone had cached long ago. In the following summer, team members Dave Rice and Charles Nelson tested the site, finding more definitive evidence of human presence in the form of chipped tool-stone remains and burned bone. Subsequent testing in 2001 by park archaeologist Greg Burtchard documented intense and repeated use for over 1,000 years, and provided charred remains of wild hazelnut, marmot, mountain goat, mountain beaver, and deer.

A single leaf-shaped projectile point was the only other archaeological evidence found during the brief time available for the 1963 survey. It lay in an exposed road-cut on the south-facing flank of Mount Rainier. Its form suggests a style widely used in Washington as much as 6,000 years ago. It is gratifying to know that our beginning work has since grown to more than 90 documented prehistoric archaeological sites in Mount Rainier National Park, firmly establishing what Allan and I always believed—that, for millennia, Indian people have used this and other Pacific Northwest uplands, and that they left a physical record of that use, if we could but have the diligence and patience to find it.

Ethnographic studies such as Allan Smith's exemplify the value of recording knowledge and insights at the earliest possible date. Much of the information contained in *Takhoma* would now be lost to the passing of the years if it were not for scholarship and care such as Allan's. Increasingly, we recognize the smallness of the planet we dwell upon and the crucial interweaving of divergent cultures. We need to understand each other. I believe that ethnography and archaeology help contribute significantly to that understanding.

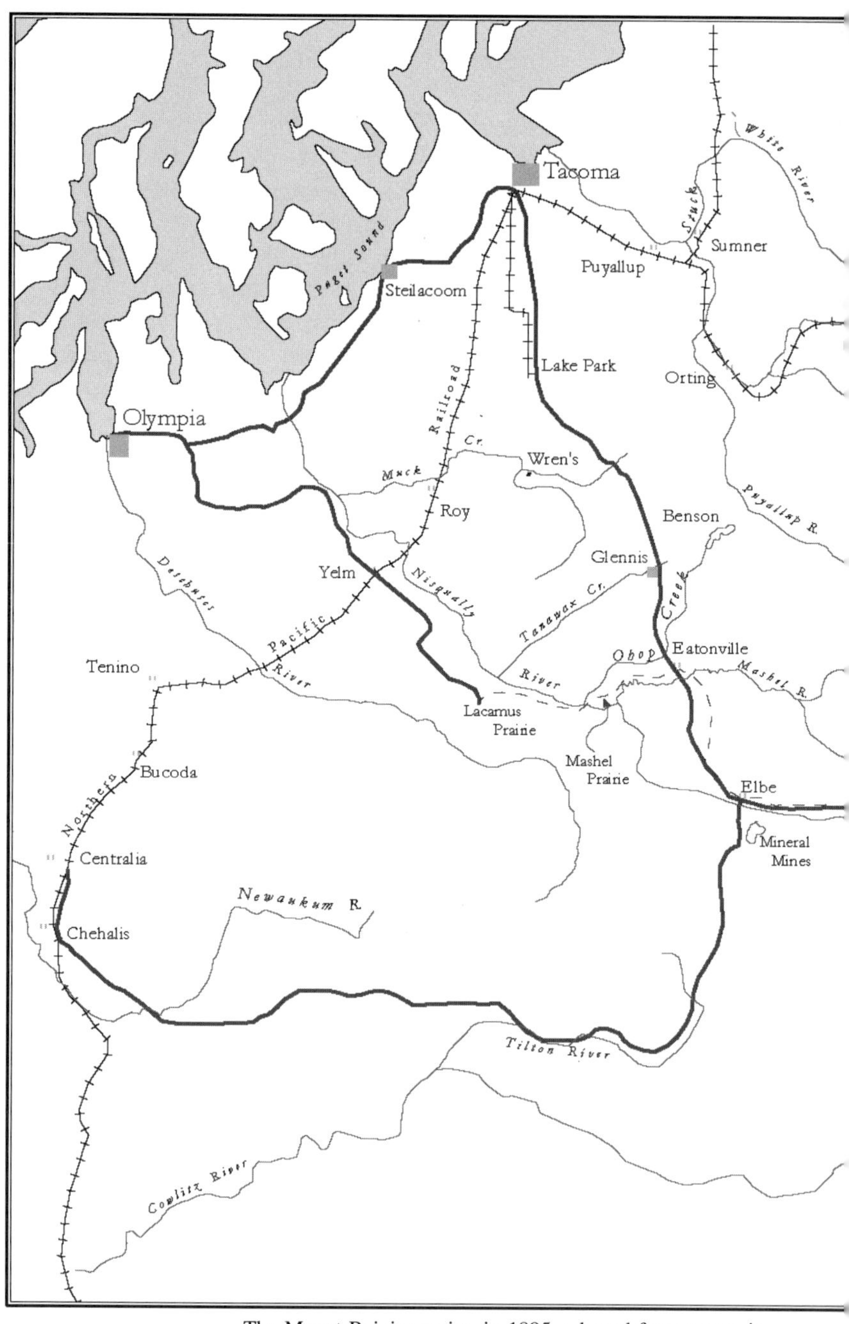

The Mount Rainier region in 1895, adapted from a map in Aubrey L. Haines, *Mountain Fever: Historic Conquests of*

Rainier (Oregon Historical Society, 1962). The modern-day boundary of the national park is indicated here.

1
Introduction

In 1963, when the decision was made by Washington State University to investigate the prehistory of Mount Rainier National Park under contract with the National Park Service, the archaeological past of the area was largely unknown. It was clear, however, that certain conditions existed that would create special problems for the research project. First, because of the rugged terrain and the heavy forest cover in much of the park, major difficulties were anticipated in locating archaeological sites. Secondly, so far as was known among archaeologists up to that time, the area did not fall within the traditional settlement territory of any Indian groups.

Taken together with the forbidding physiographic characteristics and the apparently restricted ecological potential, this suggested the probability that the area's archaeological resources would be limited or difficult to find. For these reasons, it seemed sensible to explore a frankly novel approach to investigating the national park's prehistory by carrying out the research in two well-defined phases. The first phase was envisioned as an extensive search for all informant and literature data that might serve to sharpen and make more effective the archaeological field study. The second phase consisted of the field investigation itself and a subsequent analysis of the archaeological findings in the customary fashion.

This report presents the data acquired and analyzed as the first phase of this two-fold approach.[1] However, it also aims to be more than a review of the relevant historical and ethnographic sources that normally is undertaken prior to archaeological field research. It is a prestudy attempting to detail the full range of non-archaeological elements bearing upon the prehistory of the national park. A more explicit statement of this premise and objective is presented shortly under the subheading "Research Design."

Physical Environment[2]

Basic to gaining a knowledge of traditional cultural activity in the Mount Rainier area—as reflected in its ethnography and ethnohistory no less than in its archaeology—is an understanding of the complex ecosystem of that locality and its relationship to surrounding areas. Surveyed in this section are those aspects of the physical environment that are relevant to an analysis of the ethnographic and ethnohistorical data in archaeological terms, and hence significant to the area's prehistory.

Physiography

The Cascade Range is by far the most prominent physiographic feature in the west-central part of Washington. The Cascades bisect the state north to south, interposing a chain of rugged peaks between the forested lowlands and tidewater bays to the west and the semi-arid Columbia Basin to the east. Mount Rainier National Park lies on the western flank of this range, somewhat removed from the main crest line. It is a more or less square complex of forests, streams, ridges, meadows, crags, and glacial masses encompassing approximately 377 square miles.

The park's eastern boundary basically coincides with the Cascade Divide; its other borders, in general, cut arbitrarily across lesser mountain ranges and stream valleys. The volcanic cone of Mount Rainier rises slightly to the west of the center of the national park, towering to a height of 14,410 feet and comprising about one-fourth of the total park area. Surrounding this great cone lies a mass of smaller peaks and minor mountain ranges, averaging from 5,000 to 7,000 feet in height. The lowest point, on the Ohanapecosh River in the southeast corner of the park, is 1,600 feet in elevation.

Certain physiographic details of this rugged mountainous area—in particular its major stream systems and the eastern mountain passes—must be understood if the traditional Indian usage of the region is to be comprehended. Despite the heavy forest growth, it was along the river valleys and the ridges between them that access to the present national park area was gained from the north, south, and west. From the east, however, native groups entered by mountain passes. Furthermore, both the major stream valleys and the passes were the routes by which travel east and west *through* the region was accomplished by all traditional groups.

The river systems form a basically simple pattern (see frontispiece map). The northeast quadrant of Mount Rainier is drained by the White River and its tributaries, flowing northward between the base of the cone and the Cascade Divide. The northwest part of the national park contributes its waters to the Carbon River, a tributary of the Puyallup. The Puyallup itself drains the west face of the mountain. The southwest corner of the park is dissected by the Nisqually and its confluent watercourses. Finally, from the south and southeast flanks of the mountain flows a network of headwater streams, especially the Ohanapecosh River and its secondary creeks, which form the Cowlitz River. Thus, Mount Rainier sends its waters in a radiating pattern of streams, all of which empty into Puget Sound, except the Cowlitz which reaches the Columbia River not far from the Pacific Ocean.

The eastern mountain passes of most significance in this study are those that link Mount Rainier's drainage network to the Yakima watershed in the eastern Cascades. The Yakima River is a major tributary to the Columbia River in the Columbia Basin. These passes along the crest of the Cascade Range include the following, from north to south:

Pass[3]	*Approximate altitude (in feet)*	*Location*
Snoqualmie	3,004	Between Coal Cr. (Yakima R. system) and South Fork Snoqualmie R.
Yakima	3,525	Between Roaring Cr. (Yakima R. system) and Cedar R.
Meadow	3,650	Between Meadow Cr. (Yakima R. system) and Sunday Cr. (Green R. system)
Dandy	3,750	Between Meadow Cr. (Yakima R. system) and Sunday Cr. (Green R. system)
Stampede	3,800	Stampede Cr. (Yakima R. system) and Sunday Cr. (Green R. system)
Sheets	3,450	Cabin Cr. (Yakima R. system) and Green R.
Tacoma	3,450	Cabin Cr. (Yakima R. system) and Green R.
Green	4,889	Little Naches R. and Green R.
Naches	4,988	Middle Fork Naches R. and Greenwater R. (White R. system)
Chinook	5,440	Rainier Fork of American R. and Chinook Cr. (Cowlitz R. system)
Carlton	4,100	Bumping R. and Carlton Cr. (Cowlitz R. system)
Cowlitz[4]	5,191	Indian Cr. (Tieton R. system) and Summit Cr. (Cowlitz R. system)
White	4,500	Clear Cr. (Tieton R. system) and Milridge Cr. (Cowlitz R. system)
Tieton	5,050	North Fork Tieton R. and Clear Fork Cowlitz R.

Of all these, only Chinook Pass actually lies on the Mount Rainier National Park boundary—the remainder are located at various distances to the northeast or southeast of the park (see Fig. 1.1). However, east-west routes through Carlton and Cowlitz passes, situated close to the park's southeast corner, and Naches Pass to the northeast, were at least close to the border. If this list indeed identifies all of the feasible mountain saddles for cross-Cascades travel between Snoqualmie Pass (to the north) and Tieton Pass (at the south), it is a fair measure of the area's ruggedness to note that the national park's relatively long eastern border on the Cascade Divide has only a single gap (Chinook Pass).

Another key route of importance not yet mentioned is Cayuse Pass (4,700 feet), situated immediately east of Mount Rainier between the sources of the White and Cowlitz rivers. It is uniquely oriented on a north-south axis, and not east-west like the other gaps. Cayuse Pass is located entirely within the national park boundaries, unlike the other passes. It would have been the primary route taken in north-south travel between Mount Rainier and the Cascade Crest.

Life Zones

Precipitation in the Mount Rainier region is abundant, totaling more than 100 inches per year in some areas, much of it falling as snow. Because of the area's great altitudinal range with significant temperature and moisture differences, several climatic-biotic zones—i.e., natural areas possessing distinctive plant and animal assemblages, and usually with climatic and physiographic boundaries—are represented. However, the borders between these zones in Mount Rainier National Park are not always sharply evident; they can vary somewhat in their altitudinal position depending on the directional weather exposure, the amount of precipitation, slope orientation, and other variables.

Nevertheless, the ecological features of the park can best be summarized in terms of these zones, and four are recognized. Their floral characteristics, which comprise the basis upon which the zone distinctions are drawn, are most clearly delineated by Jones (1938: 7–11).[5] In the following compilation, some data from other sources, especially faunal information, are added to Jones's formulation.

(a) Humid-Transitional Zone. This zone encompasses the lowest levels of the national park, from 1,600 feet up to approximately 3,000 feet.[6] Included here are the wide river valleys, with extensive forests typically consisting of Douglas fir, western hemlock, and western red cedar, with scattered stands of maple, alder, western yew, and black cottonwoods. The evergreen trees form a dense growth, characteristically somber and moist, with branches interlaced overhead and thick, tangled undergrowth thriving in the moister places. Fallen trees and decaying logs are extensive, often covered by mosses, ferns, and thick humus. In these forests, black-tailed deer are common, while black bear, mountain beaver (sewellel), Pacific beaver, varying hare (having white fur in winter), and whistling marmot are also relatively numerous. This zone is the uppermost range for California quail and Oregon ruffed grouse. Of the four life zones, the Humid-Transitional accounts for the smallest part of the total national park area. Indeed, some insist it only really exists in the Stevens Canyon-Cowlitz River locality near the southeast boundary (Taylor and Shaw in Kitchin, 1939: 86).

(b) Canadian Zone. Extending from approximately 3,000 feet to about 4,500 feet (or the edge of the alpine meadows),[7] the Canadian Zone also consists of dense timber, though the trees are smaller. Western white pine is common, while noble fir, spruce, Alaska yellow cedar, and western hemlock likewise occur. In comparison with the Humid-Transitional Zone, the undergrowth is thinner. The mammalian population appears not to differ significantly from that of the Humid-Transitional Zone. However, sooty grouse takes the place of Oregon ruffed grouse.

(c) Hudsonian Zone. In the higher valleys and on loftier ridge slopes, from about 4,500 to 6,000 feet or slightly higher,[8] the forests become progressively sparse and the flora is sub-alpine in character. Found here are the hardy sub-alpine (or alpine) fir, mountain hemlock, Alaska cedar, and white-bark pine. Large alpine meadows are interspersed between stands of timber and can extend to the very edge of the glacial masses. The meadows quickly burst into flowers when the last snow banks disappear in midsummer. Indian basket grass, or bear grass, is found among the smaller plants. Also in this zone are the mountain goat, whistling marmot, least hare (coney, rock rabbit, pika), sooty grouse, and ptarmigan.

(d) Arctic-Alpine Zone. This biotic association normally extends upward from about 6,000 feet in elevation. No forests are found in this zone. Here are the perpetual snowfields and glaciers. The bare, wind-scarred slopes are too frigid and inhospitable for any but the hardiest plant forms to thrive. During the warmest months, the temperatures still often fall to the freezing point; frostless days are few. In some sheltered locations an occasional twisted juniper or arctic willow manages to survive. Mosses, grasses, and sedges are by far the most characteristic types of vegetation. Even in these arctic-like conditions, however, mountain goats and Rainier white-tailed ptarmigan are sometimes seen.

Parks

Among the most striking features of the mountain flanks (and of special relevance to this prehistory study) are the so-called "parks" of the Hudsonian Zone. [In today's parlance, the "Hudsonian" is more frequently referred to as the sub-alpine zone.—Editors] These gently sloping tablelands—on divides between glacial canyons—are open meadows dotted with clumps of fir and hemlock, and with an occasional mirror-like reflecting pond or lake (Schmoe, 1925g: 8). Situated between about 5,000 to 7,000 feet in elevation, a network of parks extends around Mount Rainier, forming a ring approximately two miles in width and about 50 miles in circuit (Schmoe, 1925g: 135–36). The parks are discontinuous, however, being dissected in places by glacier tongues, stream valleys, rocky ridges, and mountain spurs.

Beginning at Paradise on the south slope of Mount Rainier and moving counterclockwise around the peak within the national park borders (see Fig. 1.1), the parks that are named and indicated on the U.S.G.S. Mount Rainier

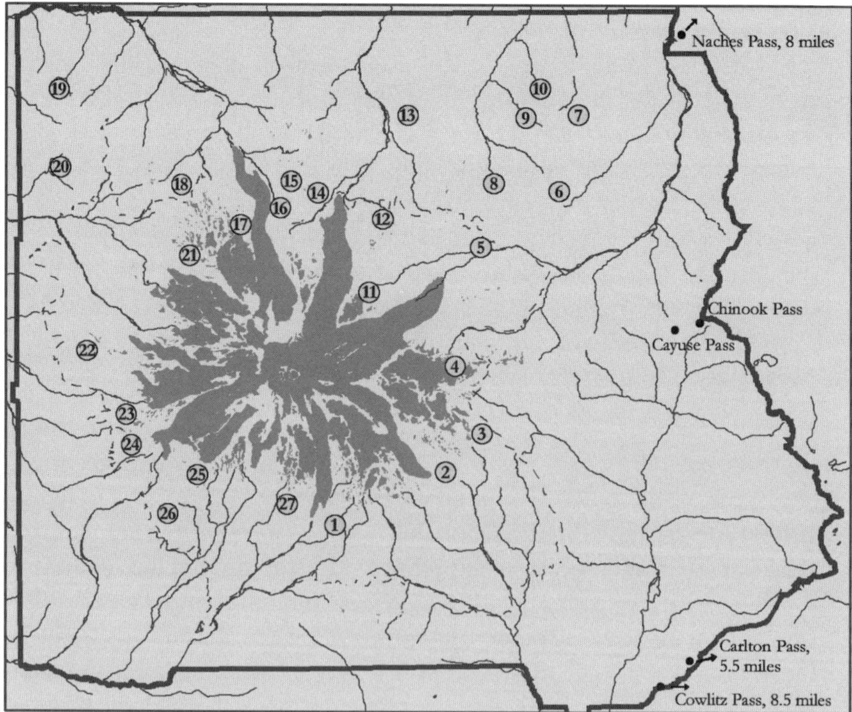

Figure 1.1. Mount Rainier National Park, indicating the principal river systems, the high altitude "parks," and the important passes within or near the national park boundaries (after Schmoe, 1925g).

National Park Quadrangle map include the following. Elevations are approximate altitudes as indicated on the quadrangle map.

1. Paradise Park (5,700')
2. Cowlitz Park (6,300')
3. Ohanapecosh Park (5,500')
4. Summer Land (5,700') (Matthes, 1916: 226; Meany, 1916: 321; Schmoe, 1925g: 103, 123)
5. Yakima Park (6,400'); A large park (Schmoe, 1925g: 121)
6. White River Park (5,700')
7. Bear Park (5,800')
8. Huckleberry Park (5,700')
9. Green Park (5,600')
10. Burnt Park (5,700')
11. Glacier Basin (6,000'); A small park (Meany, 1916: 309; Schmoe, 1925g: 103)
12. Berkeley Park (6,000')
13. Grand Park (5,300'); Extensive; miles of relatively level ground; groves of alpine fir and hemlock; deer abundant every summer (Meany, 1916: 309–10)
14. Vernal Park (5,800')
15. Elysian Fields (5,700') (Meany, 1916: 308)
16. Moraine Park (5,500')
17. Seattle Park (5,900')
18. Mist Park (5,200')
19. North Park (4,900')
20. Mountain Meadows (4,300')
21. Spray Park (6,000'); Extensive (Matthes, 1916: 230; Meany, 1916: 320)
22. Sunset Park (5,500')
23. Klapatche Park (5,500')
24. St. Andrews Park (5,700')
25. Pyramid Park (6,300')
26. Indian Henrys Hunting Ground (5,700')
27. Van Trump Park (5,700')

Tribal Classification

The traditional Indian groupings that claimed various parts of what is today Mount Rainier National Park are discussed in detail in a later chapter regarding their probable tribal boundaries. However, it is convenient to briefly identify these groupings at this point and diagram their relationships. These groups and their neighbors, and the linguistic and geographic clusters to which they are customarily classified, are listed below.

In the chart, "Groups" are geographical clusters, and "Units" are the larger linguistic divisions. The individual "tribes" within the units are cultural, geographical, linguistic, and/or political entities. The exact nature of these tribal entities and their diagnostic characteristics is a subject of much debate and not a little confusion, and is a question which need not be discussed here. At least for the present, it is sufficient to recognize that they are units customarily identified, or at least often referred to, in the anthropological and historical literature, and that they are here designated "tribes" for convenience alone. Their general locations, according to Spier (1936), are depicted in Figure 1.2.

Interior (Columbia Plateau) Group—
- *Sahaptin Unit*
  - Kittitas (Pcawanwapam)
  - Yakama (Yakima)
- *Salishan Unit*
  - Wenatchi

Puget Sound (Coastal) Group—
- *Sahaptin Unit*
  - Meshal (Mical)
  - Taidnapam (Upper Cowlitz)
- *Salishan Unit*
  - Muckleshoot
  - Nisqually
  - Puyallup

Cascades Group (extending east and west of the mountain range)—
- *Sahaptin Unit*
  - Klikitat (Klickitat)

Research Design

With this listing of the fundamental physiographic, climatic, and biotic data and the presentation of a working tribal classification, the research design of this study may now be made explicit, including the basic objectives, underlying premises, and the classes of data secured and analyzed to attain the research goals.

Objectives

The present research was a sharply focused and intensive ethnographic and ethnohistorical inquiry. It was designed to achieve three objectives, one primary and the other two secondary.

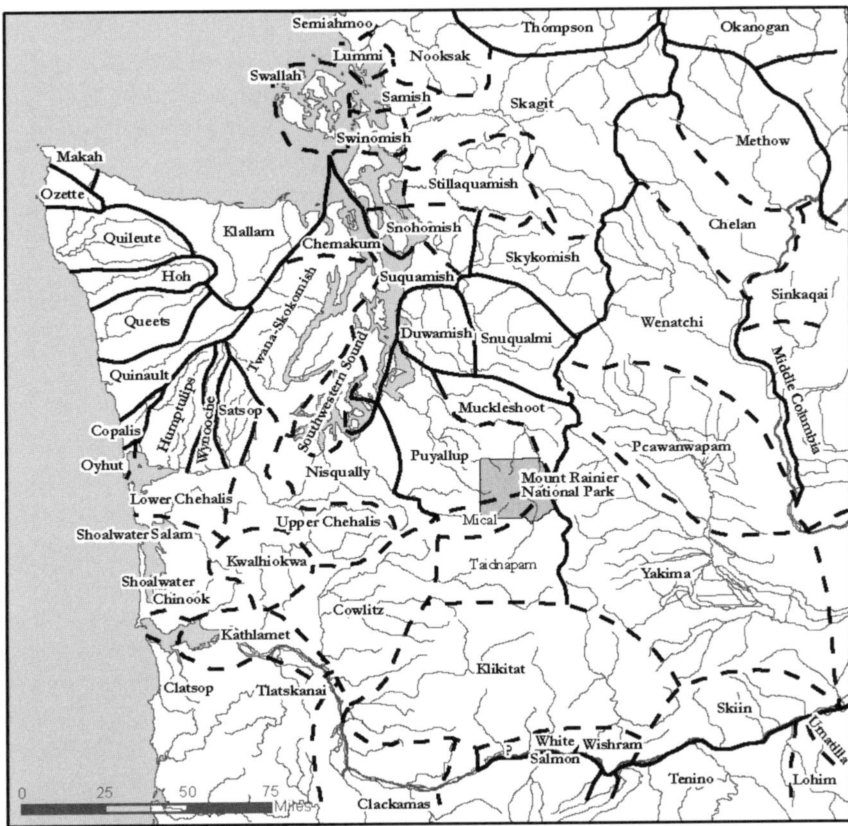

Figure 1.2. Tribal distribution in the Mount Rainier National Park area (after Spier, 1936: 42–43).

(a) The primary goal was a practical one—to define significant archaeological problems in Mount Rainier National Park, to contribute information useful for locating archaeological resources, and to provide facts for a meaningful interpretation of the archaeological finds subsequently discovered in the field search. It was thought probable that archaeological sites would be difficult to locate owing to the rugged terrain and the dense forests cloaking the lower flanks of the mountains. In an area so little known in its prehistory, the identification of meaningful archaeological problems would not be predicted *a priori*. However, a detailed ethnographic analysis of the material culture of the regional tribes—to the degree that such data could be located—may well assist materially in the determination of artifact functions.

(b) The study also was designed to serve a more general objective—to demonstrate what may be done ethnographically in the aid of archaeological research, even in a difficult situation where the native informants capable of bringing personal or traditional knowledge to bear on the topic are few, and where relevant ethnographic and ethnohistorical materials were limited. If the exercise proved successful, the possibilities of this method presumably would be satisfactorily demonstrated for adoption in other similar cases, to say nothing of the more numerous circumstances elsewhere in which richer ethnographic and ethnohistorical information are obtainable.

(c) There was an equally general, associated objective on a more theoretical level. Some years ago, as a result of field research among the Kalispel of northeast Washington, the hypothesis was generated that aboriginal patterns of land utilization in the Pacific Northwest were so extensive as to have included even areas remote from recognized settlement—i.e., localities that were difficult of access and topographically forbidding. However, this assumption has never been put to the test beyond the Kalispel scene. It appears that the Mount Rainier region not only met these geographical prerequisites, but, because of its extreme isolation, massive features, and environmental ruggedness, the national park offered an unusually rigorous test of the hypothesis. If utilization could be demonstrated for this region, the *a priori* assumption that any region, whatever its geographic characteristics, was without native use would appear highly debatable. [In the years since this report was written, a substantial number of archaeological sites, some dating to more than 4,500 years ago, have been found on all sides of the mountain. Many of these are located in the sub-alpine zone (Smith's "Hudsonian") or higher. Clearly, indigenous use of the high elevation, seemingly remote terrain is now well documented.—Editors]

Premises

Three basic premises underlay the present research. Explicitly these included:

(a) The mountainous terrain of present-day Mount Rainier National Park was known and familiar to native Indian groups; and, at least certain portions of the locality were visited and in some measure utilized by them.

(b) The national park area may have been claimed, in large or small segments, by as many as six aboriginal groups—the Taidnapam (Upper Cowlitz), Meshal (Mical), Puyallup, Muckleshoot, Nisqually, and Yakama.

(c) Specific data to test these two assumptions and to establish further facts in the matter might still be secured by ethnographic field study and by an analysis of the somewhat meager literature (primarily ethnographic and ethnohistorical).

Premise (a) is made reasonable by the native Northwest Coast and Plateau pattern of people-to-land relationships as consistently described in the ethnographic data. Premise (c) is based on the fact that a few elderly informants on Washington reservations still recall some essentials of traditional lifeways, and that some literature exists that describes various aspects of regional native activity in the national park locality. It appeared probable that enough data based on premises (a) and (c) could be secured to make the study rewarding. Premise (b), on the other hand, stands on a more complex line of reasoning and requires a more detailed explanation.

There is no serious question about the assumption in (b) for four of the six groups enumerated. The standard tribal distribution study for native groups in Washington is Spier (1936), which at the time of this study remains the most detailed and comprehensive review of the anthropological literature.[9] The assumption that the Taidnapam, Meshal, Puyallup, and Muckleshoot occupied territory now within the national park borders is supported by Spier, who assigns the Mount Rainier area primarily to the first three tribes and to a negligible extent to the fourth (see Fig. 1.2).

On the other hand, no part of the national park is considered by Spier to have been Yakama territory, which he placed wholly to the east of the national park, or to have been Nisqually country, which he locates well west of the national park. This being the case, the reasoning behind the present assumption that these two tribes may well have claimed use-rights to portions of Mount Rainier's slopes must be explained.

The Yakama

On the Spier map (Fig. 1.2), the western boundary of traditional Yakama territory coincides with the Cascade Divide (the national park's eastern border). It seems evident from Spier's data that he lacked specific information on this point, and he essentially followed a basic procedure of extending the Yakama country west to the watershed divide. This is logical, given the Plateau orientation toward boundaries. But in this instance, it seems possible that this is in error.

Four points of evidence support this latter assumption:

(a) In the Pacific Northwest, tribal limits tended to follow mountain crests. Regarding the western border of the Yakama country, however, the Cascade Divide is neither the most prominent landmark feature nor the highest. Rather, Mount Rainier just west of the divide towers 8,000 feet above the other Cascade peaks,[10] and has, in fact, a massive watershed system of its own (Matthes, n.d.). Consequently, this peak and its northeast and southeast slopes would seem to be an equally logical, or perhaps even more obvious, marker for a Yakama western boundary than the Cascade Divide.

There is a caveat, however, regarding an immediate acceptance of this revision of the Yakama border. There was a conflicting territorial principle that also prevailed in the Northwest—i.e., that the uppermost part of a drainage system tended to be claimed by a tribe that made use of its middle area. The Cowlitz and White River headwaters flow off the eastern side of Mount Rainier, before turning westward. If this drainage principle took precedence, then the eastern slopes of the mountain would have been occupied by the Puget Sound tribes laying claim to the western Cascades foothill portions of these two river drainages. However, if mountain crests were conceived to outrank this drainage principle, then the Yakama would have conceived of the eastern face of Mount Rainier as being in their country. These conflicting appraisals are diagrammed schematically in Figure 1.3.

(b) The floral and faunal resources of the Mount Rainier area may have offered more to the Yakama than to the tribal groups west of the national park. This is not to say, however, that Puget Sound groups did not utilize the upriver mountainous areas. For example, two statements made by Marian Smith regarding Puyallup land-use patterns support this conclusion. First: "Trips for hunting, as well as those for...berry picking, etc., normally followed the direction of the village system" (Smith, 1940: 24). And second: "[There was] a definite preference for the upriver route and wherever it was feasible trips were made upstream so that the loaded canoe or the products themselves might be

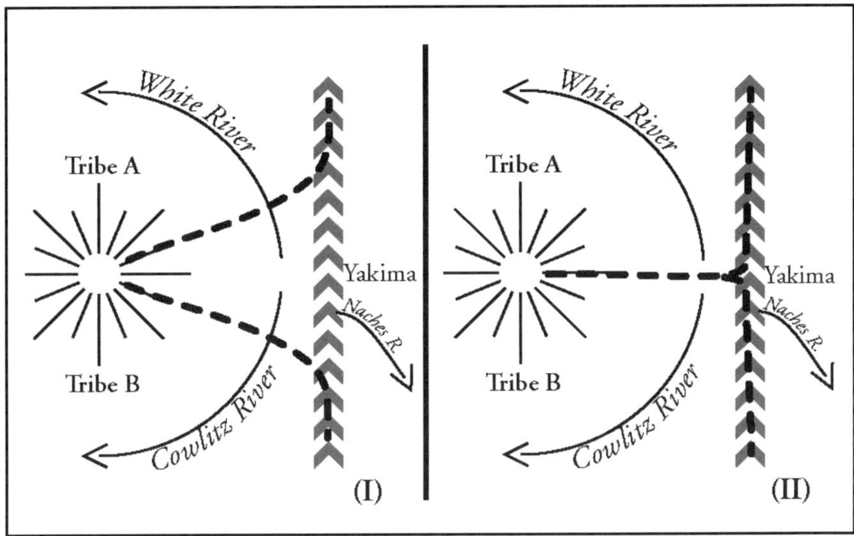

Figure 1.3. (I) Yakama territory if mountain crest principle prevailed; (II) Yakama territory if drainage principle took precedence. Because of points (b) and (c) below, alternative I is considered theoretically more probable than alternative II.

floated back to the village site" (Smith, 1940: 5). These remarks can only mean that the river forests and mountain slopes just upstream, at the very least, from villages on the western slopes of the Cascades were utilized economically by the peoples of those communities. The location of these extreme upriver villages to which these statements may apply will be described at a later point. It is noteworthy that the biota at the lower and middle altitudes of the national park area largely resembled that of the lowland rain forests utilized by western groups, but contrasted sharply with that of the dry open plains occupied by the Yakama to the east. Thus, the natural resources of the national park area might supposedly have attracted the Yakama at least as strongly as for the western groups.

(c) The Yakama were highly mobile horsemen, to whom traveling long distances was more common and presumably more congenial than it was for the Taidnapam, Meshal, Puyallup, Muckleshoot, and Nisqually with their somewhat more sedentary river orientation. Bearing upon this matter is Marian Smith's observation that as "a matter of convenience [Puget Sound] expeditions kept fairly close to the village site" (1940: 5). This suggests the possibility that the Yakama were geared to a greater utilization of distant mountainous areas than the five western tribes with their Puget Sound-Coastal cultural outlook, whose customary patterns exploited deep mountain resources only on a temporary basis.

(d) Though lying west of the Cascade Divide, the slopes of Mount Rainier seemed about as equally accessible to the Yakama as to their western neighbors. Travel to this mountainous area was no more distant from the nearest Yakama settlements as it was from the closest villages of the Puget Sound peoples. Apparently, too, Mount Rainier was as easily accessed by the Yakama traveling via the Yakima drainage through the eastern passes as it was by the five western tribal groups proceeding up the river valleys and along forested mountain ridges. It is noteworthy that the eastern portions of the Yakama trails led over relatively open, easily traversed terrain, whereas the routes of the Puget Sound groups must have been through thick timber, until they reached the open, high slopes in the national park.

Thus, despite Spier's tribal delineations, it seems methodologically sound as a research hypothesis to pursue the assumption that the Yakama used the eastern part of the national park area.

The Nisqually

The inclusion of the Nisqually in the hypothesis rests upon different considerations. The tribe's territory *vis-à-vis* that of both the Meshal and Puyallup is quite differently defined by several authors. Though Spier (1936) places the Nisqually well to the west of the national park, others see them as having made major use of Mount Rainier and assign much of the present park area to them (see Figs. 1.2 and 3.1). This significant divergence of opinion made it necessary to consider this tribe as a part claimant to Mount Rainier and to investigate their possible territorial use of the area.

Data

The data presented in this study is the result of two classes of inquiry—an ethnographic field investigation, and a search of the ethnographic, ethnohistorical, historical, and ecological literature. In summary, the specific and primary purpose of the survey was to ascertain the locations of possible archaeological sites in Mount Rainier National Park, to uncover possible archaeological problems, and to secure information to assist in archaeological interpretation. This field and library/archival research was done to explicitly identify the following:

(a) The Puget Sound and Interior tribes that claimed territory within the national park borders and their precise tribal limits within the park.

(b) The location, size, tribal affiliation, and period of use of any villages or occupation sites that were located within the national park boundaries.

(c) The economic and other utilization of natural resources in the national park, the aspects of use that might be reflected in the archaeological evidence, and the location, size, frequency of use, and tribal affiliation of temporary camps occupied during this exploitation.

(d) The precise routes of native trails that led through the national park, the frequency of use, the tribal identity of the travelers, the material objects transported over them, and the customary camping localities along these courses.

Ethnographic Fieldwork Procedures and Schedule

The Yakama Reservation, with its agency headquarters at Toppenish, Washington, was visited June 30–July 3 and again July 6–8, 1963. Superintendent Robertson was advised of my research intentions and field plans. With the permission of the tribal council, a list of potential informants was secured from the tribal rolls. This list, comprising all persons born before 1893 and resident on or near the reservation, included 113 persons.

With the special interests of the study in mind, the potentially most ethnographically knowledgeable were selected from this group with the help of Chairman Alec Saluskin of the Yakama Tribal Council, Mr. Watston and Mr. Bassett of the council office, and Dan Umtuch and Elsie Halfmoon of the agency staff. In addition, other persons, including the interviewees themselves, were queried as to possible informants. Also consulted were Edward J. Robert of Toppenish, who settled on the Yakama Reservation in 1897, and R.J. Delaney, a former reservation forester. Though both non-Indian, they had long and extensive contact with the Yakama. All of the Yakama who were identified as possible key informants were interviewed, including David Miller (born 1880), Rhoda (Williams) Yellowwash (born 1886), Alice

Ollie Spencer (born 1874), Harris W. Beavert (born 1893), Mrs. Whitefoot, and Mrs. Knockknock (Noc Noc) E. Woods (born 1880). The Yakama portion of the field information was secured from this group. Also, the Yakama districts of Toppenish, Harrah, White Swan, Medicine Valley, Fort Simcoe, and Wapato were visited in search of ethnoecological data.

It will be noted that the field investigation among the Yakama was divided into two periods. The most pressing initial issue seemed to be ascertaining whether or not the Yakama claimed a part of the national park as traditional tribal territory. If this was not the case, then my remaining fieldwork time could be concentrated on the coastal groups. But, on the other hand, if the Yakama considered the eastern slopes of Mount Rainier as tribal lands, these facts could then be compared with information subsequently secured from the coast groups. As things turned out, an appropriate follow-up period of fieldwork was conducted among the Yakama.

While at the Yakama Reservation, I learned about a Taidnapam family that still resided in their traditional territory on the Cowlitz River near the town of Randle. I visited them July 3–4, 1963, obtaining information from Mary Kiona (born 1856[?]) and her daughter Minnie Placid (born 1902), who also served as interpreter. Later, I was fortunate to get additional data from George Satanus (born 1881), a Taidnapam (with a Klikitat grandfather) who resided on the Muckleshoot Reservation.

Information about the Nisqually-Puyallup uses of the national park area was gained from informants on the Nisqually Reservation near Olympia, July 4–5, 1963. Alice Kalama and Billy Frank (born 1880), both Nisqually, and Mrs. Frank (born ca. 1890) were contacted. Efforts to locate informants who identified themselves specifically as Puyallup were largely unavailing because Puyallup tribal members were widely dispersed throughout the greater Tacoma area. A brief visit to the Puyallup locality resulted in no leads so I decided to continue to the nearby Muckleshoot Reservation, hoping that my Muckleshoot contacts might provide either specific information about the Puyallup, or the names and addresses of potential Puyallup informants. This, too, was largely unsuccessful. Fortunately, however, good ethnographic data existed for the Puyallup people (Marian Smith, 1940), unlike others in this survey. Incidentally, Billy Frank, though a Nisqually, was quite familiar with traditional Puyallup lifeways.

By this point in my fieldwork, an understanding of the native economic uses of the Mount Rainier region was fitting into a consistent pattern. Consequently, I decided that further efforts to contact Puyallup informants were unnecessary. Also, it was understood that the Meshal no longer exist as a distinct social unit, and no informants of this group were located.

Data about the Muckleshoot tribe was obtained July 5–6, 1963, from Louie Starr (born 1898) on the Muckleshoot Reservation near Auburn, Washington, and from Matilda Barr (born 1881) in Auburn. I also interviewed George Satanus, the Taidnapam-Klikitat mentioned above. From here, I returned to the Yakama Reservation, July 6–8, 1963, for follow-up interviews.

Ethnographic Fieldwork Findings

The ethnographic field results were somewhat more meager and general than had been hoped for. Many years had passed, of course, since traditional groups had utilized Mount Rainier's resources and only a few knowledgeable elderly informants yet remained. A serious effort was made to identify and consult with informants who were of sufficient age to be aware of traditional cultural practices, who were mentally alert and possessed an adequate fluency in English or who could work easily with interpreters, who had a personal familiarity with the Mount Rainier area and were willing to share that knowledge, and who possessed an "ethnographic sense," either naturally or by having worked with earlier anthropologists. In any cultural group, the number of people with such qualities is limited, but the small populations of the coastal reservations compounded the difficulty.

The number of people residing on the Nisqually Reservation numbered only 62 persons in the 1950 census, 479 persons lived on the Puyallup Reservation at roughly the same time, and 294 persons resided on the Muckleshoot Reservation in 1950 (U.S. Government, 1953: 870, 878, 933). Among these groups, the pool of individuals of the required age and qualities was understandably extremely small. Also, the relatively early date of extensive White contact in western Washington (mid-to-late 1800s) already had deeply impacted traditional native economic patterns by the time that my informants were born. This was the case, as well, for all four of Marian Smith's Nisqually-Puyallup informants, whose data was compiled in her 1940 report. Unfortunately, all four of her informants had passed away by the time of my 1963 fieldwork. Given these facts, the very limited number of truly knowledgeable informants found on Puget Sound was not surprising.

The Yakama situation was somewhat different and more informants were located, though still rather limited in number. The 1950 census estimated a population of 3,598 living on the reservation (U.S. Government, 1953:

1026). However, since this population was a coalescence of tribal groups and bands from a wide expanse of eastern Washington, only a portion of this figure were of true Yakama ancestry and who had traditionally occupied the Yakima drainage of the far western Columbia Plateau.[11] Furthermore, several reportedly well-informed Yakama were not contacted due to the regrettable afflictions that can affect the elderly—e.g., physical infirmities, deafness, etc. Contacting these people really was out of the question.

Some of the contacts that I did interview suffered from partial hearing impairment, were rather surprised or confused by the kind of questions that I was unexpectedly asking, or were reticent to share information, as can naturally occur when approached by an outsider with whom they were unfamiliar. Sometimes, too, divergent contemporary topics intruded into our conversations—e.g., personal health concerns, current Bureau of Indian Affairs issues, disputes about fishing-hunting-berrying rights, etc.

A number of the informants—e.g., David Miller, Mary Kiona, Rhoda Yellowwash, Billy Frank, Louie Starr, George Satanus, and Matilda Barr—provided quite extensive information, and I only wish I could have spent more time with them focusing on broader, more intensive ethnographical topics. I believe they and others could have developed into genuinely superior informants.

Another factor accounting for a sometimes meager acquisition of specific findings was the character of the traditional utilization of the national park area. During the historic period, Mount Rainier was rather peripheral to the primary territory of all of the groups that claimed portions of the mountain terrain. No long-term villages or other settlements were maintained within its borders, and the population centers of the tribes were located far from its slopes. Individuals, families, and groups entering the area did so either for a brief period of gathering and hunting, or incidentally as they proceeded on their way east or west between the Puget Sound lowland and the Columbia Basin.

Historically, hunting was secondary in importance to the gathering activity in the berry grounds. However, due to the passage of time, my informants often were unacquainted with the English designations for features and places in the park, and they were unfamiliar with reading modern topographic maps. Furthermore, none of the informants had visited the area in recent years, owing in part to their advanced age, but more particularly to a national park proscription against Indian berry-picking within the national park limits.[12] As a consequence, their memories of the locations of specific gathering and hunting grounds once frequented by tribal members generally had faded.

Findings from the Literature

The literature search resulted in more data than anticipated. The standard technique of placing basic reliance on primary source materials and of carefully assessing the reliability of secondary and other sources was consistently followed. Notably, prior to this fieldwork little literature research had been conducted to ascertain significant data bearing on tribal claims to the national park area and the native use of its resources. Only Spier's 1936 tribal distribution summary had really proceeded along these lines. All information derived from the printed sources is clearly identified in this report to distinguish it from the field data.

Orthography

The phonetic-phonemic transcription of native words recorded in the field research follows the method generally adopted for American Indian languages. A phonetic key appears in the table below. Accuracy was, of course, attempted in all recordings, but cannot be claimed in every instance. Knowledge of the phonetic schema of the languages in question is still imperfect. Some informants, too, had suffered dental loss, were partially deaf, or had not spoken some native terms for some time, making transcription difficult. Dialect variations apparently also abound within the language units of the area. Furthermore, dialect mixtures of various complex sorts occur on reservations and, in fact, are confusingly present in the speech of many individuals.

Smith remarks that her Puyallup-Nisqually "informants showed marked dialectical differences" (1940: xii). And Edward S. Curtis noted that among the Sahaptin bands of the Yakima River valley, from the mouth of Kittitas Creek in the Ellensburg area to the Yakima's union with the Columbia, there were many dialect variations (1911: 3). Little or no opportunity existed to check speech recordings with other speakers, or later with the same informant.

Vowels—

i = high, front, tense, unrounded
i = high, front, lax, unrounded
e = mid, front, tense, unrounded
ε = mid, front, lax, unrounded
æ = low, front, unrounded
ə = mid, central, unrounded

u = high, back, tense, rounded
v = high, back, lax, rounded
o = mid, back, tense, rounded
ɔ = mid, back, lax, rounded
a = low, back, unrounded

Semi-Vowels—

y = front, unrounded
w = back, rounded

Consonants; essentially as in English except as follows—

x = mid-palatal, voiceless spirant
q = post-palatal, voiceless stop
x̣ = post-palatal, voiceless spirant
ʾ over consonant = synchronous glottalization
B, D, G = voiceless lenis (intermediate) stops
c = English /ts/
š = English /sh/
č = English /ch/
ł = voiceless lateral
ƛ = voiceless lateral fricative
· = following vowel indicates greater length
´ over vowel = indicates stress

Where other authors, such as Curtis, employ a method of transcription quite unlike the above, which can be difficult to correlate, a transliteration into my system is sometimes placed in brackets following the original (e.g., see chapter 2). Ordinarily this is done where a linguistic point is made and a comparison of native words is called for.

Endnotes

1. In August 1963, a preliminary copy of this report was furnished to Dr. Richard Daugherty of Washington State University, under whose supervision the second phase was initiated in the summer of that year.
2. The primary data in this section was drawn from Plummer (1900), Matthes (1916), Flett (1916), Schmoe (1925c, 1925g, 1926b), Landes (1934), Jones (1938), Kitchin (1939), Writers' Program (1941), Brockman (1947), Matthes (n.d.), Standard Oil Co. of California highway map (1962), and U.S. Geological Survey quadrangle maps.
3. This list of passes is complied from U.S.G.S. quadrangles and other maps.
4. Kautz reported that Cowlitz Pass also was named Packwood Pass (1916: 93).
5. In contrast to the Jones (1938) classification, Flett (1916) earlier identified five floral zones, evidently in part because he placed special emphasis on flowering plants in

the formulation. Viewed more broadly by Jones (1938: 8–9), the Humid-Transitional Zone is regarded by him as one phase of the "Austral Region"; on the other hand, the Canadian, Hudsonian, and Arctic-Alpine zones together comprise the arctic-subarctic "Boreal Region."

6. In places on the west side of the national park, the upper limit of the Humid-Transitional zone is as high 3,500 or 4,000 feet (Brockman, 1947: 3). This well illustrates the impossibility of setting an identical, rigid altitude limit for any life zone throughout the park.
7. According to Schmoe (1925g: 130) and Taylor and Shaw (Kitchin, 1939: 86), the upper limit is about 5,000 feet.
8. The upper limit is sometimes reported to be as high as 7,500 feet and occasionally as low as 5,500 feet. Landes (1935: 1–45), Brockman (1947: 5–6), and Taylor and Shaw (Kitchin, 1939) place the upper limit at 6,500 feet. In one specific case, that of Paradise Park on the south face of the mountain, the upper border is set at 7,000 feet and the lower at 5,000 feet (Russell, 1916: 180). At 7,000 feet, the snow line, properly speaking, is reached. In certain special localities, however, permanent snow banks and ice fields remain throughout the year at an altitude of 6,000 feet (Schmoe, 1925g: 21).
9. For the Mount Rainier area, the "Indian Tribes and Languages" map compiled by Schaeffer (1958) is identical in detail to that of Spier and undoubtedly is based upon it.
10. This aspect of Mount Rainier is described in the Washington Writers' Program handbook (1941: 580): "Seen from a distance the mountain seems to be isolated, its great height dwarfing the Cascade Range on the east and the other neighboring mountains; although these peaks and mountain ranges themselves average 6,000 to 8,000 feet in altitude."
11. Hulse makes this same point (1957: 237–38).
12. This interdiction was a source of bitterness expressed by all of the Indian groups that I visited.

2

Native Toponymy

According to the informant interviews, Mount Rainier is identified as Taxó·ma by the Yakama, Taqó·ma by the Nisqually, and Taqó·b*i*d by the Muckleshoot. Curtis states that the name is of coastal Salishan origin, and adopted by the Sahaptin speaking Yakama (1911: 6, fn. 1). Other names and variants for Mount Rainier also were obtained during my study of the literature and other written records (see Fig. 2.1).

Plateau Tribes

Curtis states that Mount Rainier was known to the Yakama as Psh̓wánoapami-tah̓óma [pǎwánoapami-taxóma], meaning Psh̓wánoapam-snow peak (1911: 6, 176). This confirms my Yakama informant designation in a sense, but introduces one genuinely complicating factor—i.e., the Psh̓wánoapami modifier. As Curtis remarks, Psh̓wánoapam is the Yakama term for the Kittitas tribe, a Sahaptin people whose homeland was situated at the head of the Yakima River (1911: 15) (see Figs. 1.2, 3.2, and 3.3). They too are the pcwa′nwapam [pšwánwapam] of Jacobs (1931: 94, 220), and, following him, of Spier (1936: 17). They also obviously are the "Pschwan-wapp-am" described by the 19th century ethnographer George Gibbs, who noted that the Yakama frequently denoted the country around the north or main branch of the Yakima River by this term, meaning "stony ground" (Spier, 1936: 17); the "Indians living there sometimes assume the name to themselves."

Since Mount Rainier lies well outside of traditional Kittitas tribal boundaries as commonly designated (e.g., by Spier; see Fig. 1.2), it might be probable that by coupling the term with tah̓oma, as reported by Curtis, only the strict descriptive sense of the word is intended. That is, "stony ground" certainly would properly describe the topography of the mountain's higher slopes when free of snow.

However, contrary to this interpretation are the linguistic facts as presented by Jacobs. He explains the term pcwa′nwapam (or, pcwa′napam, pcwa′unapam, in other dialects) as containing the elements pcwá ('rock') and -pam ('people from, people of') (1931: 220). Consequently, Gibbs'

Author	Tribe							
	Yakama	Klikitat	Nisqually	Upper Chehalis	Cowlitz	Muckleshoot	Puyallup	Taidnapam
Smith (1963)	tax̣ó·ma		taqó·m̓a			taqó·b*i*d		
Curtis	pšwánoapami-taxóma		tkóbɛd	tkomɛn	nucél*i*p			
Stevens	takhóma or tahóma	takhóma or tahóma	takhóma or tahóma				takhóma or tahóma	takhóma
Longmire		Taho·ma	nebɛd ?					
Teit			tkóbɛd					

Figure 2.1. Designations for Mount Rainier. Terms in the literature are converted to my system of transcription, which are added in brackets within the main text of the present study.

translation is not strictly accurate—the word does not signify "stony ground," but perhaps "people of the stony ground." Moreover, Jacobs lists the suffix '-i,' accompanied by either a lengthening of the word final 'm' or of the vowel preceding this 'm,' as carrying the significance of the possessive (1931: 228). This strongly suggests that, though he missed the subtle long phoneme, Gibbs properly recorded the possessive form of the tribal designation. If this is the case, his full term for the mountain should be translated as "Taȟoma of the Pcwánwapam."

The significance of this seems clear enough. The Yakama regarded the mountain, or at least its eastern flanks, as falling within Kittitas territory. However, nothing was recorded in my field interviews to support this view. Since this data was unknown during the field period, no questioning was directed to this point, but the matter should be followed up in future informant inquiries. Assuming a Kittitas proprietorship of the eastern national park area, the region would still have been under the control of an Interior Sahaptin tribe. More about this will be mentioned later in this study.

For the Yakama and Klikitat, Hazard Stevens recorded the following: "Tak-ho′ma or Ta-ho′ma among the Yakimas, Klickitats…and allied tribes of Indians, is the generic term for mountain, used precisely as we use the word 'mount,' as [in] Takhoma Wynatchie, or Mount Wynatchie. But they all designate Rainier simply as Takhoma, or The Mountain" (1916: 95, fn. 1).

Len Longmire, an early resident in the southern part of the national park, stated that "the Klickitat word" for Mount Rainier was "T-a-h-o-m-a, but they pronounced it with an 'a' as in 'at' and the rest as though it has three or four 'o's' instead of one. Indian Henry told me the word meant 'highest' or 'highest hill'" (Lindsey 1933: 4).

Coastal Tribes

The literature reports a number of toponyms for Mount Rainier used by Puget Sound groups (see Fig. 2.1). Curtis states that Tkómma, in one form or another, was used by several coastal tribes as the specific name for Mount Rainier. He recorded the following list of Coast Salish designations: Nisqually "Tkóbĕd" [Tkóbɛd]; Upper Chehalis "Tkómĕn" [Tkómɛn]; and Cowlitz "Nutsélĭp" [nucél*i*p]" (1911: 6, fn. 1). It will be noted that Curtis's Nisqually form differs from that obtained by me; its terminal morph is the one recorded in my Muckleshoot gloss rather than that in my Nisqually term (see Fig. 2.1).

Hazard Stevens noted that "Tak-ho′ma or Ta-ho′ma" was the term for Mount Rainier used by the Puyallup, Nisqually, and associated peoples (1916: 95, fn. 1). He also reported that Sluiskin, his Mount Rainier guide in 1870 from Bear Prairie to Sluiskin Falls at the head of the Paradise River, knew the mountain "only as Takhoma" (Stevens, 1916: 108). Stevens identified Sluiskin as a Yakama, though it seems probable that he was a Taidnapam.

My Nisqually toponym, taqó·ma, was etymologized by Billy Frank into (ta)qó·- ('water') and -ma ('son; any young person'). This etymology is, however, quite possibly of the folk variety, for it is said to be explained by a Nisqually myth. This story relates that the mountain once was a woman who sat with the other peaks in the Olympic Range, but the other peaks decided there was no room for her there. Sent away from the range, she left with her son, sharply cautioning him not to forget taking the water. Hence, the name given to the mountain. The son, in fact, brought with him a great quantity of water, to which the many streams now flowing from the peak well attest.

James Teit suggested several possible etymologies for the Salishan designation (see Curtis, 1911: 6, fn. 1). According to one of his Indian informants, the Nisqually term tkóbĕd means 'waterer,' referring to the fact that several rivers have their sources on the mountain. This semantic analysis is consistent with the etymology of taqó·m̓a provided by Billy Frank. As observed above, however, Curtis glosses taȟóma [taxóma] as "snow-peak" (1911: 6, 176).

It must be noted, too, that the term tkómma in its several variants, according to Curtis, was applied by some tribes specifically to peaks other than Mount Rainier, and by groups as a common noun to any snow peak (1911: 6, fn. 1). A brief comment made by Theodore Winthrop, from an observation made in 1853, agrees with Curtis' contention: the Indians "call it [Mount Rainier] Tacoma,—a generic term also applied to all snow peaks" (1916: 35). Hazard Stevens also speaks to this same general point (1916: 95, fn. 1).

Since the word is apparently descriptive, it is not difficult to comprehend why it may have been applied to the most prominent mountain, or any peak, meeting the descriptive requirements in the area familiar to each tribe.

This data—from the field research and culled from the literature—seems to reveal two points of pertinence to the present subject.

(a) All terms recorded for the various tribes are clearly cognate save for Curtis's nucél*i*p for the Cowlitz and Longmire's highly suspicious

Nisqually nebɛd. Longmire had remarked: "The Nisqually name for the mountain sounded like 'Nebat' [Nebɛd?]" (Lindsey, 1933: 4). However, no support for the use of this term is known to me.

(b) The designation, according to Curtis and the evidence above, is Salishan whatever its phonetic form, not Sahaptin.

If the principle is here applicable that toponyms tend to be conservative and hence often provide evidence of an earlier occupancy by a different group (Salishan), it may indicate that the Sahaptins, who borrowed the Salishan name for Mount Rainier, were relative newcomers to the locality. This interpretation might support a conclusion that archaeological materials recovered from the eastern parts of Mount Rainier could reasonably be attributed to the Yakama only if the sites dated to the proto-historic or early historic periods.

3

Tribal Identities and Boundaries

A principal duty confronting the archaeologist is to correctly associate artifactual materials to the cultural groups known to have once occupied an area. Therefore, the identity of the tribal units that laid claim to Mount Rainier and its vicinity are of key importance in this study, as are the precise locations of tribal borders, and any changes that may have occurred in the composition of tribal units or their territorial limits through time. Thus, an extended effort was made in the ethnographic and literature inquiry to secure data about these questions.

In the Pacific Northwest, there are special difficulties in determining both tribal identifications and boundary locations. This explains why even early researchers, working with the excellent informants available at the time, sometimes found it difficult to make clear and consistent statements about these matters. Since even the complications are of archaeological interest, it is useful to catalog and discuss them here.

Problems in Boundary Definition

Seven **(1–7)** socio-economic characteristics of the traditional native populations in the national park region are relevant in the present context.

(1) Utilization of the National Park

The traditional use of the mountainous terrain in the national park has been mentioned briefly in chapter 1, and will be the subject of chapter 5. Therefore, it only needs to be noted here that tribal activity was seasonal, annual, of short duration, and primarily involved collecting and hunting.

(2) Political Independence of the Plateau Band

The territory east of Mount Rainier is normally assigned to the Yakama. Sometimes, early writers regarded the Yakama as a segment of a notably larger population grouping of an important cohesive sort. But, on the other hand, some evidence also exists that the term "Yakama" might be an anthropological artifice, and that they should be split into at least two groups if it is to conform to native thinking. These difficulties of tribal definition arise because of the tenuous nature of the political bonds that united the geographically separate Plateau bands.

Klikitat

Sometimes, writers have classified all of the Sahaptin speakers of the eastern Cascades slope as a single group, customarily designating them as the "Klikitat" (or Klickitat). This broad classification included, among others, the Klikitat proper (x̣wałx̣waipam), as usually now defined, the Yakama, and even the Kittitas.

> This tendency was observed by Jacobs, who gave explicit testimony on this point: "[The term] Klikitat has suffered confusion in popular usage. While used most often for the x̣wa′łx̣waipam of the Lewis, White Salmon and Klickitat rivers, it has been applied frequently to the adjacent sk̓i′n and Yakima bands, while the upper Cowlitz ta′iDnapam…are very often termed Cowlitz Klickitats" (1931: 96).

Examples of this broad, all encompassing usage of the designation "Klikitat" include the following:

> Haeberlin and Gunther stated that the Klikitat lived just east of the Muckleshoot and Nisqually tribes, and that their country "extended south to the Columbia River and eastward [westward?] to the mountains" (1930: 9–10). Since it was Yakama territory that lay east from the Puget Sound tribes mentioned, these authors quite obviously employed "Klikitat" in its wider usage (see Fig. 3.1).
>
> Ballard identifies the occupants of the Naches River valley, the "naxtce′spam," as the people "commonly called Klickitat" (1929: 147, fn. 160). (The Naches valley actually is in the northern territory of what is now customarily assigned to the Yakama.) Evidently, Ballard followed Haeberlin and Gunther's broad usage of the "Klikitat" term.
>
> Likewise, at least on one occasion, Marian Smith apparently coalesced the Klikitat, Yakama, Kittitas, and even the Taidnapam under the Klikitat designation (1949: 344).

In the present study, however, I will use the term "Klikitat" exclusively to refer to the smaller group known to my informants as the x̣ʷə́ɬx̣waipam, who resided on both sides of the Cascades to the south and southwest of the Yakama (see Figs. 1.2 and 3.3). This conforms to the usage of Jacobs and Spier (Jacobs, 1931: 94, 96; Spier, 1936: 24–26, 42–43).

The relevant point in this discussion is this—whenever the term "Klikitat" is employed in the literature to identify groups making use of the national park resources, it need not be assumed that it is those people known by the narrow designation. Bands designated more commonly today as Yakama (or even Kittitas) may have been the actual ones involved.

Yakama

As with "Klikitat," the term "Yakama" has been interpreted by different authors as a grouping of varying magnitude. This is largely due to the views of the natives themselves, who have had differing definitions of who the Yakama are. It is convenient here to regard the "Yakama" in terms of *minimum*, *median*, and *maximum* definitions of group size, and to organize the discussion on that basis.

In the *minimum* sense, the term Yakama embraces only those groups residing on the middle section of the Yakima River below Union Gap. This would include the people on the tributaries in that locality, too. However, the adjacent Naches River people to the northwest are specifically excluded.

This clearly was the view of my Yakama informant David Miller, who volunteered a list of tribes in the Yakima vicinity. Miller stated that the Naches (nax̣číspəm)[1] were separate from the Yakama, as were the Wenatchi (w*i*náčapəm at w*i*náčə), the Kittitas (pⁱšwánapəm), the Klikitat (x̣ʷátx̣ʷaipəm), the sk̓inƛ̓a at Wishram, and the wayə́mpəm at Celilo Falls. The Naches (Yakama: nax̣čís) were said to have been especially favored with bitterroot (Yakama: piyáx̣i) and maintained an important willow weir for catching salmon.

Curtis's early classification agrees with Miller's view (Curtis, 1911: 3–4, 160). Curtis reported that the bands known as the Yakama to the Salishan tribes to the north were located in the Yakima River valley below Union Gap. Similarly, Jacobs clearly excluded the Naches people from his Yakama classification (Jacobs 1931: 95–96). However, Jacobs included the Naches with the Kittitas, rather than considering them a separate tribal unit.

A *median* view of the Yakama, on the other hand, identifies a somewhat larger grouping, including all of the bands residing in between the Kittitas people of the upper Yakima River and the Klikitat to the south. More specifically, the Naches would be a part of this Yakama tribal definition. This *median* classification has been presented for some time.

> In 1854, George Gibbs, as quoted by Leslie Spier, identified the people of the Naches valley as Yakama, as did Mooney writing in the mid-1890s (Spier, 1936: 16). Curtis also lists the Nahˀchish-hlama [naxčišłama], on "Nachess creek," as being among the Yakama bands, correlative with the Síha-hlama [síhałama] on the Yakima River between Wenas and Umtanum creeks, the Wínas-hlama [wínasłama] on Wenas Creek, and others (1911: 16).
>
> After reviewing the literature at some length, Spier recognized the Yakama as being of this *median* degree of inclusiveness: "I am reserving the name Yakima for the Sahaptin bands occupying the greater part of the middle Yakima River and its tributary streams to the west [including the Naches River]" (1936: 16).
>
> On the basis of his field research, Verne Ray likewise adopted this definition of the Yakama—clearly identifying them as a single people residing on the Naches River and downstream on the main Yakima River from Union Gap (1936: 115) (see Fig. 3.2).

Regarding examples of a *maximum* definition, the Yakama once were thought by some to include not only the groups on the Naches and middle part of the Yakima River, but also either the Kittitas, or part or all of the Wenatchi. (In addition, the Kittitas are sometimes linked with the Wenatchi in a single group, quite apart from the Yakama.)

> As early as 1854, Gibbs identified the Yakama as occupying "the country drained by the river of that name." He divided them, however, "into two principle bands, each made up of a number of villages, and very closely connected; the one owning the country on the Nahchess and lower Yakima [i.e., essentially a *median* view of the Yakama as expressed above], the other upon the Wenass and main branch above the forks" (Spier, 1936: 16). Spier identified the "forks" as referring to the junction between the Yakima River and Wenas Creek (1936: 16). This latter group, as identified by Gibbs, is plainly the equivalent of the contemporary Kittitas.
>
> In 1857, Robie saw this situation in the same light, though he also included with the Lower Yakama a number of Columbia River groups which are of no concern to this study (Spier, 1936: 16).

Thus, including the Kittitas with the Yakama was a classification presented in the mid-19th century. The view that the Wenatchi and Yakama were to some degree united also was revealed in the testimony of my Yakama informant, David Miller, even though he regarded the w*i*náčəpəm at w*i*nácə as a tribal entity distinct from the Yakama. Without question, these are the people referred to in the literature as the Wenatchi. The following data testifies to their identification.

> Ray recorded the Sahaptin name for the Wenatchi as "winȧ′ca, 'waters (large stream) flowing out'" (1936: 122).
>
> Teit stated: "The name Wenatchi is, with little doubt, of Yakima origin, probably from Wina't.ca (river issuing from a canyon), referring to the Wenatchee River" (1928: 90).
>
> Curtis considered the Wenatchi as a "group of small tribes" or bands, and referred to them as the Winátsh̉apam [winátšapam]. This term, he said, was the Yakama word designating the band resident at Winatsh̉a, the fishery at the forks of the Wenatchee River (1911: 60, 160, fn. 4). These peoples were known to the Klikitat, Curtis reports, as the Winắtsh̉a-pŭm [wihátšapəm] (1911: 161).
>
> Summarizing an observation of Curtis, Spier adds: "The band at this place called themselves Sĭnpŭskqóisoh̉, whence the name Pisqouws [sic] of early writers" (1936: 14). This makes intelligible the statement of Gibbs that the "name of the Pisquouse [the Wenatchi term for themselves]...properly refers to a single locality on the Wenatchee river, known to the Yakimas as Winatshapam" (Spier, 1936: 14).

Although my Yakama informant considered the w*i*náčapem to be a separate and distinct tribe apart from the Yakama, he also remarked that they were "under the Yakima." This is a curious statement, unless he was thinking of post Walla Walla treaty council times, when U.S. government negotiators in 1855 had assigned the Wenatchi to the tutelage of Chief Kamiakin of the Yakama proper. However, the Wenatchi were a Salishan-speaking group, and clearly an independent and separate unit from the Plateau's Sahaptin speakers. Nevertheless, the Wenatchi at an earlier time apparently had claimed the lower Yakima valley and the adjacent Cascade foothills; consequently, the existence of mixed Yakama-Kittitas and Wenatchi groups on the Sahaptin-Salishan language border might be expected. The presence of just such groups is described later. However, what is difficult to explain is the apparent inclusion of the *wenatchi proper* within the political sphere of the Yakama, as my informant and some others would have it.

For example, in 1854 Gibbs wrote: "The Pisquouse [Wenatchi] themselves...are so much intermarried with the Yakimas that they have almost lost their nationality" (Spier, 1936: 14).

Furthermore, Hodge defined the Yakama as formerly being situated on both sides of the Columbia and on the northerly branches of the Yakima *and the Wenatchee* (1910: 983; italics mine).

In the present context, an odd and obscure note by Nisqually-Puyallup researcher Marian Smith also is of some interest. Under the rubric "Sahaptins," Smith stated:

> The term tai′dnapab referred to peoples, *of whom the Wenatchee were one*, who lived all along the eastern slope of the mountains, keeping close to the foothills. These were said to have reached as far south as Klickitat territory and their language was known to differ from that of the true tóbcadad [Kittitas, Yakama, and Klikitat] who lived farther east. (1940: 19; italics mine)

Evidently, Smith's west-side informants regarded the Wenatchi as Sahaptin in speech, unless she misunderstood their intent.

Finally, Mooney and Curtis advocated the joining of the Kittitas and Wenatchi into a single tribal unit.

> Mooney reported that the Kittitas "were chiefly of the Piskwaus [Wenatchi] connection" (Spier, 1936: 16). He specifically identified the Wenatchi bands as residing about the headwaters of the Yakima River, on the Yakima River in the vicinity of Ellensburg, and perhaps even in the Selah Creek area (Spier 1936: 15). These groups, however, are normally regarded as Kittitas.
>
> Curtis considered the Kittitas as being a band of the Wenatchi (Spier, 1936: 14). This same author also put the situation in reverse: "related to these [Wenatchi] bands were those of the upper Yakima river, beginning with the Kĭ́titasȟ [Kittitas], on Kittitas Creek" (Curtis, 1911).

Spier would explain these remarks concerning the relationship of the Yakama-Kittitas and Wenatchi as garbled confusions, probably applying not to the Wenatchi proper, but only to that group "at the southern extremity of their range" where intermarriage with Sahaptins had occurred (1936: 14). But, unless extreme confusion or even down-right errors of information are assumed, this assumption would seem not to explain satisfactorily all of the above.[2]

The Band

The truth of the matter seems to be: (a) the basic territorial unit was the small band; and (b), how these were united into groups of larger dimensions may well have varied from time to time, and may have even differed at any one time in the view of the different groups according to their particular criteria. This brings us to a consideration of the essential nature of the band.

In the first place, each band had a recognized geographical locus, the name of which it bore. As Curtis reports, each Yakama band regarded the Yakima valley, or some particular portion of it, or one of the small lateral streams, as its proper home. As a rule, this area was occupied only during the winter (1911: 4, 6).

Secondly, each band was a political unit, either wholly or essentially independent from all other bands.

> As long ago as 1857, Robie recognized the political independence of the Yakama groups, noting that they were "made up of a number of small bands or villages acknowledging the authority of one or more chiefs or principal men" (Spier, 1936: 16).
>
> Similarly, Curtis remarked that at the time of early white exploration, the Yakima River watershed from its mouth up to the vicinity of Kittitas Creek was occupied by small Sahaptin bands (1911: 3–4, 160). These bands were loosely bound together. However, several geographic divisions existed, each with a certain cohesiveness. The component bands of each division occupied their respective territories to the exclusion of the others, but all bands of a single division regarded themselves as closely related. The bands known as the Yakama to the Salishan groups to the north were located in the Yakima valley below Union Gap, "just east of the mouth of Ahtanum Creek." The term Yakama was extended early in the period of white contact to include all bands of the Yakima valley. In any event, each Yakama band had its own chief, though in several cases headmen are known to have extended their influence so as to politically control several adjacent and closely related bands.
>
> From his survey of the literature, Spier sensed the problem of whether the so-called Yakama (i.e., the *median* definition group) really formed a single tribal unit. He summarizes the situation thus: "It is questionable whether the groups denominated Yakima and Klikitat are to be considered single political entities, 'tribes.' They seem rather to have been loose aggregations of bands of somewhat

> diverse origin which have come to be called by these group names.... Still, we can do no better at the moment than to map these larger groups, leaving a more strict presentation of tribal and band divisions to future field ethnologists" (Spier, 1936: 16).

Conclusion

It might seem arbitrary to speak at all of there being a "Yakama tribe" given the following two observations: (a) no political units above the band level (or at least no "stable" long-term units of greater magnitude) seem to have existed in the region; and (b) no sharp linguistic and cultural breaks appear to have prevailed, even between Sahaptins and Salishans, to create recognizable tribal entities on a non-political basis. However, a "Yakama" tribe has in fact been recognized for some time.

What is more, evidence exists to indicate some feeling of special affinity among the several bands classified here as *minimum*-definition Yakama, and perhaps even among those which comprise the *median* definition of Yakama. Curtis, for instance, records the native view that hunting and collecting territories were the common property of several bands (1911: 160). Rather than debating the issue further—in the absence of additional data, it appears to be unresolvable—we shall simply assume the existence of some as yet imperfectly defined bonds between the bands, and adopt the convenience of identifying a "Yakama" tribe at the conventional *median* definition level. This at least has the virtue of consistency with the common, present-day usage of the term "Yakama."

In the present context, the significance of this somewhat complex state of affairs—in which both the "Yakama" and "Klikitat" have been defined in different ways—is evident in regard to a study of Mount Rainier National Park. If it can be demonstrated that people from the eastern flanks of the Cascades journeyed west into the national park, the only precise way of identifying the groups involved would be by band unit.

In theory, of course, band identification in these cases could be ascertained by knowing where their winter villages were situated in the Yakima, Naches, Kittitas, or even Wenatchee localities. But unfortunately such precise information ordinarily cannot be achieved—neither my informant data nor the literature search normally provided such identifications. It can only be postulated that if the "Yakama" are designated as having utilized the national park's resources, it might be likely that the band or bands closest to the park boundaries were those primarily involved, specifically perhaps the Naches.

(3) Autonomy of the Coast Village or Village Cluster

The Puget Sound village normally was politically autonomous. At most, as Marian Smith reported, the personal character of a leading man in a village might exert a loose and temporary influence over a neighboring community or a few other villages (1940: 6).

> Curtis earlier spoke to this point in general when he wrote: "A host of small bands of Salish Indians inhabited the country surrounding Puget sound, its islands, and the valleys of its tributary streams.... All spoke variations of what is known as the Nisqually dialect..., yet in spite of the close linguistic, geographical, and cultural relationship there were no political ties among them" (1913: 14).
>
> Curtis, however, also presented a more precise observation, noting that these small independent Coast Salish communities would cooperate together so far as necessary in time of war and subsistence efforts, or as "social instinct" demanded (1913: 67).
>
> In reviewing the status of political bonds among the Puget Sound Salish, Marian Smith noted their lack of a "formal paraphernalia of political organization," and to the absence of "any political institution which might have nourished...[the concept of the geographical drainage system] into a hierarchic, territorial union." She concluded that the "amount of actual unity achieved by the people of the Puget Sound drainage was negligible" (1940: 3–6).

Conclusion

Clearly, tribal classification in a larger political sense did not apply to the southern Puget Sound Salish. As with the Yakama, a proper identification of the Coast Salishan groups residing adjacent to the national park vicinity and making use of its resources would be by village unit; this was the largest geographical and political entity traditionally recognized.

Beyond this point, however, the situation is more complex than even in the Yakama case. When ethnographers have categorized coastal villages into larger entities, the results have differed widely according to the principles followed and the data applied. But these different formulations may, in fact, reflect a native view that villages should be clustered differently according to the nature of the criteria applied—consequently, a particular "tribal" designation may be applicable to a few adjacent villages, or to a different

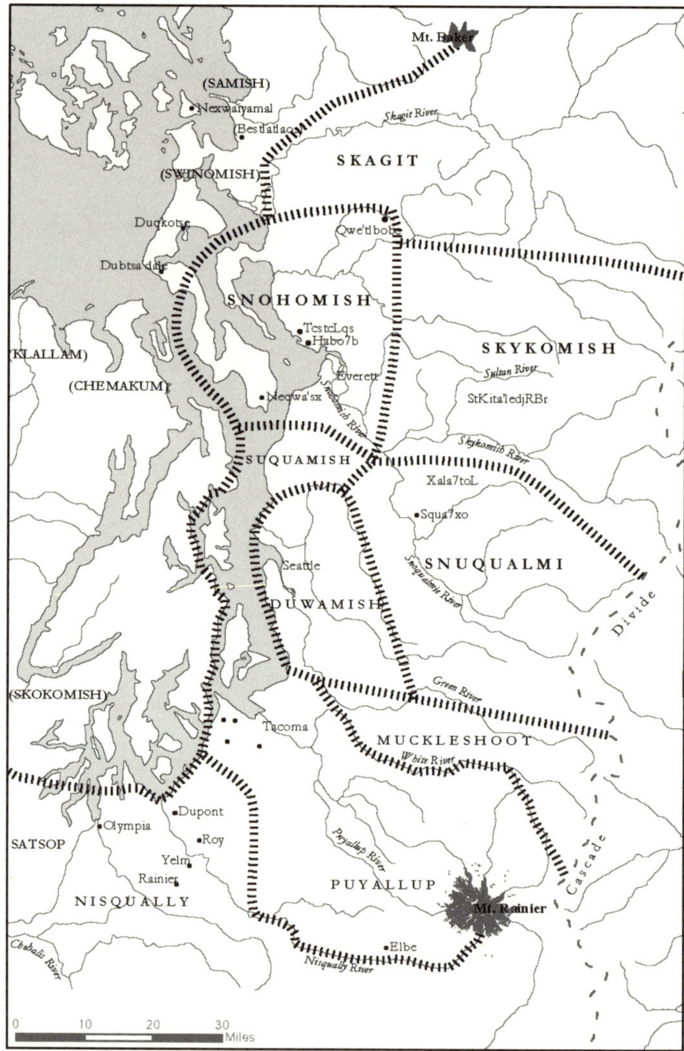

Figure 3.1. Distribution of Puget Sound tribes (after Haeberlin and Gunther, 1930). Here, Mount Rainier is assigned entirely to the Puyallup, save possibly for the southeast face.

arrangement of communities, or even to much larger clusters of settlements. In short, it is not always obvious which precise village or group of communities is referred to under a "tribal" term.

Although data is lacking for the small "Sahaptin" villages located west of the Cascade Divide—such as the Taidnapam on the upper Cowlitz River—presumably they followed either a band organization like the Yakama, or the independent village principle of the Coast Salish. In any event, they may be presumed to have possessed no more of a complex social unit than that of the groups surrounding them.

(4) The Concept of Boundary in Mountainous Areas

Agreement was found among my informants on these two points: (a) tribal limits corresponded to the crests of mountain ranges; and (b) these delineations in the deep mountains were considered more theoretical than a matter normally of serious concern. In practical terms, they regarded mountain boundaries as merely a reflection of the fact that a group could more or less effectively exploit the natural resources of those slopes that faced toward their tribal villages or localities, but not those mountain fronts that faced away from their settlement areas. Thus, rights to exploit natural resources on the mountain flanks basically belonged to those groups that resided down-slope from them.

A Nisqually informant, for example, placed the boundary between Nisqually and Yakama territory at the top of Mount Rainier—hence with the western flanks being exploitable by the Nisqually, and the eastern slopes by the Yakama. My Muckleshoot informants saw no clear and definite border between their country and that of the Yakama; the territorial boundaries were not an issue of great concern. The literature search generally supported these views.

If tribal people in earlier times had adhered to more rigorous boundary definitions and stronger proprietary attitudes, the informants claimed to know nothing about this. Perhaps, the opinions of my informants were slightly more relaxed than those of earlier tribal peoples as recorded in the literature.

Yakama

Clearly, the various Yakama bands shared hunting and gathering grounds within Yakama territory. Curtis avers that each of the cognate bands of the Yakama was master of the locality where its winter camp was made, but possessed a right to use common tribal grounds for hunting and fishing, and for gathering berries and roots (1911: 160).

Figure 3.2. Territory of the Yakama and neighboring Plateau tribes (Ray, 1936).

Considering the Yakama area as a whole, however, traditionally the tribe might have possessed a somewhat stronger feeling of ownership toward their territory than perhaps my informants' testimony would indicate.

> According to Ray: "Proceeding [east] from the Umatilla to the Yakima and Wanapam and thence to the Columbia a gradual diminution in tribal emphasis is observed, with complete disappearance for some distance [east] beyond that point. Illuminating is the former

> Yakima feeling of responsibility for the safety of any member of another group while he remained within Yakima territory. When the visitor was ready to leave he was given safe convoy to the Yakima boundary, Satus Pass, for example, beyond which he was upon his own responsibility. Also, scouts were stationed at many strategic points, in the interests of the group as a whole" (Ray, 1936: 115).
>
> Ray further observed: "The hunting territory of one [Plateau] group might be quite open to use by another even though the bounds be highly specific. This freedom of use was the rule among many of the Salish groups. But among the Yakima, for example, outsiders were required to obtain formal permission from a chief before hunting grounds might be used and even then the length of time was definitely limited" (1936: 119–20).

But this appears to be less of a contradiction to my informants' position than it would first appear.

> Ray adds: "far back in hunting territory or far out in desert root digging grounds, boundaries sometimes completely faded out" (1936: 117). Furthermore, Ray made no attempt to make a demarcation of the Yakama-Klikitat border on the upper course of the Klickitat River. Even his boundary between the Yakama and Kittitas in the Cascade foothills is left somewhat shadowy (see Fig. 3.2).

Puget Sound Tribes

Information available for the groups west of the Cascade Divide generally supports my informants' views. West of the mountains, however, land-rights considerations are seemingly complex, and can evidently be best understood by introducing a zone concept into the discussion. Three zones running roughly parallel to Puget Sound on the west and the Cascades to the east—(a) coastal, (b) interior, and (c) mountain[3]—may be recognized on the basis of the documentary material

In the "coastal" unit, where natural resources often were highly localized, a lively concept of territorial possession prevailed. In the "interior" unit (b), between zones (a) and (c), the notion of land ownership seems to have been little developed. However, in the "mountain" zone (c), comprising the western slopes of the Cascades, a stronger consciousness of territorial use could prevail. This feeling of ownership, perhaps, was not so much due to the economic resources available in the area, but was a reaction to the nearby presence of Sahaptin groups east of the Cascade Divide. The following data extracted from the literature can be understood in its apparent contradictions by reference to this zonal concept.

> In regard to the Puget Sound groups as a whole, Marian Smith states: "Movements were not restricted because of land ownership: the main considerations which determined them were always (a) convenience and (b) the state of feeling, whether friendly or inimical, which existed between travelers and the persons they might expect to encounter. However numerous other causes for disagreement were, there were no quarrels over land" (1940: 24).
>
> And again Smith generalizes: "boundaries in this and adjacent areas are arbitrary," and "divisions overland, between groups cross-country from each other, were seldom...marked [as they sometimes were along the sea coast by rocks, islands, etc.], there being little or no interest in land boundaries of this sort" (1941: 197–98).

Clearly in the two preceding statements, Smith speaks of conditions that prevailed in the intermediate or "interior" zone (b). (Even here, however, at least a loose and oblique concept of territoriality was held by Puget Sound groups, in the sense that the villages along a single major stream drainage were thought to be combined together in a supra-group unit of an unstructured sort. What underlay this notion is not clear, but it may well have been due to a realization of a commonality of interest, and also was a reflection of a higher rate of inter-village social contacts than would occur between villages of different drainages.)

For the villages in the "mountain" zone (c), which consisted, so far as the Nisqually and Puyallup were concerned, of five up-river communities that Smith designates as 9–11 and 25–26 in Fig. 3.6, a somewhat different situation prevailed than in the "interior" zone.

> Smith describes the situation as follows: "the extreme easterly, up-river groups...had a rather definite idea of what may well be called 'hunting territories.'" These "large land units...were aggregates of smaller units hunted over by family groups" (1940: 24–25).

The fact that people in the "mountain" strip felt more strongly about territorial ownership than in the "interior" zone is explained by Smith as due to the influence of Sahaptin neighbors east of the Cascades (1940: 25). This explanation seems logical.

Although it cannot be demonstrated with the data at hand, it may be supposed that a similar situation prevailed among the Muckleshoot, a major portion of whose territory lay within the "mountain" zone. For some reason, it evidently also existed among the Snohomish, even though their territory failed to extend eastward beyond the Cascades foothills.

> Speaking of the Snohomish specifically, Haeberlin and Gunther reported: "In summer...[they] left their large winter houses to go hunting and fishing. They did not leave their own lands, unless they had friends or relatives elsewhere. Although there were no sharp dividing lines between the territory of neighboring tribes, it was taken for granted that a person straying too far into the country of another tribe was looking for trouble" (1930: 10).
>
> On another occasion, when referring to all Puget Sound groups, Haeberlin and Gunther stated the situation slightly differently: "Fishing, hunting and berry picking grounds were tribal property. One tribe could ask permission to use the territory of another, a favor which was rarely refused. If, however, a tribe used the territory of another tribe without asking permission, the act was regarded as an invasion and war might follow" (1930: 12).

It seems apparent that a zone concept as I described above introduces a certain measure of consistency and reason into the otherwise somewhat contradictory data from Marian Smith and from Haeberlin and Gunther. How may it be brought into harmony with the statements of my Puget Sound informants? Evidently these latter were expressing mostly an "interior" zone attitude in the matter of territorial possession. At any rate, it is the concept of upstream villages controlling the upper reaches of the rivers taking their source in the Mount Rainier area that is most important in the present connection. However, the ethnographic and literature data does not permit the drawing of sharp "tribal" limits in the eastern, upriver segments of these coastal "tribal" territories.

The attitude of the Taidnapam may be assumed to have been similar to that of the upper Nisqually and Puyallup villages, since their geographic position was in the "mountain" zone. The eastern Sahaptin influence among them presumably would have been at least as strong as with the uppermost Nisqually and Puyallup.

In one aspect regarding territorial concepts, the upriver-most Puget Sound villages described by Smith seem genuinely peculiar—the territory over which they together hunted "was divided into tracts lying *between* the rivers" (1940: 24; italics mine). For example, the two southerly Puyallup River villages (nos. 9–10 in Fig. 3.6) claimed the area "between the Carbon and the Nisqually." This appears to mean that "tribal" territory here basically extended from river to river, not from the drainage crests. This interpretation seems to contradict Smith's general insistence that hill and mountain crests marked "tribal" limits among Puget Sound groups, and of Kroeber's comment to the same point that Smith cited with approval. However, it agrees, Smith points out (1940: 24, fn. 1), with Haeberlin and Gunther's mapping of the area (see Fig. 3.1). On the other hand, Smith seems to make some subtle distinction between "hunting territory" and "tribal territory" limits, as though the former would not necessarily coincide with the latter where the outer borders of an area claimed by a "tribal" group are considered.

Conclusion

The data leads to these conclusions. Since the Mount Rainier area is notably mountainous, it is expected that, if the Yakama claimed any part of it, their borders would be difficult to define with precision. On the other hand, the fact that the coastal groups had a somewhat greater definiteness may be anticipated, inasmuch as a number of their villages were situated in the "mountain" zone. And finally, where Coast and Plateau groups possessed a common border, this likely would have been more defined in the minds of the Coast people than in the view of the Yakama.

(5) The Joint Exploitation of Mountainous Terrain

It has been observed that some authors have reported a relatively clear concept of tribal territory, territorial ownership, and exclusive use-right in geographical areas neighboring Mount Rainier. However, so far as mountain berry grounds and, by implication, mountainous hunting areas were concerned, my informants were unanimous in their assertion that in actual fact these places were free for all to use.

The Yakama informants often insisted that members of several tribes were to be found jointly harvesting and drying berries in one area, and these intertribal contacts were cordial, all the more because of intertribal marriages. To the same point is the Nisqually statement that Potato Hill (just beyond the extreme northeast Skamania County border in sec. 24, T. 10 N., R. 10 E.) was in Yakama country, but the Yakama allowed any Indians to harvest berries there who wished to. Similarly, in the view of Satanus (a Taidnapam), the Taidnapam and Yakama were free to enter each other's territory.

Rhoda Yellowwash (a Yakama) mentioned a pertinent incident in this regard. One year when berries failed to appear in the Mount Adams area where her family customarily secured their supply, she went instead with her mother and sister to the "Gold Hill" berry patch to pick blueberries and huckleberries, and they remained there for some weeks. She said they were on the Cowlitz River (Yakama: qau*il*ʹc), close to a traditional salmon-fishing place, which she believed was in Taidnapam country. (Presumably, this locality is not the Gold Hill located on the upper American River, a tributary of the Bumping River that in turn flows into the Naches River. On quadrangle maps, however, I was unable to locate a "Gold" Hill in the upper Cowlitz drainage, though there is a "Coal" Creek Mountain. This would have been in Taidnapam territory.)

> Marian Smith, however, reported something less than a peaceful, sharing interaction. She claimed that "alien threats to the Puyallup-Nisqually came…over land from the east." And she mentioned that these tribes held the Sahaptins in some fear (1940: 151).
>
> In regard to Curtis, on the other hand, he reported that the Yakama had been at peace with all tribes within the memory of the oldest men (1911: 14). The only tradition of warfare is a doubtful one telling of ancient hostilities with the Nez Perce for the purpose of obtaining slaves.

Likewise indicative of peaceful interaction was the Nisqually avowal that the Bear Prairie vicinity berry grounds were situated in Nisqually territory, but that "lots of Coast Indians used to pick there." However, according to the Nisqually informant, the Yakama never came over to the west side of Mount Rainier for hunting, berrying, or for other reasons; nor did the Nisqually ever visit the eastern slopes of Mount Rainier. The top of the mountain was considered the boundary between the territories of these two groups. However, this clearly might be due to the significant traveling distances involved and the difficult mountainous terrain that lay as a barrier between the territories of the two tribes.

The Muckleshoot informants, on the other hand, held that no sharp line existed to demarcate a boundary between their country and that of the Yakama: both used the mountains between their territories. Similarly, the Yakama reported that they were free to visit the Taidnapam country to fish for salmon; no permission had to be secured. Mary Kiona (a Taidnapam) confirmed that the Yakama came over to Taidnapam country to fish.

Some data exists in the literature bearing on these observations.

> Although Curtis avers that there was "constant internal strife (rather thieving and assassination than war) among the Puget Sound Indians" (1913: 14), he also reported that the Nisqually plains at the head of Puget Sound furnished the chief supply of acorns for the Sound tribes (Curtis, 1913: 58). Since these nuts were a highly regarded food, "thither in the fall came canoes from all points on the neighboring waters and even from the Strait of Juan de Fuca." The Nisqually plains are at some distance from Mount Rainier National Park, but the example does testify to the positive attitudes of Sound tribes toward sharing natural resources in abundant supply.

Other information gained by Marian Smith regarding the Puget Sound groups seems somewhat internally inconsistent in certain details. Its general import appears to be as follows (1940: 25–26):

> The villagers who lived along the coast or at least away from the mountains allowed free use of their hunting lands and berry grounds to other villagers. On the contrary, however, each upriver village held its individual hunting territory for itself so far as the members of other *upriver* communities were concerned.[4]
>
> But in contrast, according to Smith, these same upstream villages "shared their berry picking, etc., grounds in exactly the same fashion as other friendly villages of the area,"—i.e., apparently, welcoming all comers. She adds: "Expeditions for vegetable products...were undertaken regularly in summer and by large groups from several villages" (1940: 26). If this latter interpretation of Smith's data is correct, it generally agrees with the evidence from my informants.
>
> However, Smith pertinently added: "Berry and root patches frequently lay on high spots inland from the river beds and for the peoples of these valleys contacts at such locations were...sporadic" (1940: 26).

Movement specifically from the Plateau into Coastal territory in the national park area is explicitly attested to by Jacobs: "natives traveled into and across the mountains each year to hunt and collect berries" (1937).

Haeberlin recites a traditional myth-narrative that is suggestive regarding tribal land access (1924: 417–18). The story was told by Henry Sicade, a Nisqually (see also Haeberlin and Gunther, 1930: 43). It involved two mythical brothers, Enumclaw and Kapoonis:

> The brothers "lived somewhere to the east of the present town of Enumclaw." They "were great hunters and traveled far and were often gone for many month," hunting and seeking guardian spirits. Sometimes Kapoonis "took long trips alone. At the head of the Cowlitz River he took baths every day at dawn and at dusk and in this way he finally acquired a great fire spirit....In friendly rivalry the brothers sat on the rocky ridge to the south of Tacoma [Mount Rainier] facing the setting sun, and they agreed to test their powers. Enumclaw pointing to a great white rock across the ravine, offered to throw stones to the left of the rock...with such force that the ridge would tumble down.
>
> "Kapoonis agreed to do likewise, throwing to the right of the rock. The contest raged with such terrific force that in a short time only a sharp rock stood high in the air where the ridge had been. This rock is known now as Saw Tooth Rock and stands somewhere to the south...of Longmire's Spring."[5]

The pertinent points here are that the mythical brothers "lived somewhere to the east of" Enumclaw, which surely must refer to the White River valley, and hence they were from traditional *Muckleshoot* territory. Kapoonis, however, journeys to *Taidnapam* country at the "head of the Cowlitz river," evidently the Ohanapecosh River, or possibly Chinook Creek, a tributary of the Ohanapecosh. Granted, caution must be exercised in extrapolating from a myth, but it is interesting that no issue is made of the brothers traveling into the territory of another group, and there is no intimation that any hostility might be incurred on such a journey.

The same point can be made regarding the area around "Saw Tooth Rock...south...of Longmire's Springs." Perhaps this is High Rock, on Sawtooth Ridge, 6-1/4 miles southwest of Longmire. High Rock stands just south of the upper reaches of the Nisqually River in T. 14 N., R. 7 E. This would be in *Nisqually* country. In fact, irrespective of the precise location of "Saw Tooth Rock," this area is Nisqually territory in any case.

Conclusion

Hence, to draw sharp boundaries regarding tribal limits would be in a sense arbitrary, if thought of in terms of contemporary political borders. If it is understood, however, that the borders represent in some part merely the limits of a use-area—with some uncontested overlapping in those districts convenient to two or more tribes, and with other parts in the depths of the mountains little used by any tribe—then boundaries serve the purpose of indicating at least the tribe that made the more frequent incursion into an area. Based upon the general informant data, the tribal bounds within the national park may be estimated as indicated in Figure 3.4.

(6) Intertribal Marriage

Intermarriage between tribal groups in the Pacific Northwest was common. This raises the question as to what extent intermarriage was a custom among those groups holding territorial claims to the national park area, and the degree to which this practice affected the delineation of tribal boundaries.

> Speaking in general terms, Marian Smith stated that on Puget Sound, "every effort was expended to increase…marriage with distant villages." This was desirable because it extended the kin group and allowed persons to move more widely with safety. "Wanderers, however far afield and for whatever purpose, sought out groups in which they could claim relationship and the trail or direction they took was usually dictated by that possibility" (1940: 32–33, 166).
>
> Haeberlin and Gunther speak to this same general point. They aver that every Salish community on Puget Sound was to a considerable extent heterogeneous owing to the practice of tribal exogamy and patrilocal residence (1930: 7).

The specific question about the affects of intertribal marriage on tribal relations may be examined conveniently in terms of the following four intermarriage possibilities—Puget Sound to Plateau, Plateau to Puget Sound, Intra-Plateau, and Intra-Coastal.

Puget Sound to Plateau

No evidence (either from the informants or the literature) is available to demonstrate that Puget Sound persons in any "considerable" numbers intermarried and resided with Plateau bands east of the Cascades. Evidently it occurred to some slight extent, however, at least for women.

> This is indicated by an observation from Marian Smith: "the data carry no single instance of a male from the Sound moving permanently into Sahaptin groups. Women did, but not men" (1940: 23).

Plateau to Puget Sound

On the other hand, there is considerable information attesting to Plateau persons marrying into Puget Sound groups. It is clear that along the western flank of the Cascades, where Sahaptin and Salish bands frequently interacted, the population often was highly mixed.

> In connection with his linguistic studies, Jacobs gave some attention to this question: "Arthur C. Ballard...told me that he thought there were some small Sahaptin speaking bands, or at least rather numerous speakers of Sahaptin, living in several river valleys immediately west of the Cascades and north of the upper Nisqually mica'l [Meshal] tribe. In the lack of a single field or historic note from such unidentified and problematic persons, it may be suggested that if they do exist as persons or as independent groups we may expect to find them speaking dialects akin to mica'l...; the report of their existence may be interpreted as evidence of numerous Sahaptin speaking persons resident in Coast Salish upriver villages; the upper Nisqually mica'l themselves...give evidence of substantial and recent drifts of Sahaptin (pcwa'nwapam) speech from east of the Cascades into the timbered Salish speaking country west of the Cascades. The Sahaptins of the wooded western Cascades river valleys, whether they be eastern Nisqually, eastern Cowlitz or Lewis river residents, are not modern representatives of spectacular mass incursions or migrations into Salish territory. It is probably that generations of quiet friendship, intercourse and intermarriage of Coast Salish speakers and Sahaptin speakers effected a gradual northwest Sahaptin advance. The Sahaptins of the eastern slopes of the Washington Cascades, the Yakima and pcwa'nwapam [Kittitas], were wont to seek mates among their Coast Salish friends beyond the Cascades passes; the entire Sahaptin advance may have been caused by such a slow infusion. It is possible that much of the blood and culture of the Upper Nisqually, upper Cowlitz and other coastal up-river bands continued to possess a large Coast Salish content, while speech boundaries moved westwards and northwards imperceptibly, at Salish expense. Certainly neither Coast Salish nor Sahaptin natives themselves mention, in narrative or myth, a movement of Sahaptins; they have no appreciation of such an advance, though we are obliged to postulate it" (1931: 95–96).

Jacobs made the same points in a later publication:

> "The frontiers of interior, eastern or up-stream dialects advanced at the expense of the frontiers of coastal, western or downstream dialects. Paradoxically, economically less favored communities seem to have expanded the area of their speech at the expense of the area of more favored communities.... There must have occurred gradual changes in the percentages of speakers of one or another language in smaller bilingual upriver border villages; in a bilingual border village the percentage of upriver dialect speakers increased, the percentage of lower river dialect speakers diminished. The changing percentages reflect the greater attractiveness of certain locations and the large numbers moving in such directions.... At the heads of several Salish speaking rivers in Washington may be found smaller bilingual villages, some of whose speakers are Sahaptin. Along the same and other rivers the small headwater villages are largely or completely Sahaptin in speech; this appears on the Upper Nisqually Meshal Creek, on the Upper Cowlitz and probably on the Upper Lewis."

In sum, Jacobs observed:

> "Speech drifts were mainly [through intermarriage and] in the directions of wealthier or more attractive communities via the more thinly-populated river highways.... When a more attractive community lay far across a mountain trail no particular concern would be felt because the natives traveled into and across the mountains each year to hunt and collect berries; they were already familiar with the route. The mountains provided less barrier to speech drifts than did populous waterways" (1937: 55, 57, 70, 73–74).

The linguistic data led Jacobs to suspect that even in pre-Taidnapam and pre-Meshal days, intermarriage occurred between east-Cascades groups of what was later the Yakama-Kittitas area and west-Cascades tribes in the recent Taidnapam and Meshal territories.

> Jacobs suggested that a gradual population movement by intermarriage "westward over passes of the Cascades into the [more attractive] Coast Salish Upper Nisqually and Upper Cowlitz villages" explains best an anomalous Interior Salish linguistic trait in the Coast Salish language of the Lower Cowlitz. He concludes that "an especially long stream like the Cowlitz, more thinly populated

> along its extensive upper reaches than other Coast Salish speaking rivers, might be somewhat more receptive to advancing speech drifts than shorter and more densely populated rivers; other Washington streams flowing from the western slopes of the Cascades are shorter than the Cowlitz and have no long thin line of lightly populated upriver house clusters. The upper Cowlitz was at once the most isolated Coast Salish stream of Western Washington and the territory most exposed to speech drifts due to numbers of intermarriages from peoples living east of the Cascades. The interior trait of speech that gained ground first in upriver Cowlitz homes spread down the river for the usual reasons, until all of the Cowlitz had the interior trait; later, when Sahaptin speech occupied the Yakima-Kittitas region, the process of diffusion continued until at the time of the end of native history a fair fraction of the Cowlitz had become Sahaptin in speech" (1937: 72–73).

My own field findings and other specific statements in the literature concerning individual tribal entities offer at least partial confirmation of Jacobs' hypothesis. Marian Smith, too, secured evidence indicating that "for several generations at least, [there has been] a constant trickle of Sahaptins into the Sound country, an infiltration accomplished by intermarriage rather than by any group migration" (1940: 21–23, 151).

Both men and women from Sahaptin groups married into Coast groups and took up residence among them. The more interior of these groups apparently were proud of their east-of-the-mountains connections. The Sahaptin thrust westward over the Cascades occurred not only into the upper Nisqually, where Jacobs locates the Meshal Sahaptins, but also both north and south of this valley. North of the Nisqually drainage, the Sahaptin incursion into the upper Puyallup watershed probably was in numbers even more significant than on the upper Nisqually.

> As Smith noted: "Down the length of the [Puyallup] river as far as Clarks Creek ([village no.] 6 [see Fig. 3.6]) there were family groups, which spoke only Sahaptin, although individuals of the down-river groups were apt, in addition, to understand Salish. In the extreme up-river Puyallup villages (9–11) the proportion of Sahaptins was fully as great as among the bacálabc on the upper Nisqually. The attitude of the Salish toward the newcomers was one of complete acceptance...the process did not violate the accepted pattern of inter-village marriages."

Moreover, Smith explained that there seemed reason to believe that Sahaptins also had extended west of the Cascades among the White River Muckleshoot and the Snuqualmi (1940: 23). A bit of evidence for the occurrence of some intermarriage between the Muckleshoot and Yakama, at least the Naches River group, is known to me. This is the statement by Ballard that Naches River descendants lived among the Green River people, who, according to my evidence, were Muckleshoot (Ballard, 1929: 147, 160 fn.). Smith also noted that Sahaptins resided in drainages to the south of the Nisqually valley.

> The Tenino (tanai′no), she reports, were a "Sahaptin or bilingual group living…in the foothills [on the Deschutes River or Skookumchuck River] somewhere between Bald Mountain and the present town of Tenino. They were closely connected with the Mashell Creek…group of Nisqually and probably also with the Upper Chehalis" (1940: 19, 21–22, fn. 2).
>
> Smith also made the interesting observation: "There are many cases remembered in foothills villages in which husband and wife could barely converse on the most simple subjects; children of such unions spoke either language, but seldom both" (1940: 22).
>
> There seemed, she observed, "to have been two streams of Sahaptin influence into the Puget Sound Area. One from the Yakima, which touched the upper Nisqually and through them the middle Puyallup. The other which came west from the Kittitas region in the neighborhood of Ellensberg [sic] and spread north and south to the Snoqualmie, the White River [Muckleshoot] and inland Puyallup peoples" (1940: 23).
>
> These influences were so great, Smith reports, that the Nisqually and Puyallup themselves recognized it, attributing many inter-village cultural differences, "whether correctly or not, to contacts with east of the mountain Sahaptins" (1940: 44).

Ballard records a purported inter-tribal marriage in one of his "Upper Puyallup" tales (1929: 85). In this account, when "Klickitats" come to the Nisqually River country to trade with the Puyallup, a woman of the latter tribe is said to have a Klikitat husband. Ballard's Klikitat tribal identification may be accurate, but in a footnote he remarked: "the Naches River people (naxtce′spam) [are] commonly called Klickitat" (1929: 147, 160 fn.). As already noted, however, the Naches are customarily regarded as Yakama, not Klikitat. It would appear more probable that a Yakama Naches would be involved in such a marriage arrangement rather than a true Klikitat. If this is the case, travel and contact through the Mount Rainier area, possibly via Chinook Pass, the Ohanapecosh valley, and the Nisqually River, can legitimately be postulated.

Ballard also recorded a mythical tale relating to Coyote in the Naches valley, narrated by a person identified as a "Yakima-Puyallup" (1929: 147–50). Furthermore, a Puyallup or Nisqually informant of Smith's reported having had a maternal grandfather who was half Yakama, and who lived much of his life among the Puget Sound Salish (1940: 202).

Likewise of further interest regarding the Sahaptin drift west of the Cascade Divide is the fact that, according to Teit, in "early times there was probably a little intermarriage between [the] Wenatchi and some of the Coast tribes, particularly the Snuqualmi" (1928: 110). The Snuqualmi, of course, occupied the territory immediately to the north of the Muckleshoot (see Fig. 3.1).

Quite possibly, this general intertribal marriage pattern in the western Cascades helps to explain why tribal bands that claimed the Mount Rainier area and its vicinity had allowed such free use of their territory. For the most part, it appears that the users from other tribes were related to them consanguineally or affinally. This kinship evidently permitted considerably more traffic through the mountain passes and the national park peripheries than otherwise might have been permissible. Had this relationship not prevailed, possibly the more rigorous definition of tribal territory, as described by some authors, might have been in effect even in this remote and rugged area.

Intra-Plateau

In view of the apparent gradual expansion of Sahaptins westward over the Cascades through intermarriage in recent times, it is of interest that the Yakama also intermarried with Sahaptin and Salishan groups to the north.

> Regarding the Yakama, Curtis noted: "in a great many cases one wife was from some neighboring tribe or band, for there was much intermarriage with kindred bands of Sahaptins, as well as with eastern Chinookans and Interior Salish bands above Priest Rapids on the Columbia" (1911: 9).
>
> Curtis also remarked that since early times, the Wenatchi, whose territory extended from the Wenatchee River to Lake Chelan, were on intimate terms with the Yakama bands and were much intermar-

> ried with them (1911: 60). As a result, many Sahaptin words were incorporated into their language. In fact, remnants of the Salishan bands on the upper Yakima River appear to have adopted the Sahaptin tongue.
>
> Likewise, Teit felt that at least some of the Yakama, especially those close to the mountains and in the northern part of Yakama territory, were somewhat mixed with the Wenatchi (1928: 95, 124).
>
> On another occasion, Teit went so far as to contend: "It seems that there was a great deal of inter-marriage at one time between the Wenatchi bands on the Yakima River and the Yakima. It is likely that part of the Wenatchi inhabitants of the Yakima were absorbed by the Yakima" (1928: 110).

This is interpreted as the result of relatively late Yakama diffusion into an area formerly occupied exclusively by the Salish-speaking Wenatchi.

Intra-Coastal

Intertribal marriages also occurred among the Puget Sound groups themselves, for the practical reasons delineated by Smith earlier in this section.

> In addition, Smith noted the Nisqually and Puyallup viewpoint that the "peoples of the entire Puget Sound drainage down to and including the Skagit River, plus the Skokomish, Chehalis, Upper Cowlitz and, possibly, Lower Cowlitz countries belonged to the same group. This was practically the same region over which marital relations spread. To it should also be added certain poorly defined groups of Sahaptin-speaking peoples near the Cascade range" (1940: 151).

No catalog of known cases of intermarriage between Puget Sound groups will be attempted here, but it might be added that Smith noted an instance in which a White River (Muckleshoot?) man married a Nisqually woman (1940: 67).

Conclusion

Intertribal marriage doubtlessly helped contribute to the blurring of tribal boundaries in areas. At the least, it reduced the tendency of a group to hold its tribal territory economically inviolate from members of at least some other bands.

(7) Tribal Boundary Changes Through Time

It finally is necessary to introduce diachronic considerations into this discussion. On the basis of the present evidence, two types of event sequences have resulted in boundary changes in the geographic area under discussion—intertribal marriage, and the actual migration of larger social groups. Both of these phenomena create difficulties in regard to clearly defining tribal boundaries in the Mount Rainier locality. Sometimes, it may be supposed, these two phenomena were even in operation together, the end result being due to their combined effects.

It is not difficult to comprehend how continual and extensive intermarriage between groups can in time measurably obscure tribal boundaries. But the effect can be even more pronounced than this. Where the flow of spouses is largely unidirectional between two tribes, it may, in fact, finally result in markedly altering the linguistic, cultural, and ethical orientation of the group receiving the spouses. In fact, tribal ties may even shift. Consciously or covertly, a group may simply disavow its earlier bonds and regard itself as an independent entity, or, alternatively, it may assimilate itself into the group whose language and cultural characteristics it has been gradually embracing.

Change by Intermarriage

The example of the Yakama themselves may well best illustrate the first of these alternatives—i.e., an intertribal marriage flow resulting in a changed tribal unit. On the basis of his informant data and the records of the Lewis and Clark Expedition, Teit suggested that the Yakama have not always occupied the homeland to which they now are affiliated.

> Teit reported that a distinct group of Wenatchi or possibly a subdivision of another band "lived south of the Wenatchi Mountains, on the north Yakima, with headquarters around Ellensburg or possibly lower down. This division is said to have been large at one time, and commanded the Snoqualmie, Yakima, and all the principal passes through the Cascades, including those to the Cowlitz country. Some of these people are said to have lived still farther south at one time, on other branches of the upper Yakima and the Klikitat River; but they intermarried so much with Yakima that they became absorbed by the latter. They may possibly have formed a division by themselves, and were probably the original inhabitants of the upper and central parts of the Yakima country" (1928: 95).

Jacobs similarly reported:

> "Southeastern Washington Sahaptins may have married into these [Salish] villages [in the mid-Columbia area] and also sometimes into even smaller villages west of the middle-Columbia...located along the attractive eastern foothill Cascades streams such as the Naches, Tieton and Yakima. The Kittitas and Yakima dialect regions of today may have been well sprinkled with Sahaptin speech, if not dominated entirely by Sahaptin, at a time when some Salish communities still survived along the middle-Columbia south of Ellensburg" (1937: 70, 72).

These observations make it clear that Jacobs sees an earlier Salish population occupying today's Yakima River country that was absorbed and superceded as Yakama. Jacobs, like Murdock and Ray, saw no evidence for an important trans-Columbia migration, nor even for a true migration of Sahaptins into the Yakama area.

The same situation may have been experienced by the Taidnapam, as is suggested by the data presented in the preceding section. Jacobs concludes that it was probably drift by intermarriage that brought the Sahaptins into the valleys west of the Cascade Range and Mount Rainier National Park (1937: 69, 71). Also, the Meshal apparently were experiencing a changing sequence at the time of first White contact. The Nisqually, to judge from my informant, still regard the Meshal as Nisqually, whereas, if Jacobs is correct, they may have thought of themselves in recent times as being separate and distinct from the Nisqually, and more closely aligned to the Sahaptins to the east of the Cascade Divide.

Change by Migration

Secondly, the actual movement of a population of significant size—a true migration—may plainly alter boundaries.

> Alternatively to the views of the Yakama presented above, Curtis regarded the various loosely-united Sahaptin bands of the Yakima watershed, from Kittitas Creek (in the Ellensburg area) to the Yakima River's confluence with the Columbia, as westerly extensions of Sahaptin speakers probably representing "many successive migratory movements from a former home on the Columbia River" (1911: 3).

> Teit also speaks of the Yakama moving across the Columbia River "into the mountains north of...[the river], whence they gradually moved into the central Yakima valley, and spread up and down that stream." Possibly they first settled in the "country south of Naches (Na′xtcEs)" (1928: 97–98, 101, 103, 106, 108). The area was at the time Wenatchi or Middle Columbia Salish country. Teit, in fact, noted that in the entire "upper Yakima country next to the mountains[,] places have both Yakima and Wenatchi names." Teit speculated that this movement "may have occurred about two hundred years ago," and that the western part of the area, "near the mountains west of Yakima," may have been still in Salish (i.e., Wenatchi) hands as late as 1830. The Lewis and Clark documents were believed to support this view.
>
> Spier accepted Teit's evidence, commenting that the Wenatchi "were in part forced northward from their holdings in the upper Yakima valley and the area to the south, and in part absorbed by the newcomers." From his review of the literature available at the time, Teit concluded: "It is not clear in how far the upper Yakima valley was Wenatchi territory during the early nineteenth century. If I read the source material rightly, this was then predominately Sahaptin country. It seems credible that there were Wenatchi still there in isolated families, or intermarried with Yakima-Klikitat, or speaking the language of these Sahaptins. I have accordingly drawn the southern Wenatchi boundary somewhat arbitrarily on the Wenatchee-Yakima divide" (1936: 14; for Spier's boundary, see Fig. 1.2).

Across the Cascade Divide, a similar mass change is reported to have taken place.

> Teit writes: "After the depopulation of the Cowlitz..., about 1829, large numbers of...[Klikitat] moved into the Cowlitz valley. It seems that the Cowlitz were the principal people with whom they traded in the west, and they were most friendly with them. About this time, or probably earlier, bands of Klickitat, possibly exploring for a new country and trading, and other bands of mixed Klickitat and Cowlitz bent on raiding and war, had begun to make excursions north, following the west side of the Cascades back of the more populous areas of the Coast tribes, going as far as the Mount Baker region.... They soon gave up the northern expeditions...those who

> remained west of the Cascades, in the Lewis and Cowlitz districts, made their headquarters around Silverdale [Silver Lake?], and became known as Tai′tnapam or Wanukt" (1928: 99).

Thus, Teit felt that the origin of the Taidnapam was due more to migration than intermarriage.

> However, Boas observed that Jacobs' field information failed to support the notion of a genuine migration into the Taidnapam country: "So far as their memory goes they [the Taidnapam] have been associated with the upper Cowlitz.... the 'upper Cowlitz' (Wanukt) are Sahaptin in language; although the old Cowlitz are undoubtedly Salish." Boas concluded: "I presume that the lack of a migration legend indicates that the people are descendants of the early Salish inhabitants who have changed their language" (in Teit, 1928: 99–100).

Of comparative interest is the report by Teit that a similar movement westward over the Cascades occurred slightly to the north of Mount Rainier.

> Teit contends: "a considerable number of interior people... crossed the Cascades and settled in the Snuqualmi country.... After intermarrying more or less with the Snuqualmi, and becoming to some extent incorporated with them, part (or the remnants) of these people...moved down and settled among the Snohomish about five or six generations ago.... The names of the seven head men...show these emigrants to have been interior Salish.... These people were probably Wenatchi" (1928: 108).

Conclusion

Whether the affinities of a band or village were altered through time by intertribal marriage or by true migration, it is apparent that the boundaries as they may be drawn for recent times are not necessarily those of an earlier period. And it is equally plain that, though archaeological evidence may be discovered in the national park areas assigned in this report to the Yakama, Taidnapam, Muckleshoot, or others, they may not surely be attributed to these groups if the artifacts are of any substantial antiquity.

Boundary Data

We may now examine more specifically the identity of those groups in the protohistoric and early posthistoric periods that claimed portions of the Mount Rainier locality, and also outline their use areas.

Yakama

Delineating the "western" limits of Yakama territory was one of the primary concerns in this study, consequently my Plateau informant and literature research mainly focused on this geographical part of the tribal area. According to Rhoda Yellowwash, both White Pass and Naches Pass were considered to be in Yakama country. She asserted that Yakama tule tipis were to be found "way up in these passes." Moreover, the Yakama frequented the eastern slopes of Mount Rainier without feeling that they were wandering beyond the borders of their country.

> The earliest record of tribal distributions in the Pacific Northwest known to me, Horatio Hale's 1841 map,[6] provides data that is not contradictory to this view (1846, 196–97). On the map, Mount Rainier is explicitly within Sahaptin territory. Hale divided this vicinity of the Cascade Range between two groups: the "Kawelits" to the west of the mountains, and the "Walawala" to the east. The former clearly are the "Cowlitz," and presumably the Upper Cowlitz (Taidnapam), since the Cowlitz proper, located further down the Cowlitz River, were non-Sahaptin in speech. According to Hale, the "Walawala" included the "Yakemas" on the Yakima River, "Peloos-es," "Wallawalla," and others (1846: 213).
>
> Precisely where the line fell between these two Sahaptin groups—i.e., the "Kawelits" and the "Walawala"—is not shown on the map. Hence it must be supposed in Hale's view that Mount Rainier was either on the extreme western edge of "Walawala" (i.e., evidently the Yakama specifically) country, or on the northeastern limits of "Kawelits" (Taidnapam) territory. No specific reference to Mount Rainier is made in Hale's descriptive material to clarify this situation.
>
> Jacobs, on the other hand, disagreed with a point of view that the Yakama's western border extended to the flanks of Mount Rainier (see Fig. 3.3). On his tribal distribution map, Jacobs plotted the northwest boundary for the Yakama well to the southeast of Mount

Rainier. Instead, he had the Kittitas (Pcwa′nwapam) claiming the eastern Cascade slopes east of Mount Rainier (1931: 94). It is not clear whether Jacobs himself secured field data bearing on tribal limits in this area, nor is there evidence that he specifically searched the literature for information on the subject. Perhaps his map is, therefore, diagrammatic and should not be interpreted as providing really useful information on Yakama tribal boundaries in the national park area.

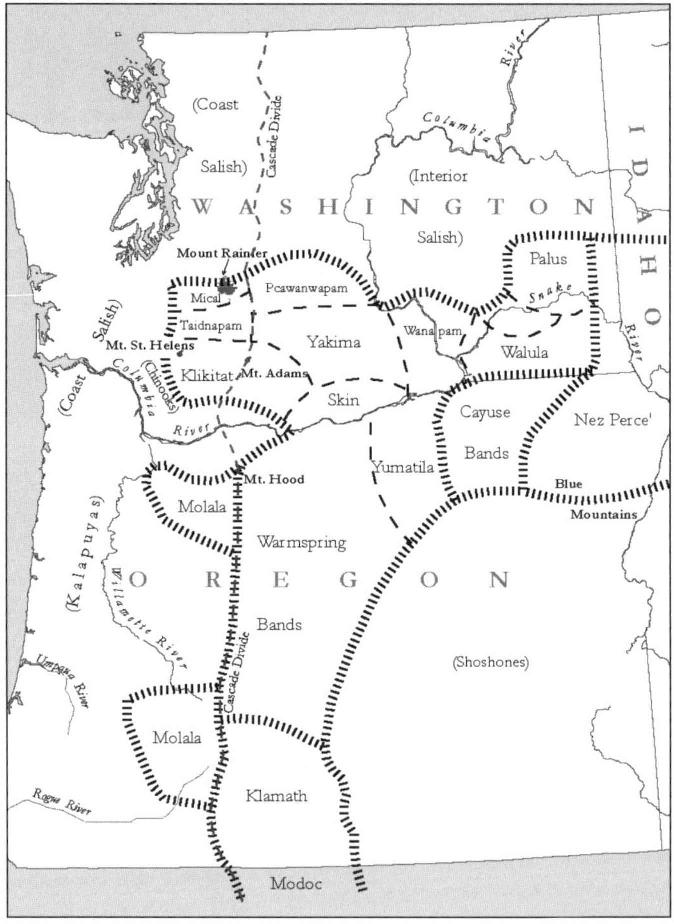

Figure 3.3. Territories of the Yakama, Kittitas (Pcwa′nwapam), Meshal (Mical), Taidnapam, and Klikitat in the mid-19th century (after Jacobs, 1931). Jacobs excluded the Yakama and Taidnapam from the Mount Rainier area, the southern slopes of which are assigned exclusively to the Meshal.

> Ray (see Fig. 3.2) marked the Yakama border at the Cascade Divide (along much of today's eastern park boundary), and thus plainly east of Mount Rainier. Other observations can be made regarding Ray's map. The northern boundary between the Yakama and Kittitas tribes lies along the Naches River-upper Yakima River divide, thus Ray designated the Naches River population as clearly being Yakama. The boundary between the Yakima and Klikitat to the southwest is along the Klickitat River from just below the mouth of White Creek northwest to the latitude of Mount Adams. Above this point, Ray did not attempt to demarcate a line between the Yakama and Klikitat (suggesting dual use of the eastern slopes of Mount Adams by both groups). And finally, Ray includes Mount Rainier National Park in "Coast Salish" territory (1936: 119). I would point out, however, according to Ray's field research, that only the Yakama of any Plateau group were in a position to make use of a part of the national park area.
>
> Spier reserved "the name Yakima for the Sahaptin bands occupying the greater part of the middle Yakima River and its tributary streams to the west...labeling those in the upper Yakima Valley" as Pcwa′nwapam (Kittitas) (1936: 16). As indicated by the list of Yakima bands enumerated by Spier and their individual territories, the courses of the Naches and Tieton rivers, which take their source in the Cascades east of Mount Rainier Park, fall within the area assigned by Spier to the Yakama (see Fig. 1.2). This means, if any tribe seated primarily to the east of the Cascades controlled any part of the national park area, it would be the Yakama. Unfortunately Spier did not specifically discuss the western borders of this tribe. His tribal distribution map, however, places the Yakama boundary along the Cascade Divide.

If the *median* definition of the Yakama is allowed, it may be concluded, primarily from the Ray and Spier data, that the western border of Yakama territory extended to at least the Cascade Divide, and, according to my informants, slightly beyond to include the eastern slopes of Mount Rainier. This locality clearly was distant from the Yakama's main population centers, therefore it seems probable that Verne Ray gave little or no specific attention to this boundary. Certainly the published data that was available to Leslie Spier did not include definitive statements regarding this matter, consequently Spier's view appears to be based on the general Plateau hypothesis that tribal limits coincided with mountain ridges wherever possible. On the other hand, my informant inquiry was directly explicit, and, while the number of sources were somewhat meager, it seemed to show an extension of Yakama territory west beyond the Cascade crest. Tentatively, the Yakama boundaries are shown in this position in Figure 3.4.

Of comparative interest are the Salishan Wenatchi to the north of the Yakama, who also occupied an eastern Cascades foothills country. The Wenatchi are reported by Teit to have held not only "all the country on the west side of the Columbia to the Cascades" but even to have claimed territory "a little beyond [the Cascades] in some places" (1928: 93). Hence, as a comparative case, it would appear that in the view of the Wenatchi, the

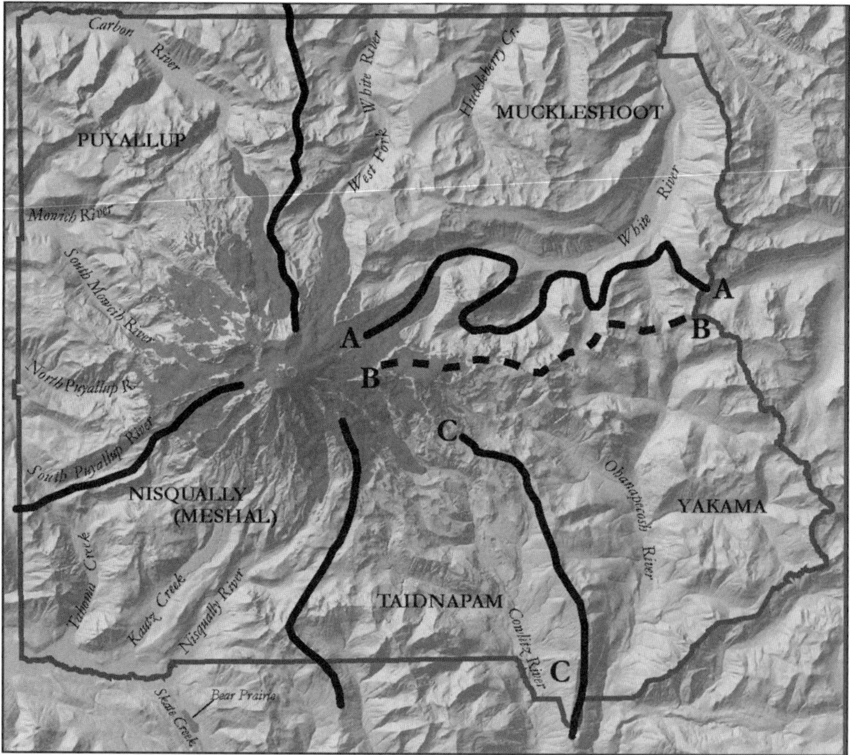

Figure 3.4. Tribal map of Mount Rainier National Park. Boundaries are close approximations based on my research and field data. The Ohanapecosh-White River divide (dashed line B-B) seems to have separated the Taidnapam country to the south from that of the Muckleshoot to the north, based on the evidence gathered for these two tribes. Nevertheless, the Yakama clearly made extensive use of the area between A-A and C-C, and claimed this as their own. Boundary A-A is especially indefinite and may well have actually fallen somewhat to the north of this position (base map: U.S.G.S. Mount Rainier Quadrangle).

Cascade Divide did not coincide with their tribal boundaries. Interestingly, no conspicuous mountain mass (such as Mount Rainier) stood as an attraction west of the Cascade crest, yet the Wenatchi crossed over to utilize resources in some parts of the westward flowing watersheds.

Taidnapam

My informants, Mary Kiona and Minnie Placid, indicated that the Taidnapam claimed the Tatoosh Range (Taidnapam: nq́ot) on the south central border of the national park and up to Mount Rainier itself. Furthermore, George Satanus averred that the boundary between the Taidnapam and Yakama in this area was on line with the summit of Mount Adams to the south. No statements, however, supporting this data have been found in the ethnographic literature.

> George Gibbs in 1854 considered the "Tai-tin-a-pam" to have been a band living apart "in the country lying on the western side of the mountains, between the heads of the" Cowlitz River and the north fork of the Lewis River near Mount Adams (Spier, 1936: 26).
>
> Similarly, Curtis regarded the Taítnapŭm [taítnapam] as a small tribe, cognate to the Klikitat but distinct from them, that occupied the head of the Lewis River (1911: 37). Curtis noted that the Yakama called them the "taítnapam" (1911: 160). As Spier remarks, however, there is a suspicion that Curtis is here merely following Gibbs (Spier, 1936: 26). In any event, both Gibbs and Curtis locate the Taidnapam somewhat further south than my data indicates, and basically beyond the southern limits of Mount Rainier National Park.
>
> Jacobs, too, assigned the upper Cowlitz River to the Taidnapam, whom he described as an independent band of fair size (1931: 95). However, his rather diagrammatic map terminates their country before it reaches the headwaters of the Cowlitz system, thus excluding the group entirely from the national park area (see Fig. 3.3).
>
> Spier followed Jacobs in assigning the upper Cowlitz drainage alone to the Taidnapam (1936: 26). But his tribal distribution map, in contrast to Jacobs', extends this tribe's country up into the southeast corner of the national park (see Fig. 1.2).
>
> On the basis of her field data from Nisqually-Puyallup informants and perhaps the published literature, Marian Smith did not consider the Taidnapam as a distinct and separate group; she apparently assigned their area to the Klikitat. She defined this latter group

> as the "Sahaptin-speaking people of the country of the headwaters of the Cowlitz and Yakima rivers and of the Klickitat River" (1949: 344). Thus she obviously sees the southern portion of the national park as falling within Klikitat territory, instead of being Taidnapam country, or even as Yakama territory, or as a dual-use Taidnapam-Yakama area on the southeast (as my survey indicated was actually the case).

In connection with this Taidnapam question, it is of interest to examine the example of Sluiskin, an Indian guide who led Hazard Stevens and P.B. Van Trump up to the slopes of Mount Rainier in August 1870. The latter two then made the first confirmed full ascent of Mount Rainier, using recently developed European Alps style climbing equipment (Stevens, 1916: 108–30).

The excursion began when James Longmire, an early explorer of the Mount Rainier area, guided Stevens and Van Trump (Puget Sound residents) and E.T. Coleman (an experienced British climber from Victoria) from Yelm Prairie up the Nisqually River. When reaching the Horse Creek vicinity, several miles past today's Nisqually park entrance, Longmire led the party on an Indian trail into the uplands away from the Nisqually River. They proceeded a few miles southeast to camp in Bear Prairie, a sizeable opening in the burned over forest. From there, seeking an Indian guide, Longmire and Stevens continued southeast down Skate Creek to a Taidnapam village site on the Cowlitz River, near present-day Packwood. (The 17 or 18 mile-long Bear Prairie-Skate Creek trail was an important route between Meshal-Nisqually territory on the upper Nisqually and the Taidnapam's country on the upper Cowlitz. It was an easier route in comparison to proceeding through the heavily timbered hilly terrain on either side.)

On the Cowlitz, however, Longmire and Stevens found only a solitary family camped there at that time (i.e., Sluiskin's), but they were hospitably received. After securing Sluiskin's services and making arrangements for him to shortly join the climbers back at Bear Prairie, Stevens and Longmire returned up the Skate Creek trail to the meadow encampment. As previously agreed upon, Longmire's services were ended and he returned toward his Yelm Prairie ranch.

After Sluiskin arrived, they set out. He guided the climbers up "the almost perpendicular height immediately back or east" of Bear Prairie. After reaching the top of this steep forested terrain in the Lookout Mountain area, they proceeded along a "high, backbone ridge of the mountains," eventually onto the western end of the Tatoosh Range. They passed along Tatoosh ridges to the Reflection Lakes vicinity, and then continued north up Mazama Ridge (not far east of today's Paradise visitor center) to Sluiskin Falls at the edge of Mount Rainier's steep slopes. Meanwhile, Coleman had fallen behind, and would not participate in the summit attempt.

Throughout their traveling, they had kept "to the highest backbone between the headwaters of the Nisqually and Cowlitz rivers." Apparently, the first part of the trek up the "perpendicular height" from Bear Prairie had been bushwhacking; there was no Indian path there, as Stevens notes (1916: 109). However, when reaching the summit ridge, they had encountered a north-south Indian trail on the mountain crest. Sluiskin often had camped in a grassy hollow two miles away on this ridge trail; the party soon passed this site (1916: 110).

After they had proceeded to Sluiskin Falls and encamped, Sluiskin had refused to proceed further, and concernedly advised the climbers about the many grave dangers they would encounter on the high glaciers and cleavers. After Stevens and Van Trump successfully returned from their harrowing trek to Mount Rainier's summit (August 17–18, 1870), they rejoined Sluiskin, who clearly was relieved about their return. Van Trump, however, had fallen late during the descent and was injured.

On the morning of August 19, they set out south along Mazama Ridge, but Van Trump soon had to be left behind in as comfortable circumstances as allowable (a day later, Sluiskin returned to retrieve him by horse down the Nisqually River). Where the Mazama Ridge-Tatoosh Range trail reached Tatoosh Creek, Stevens insisted that they leave the Indian path and bushwack down the Tatoosh valley to the Paradise River and on to the Nisqually River. Sluiskin showed extreme reluctance for doing so, and, while descending, he attempted by guile to divert Stevens back up to the mountain trail to the south.

Once the Paradise-Nisqually river junction was reached, however, Sluiskin once again took over leading, being familiar with "with every foot of the country," as Stevens admiringly reported (1916: 128). Quite obviously, Sluiskin was following a trail evidently little used, and certainly obscure to Stevens. With Sluiskin's skillful guidance, they expeditiously proceeded to Bear Prairie Point and thence south to Bear Prairie, rejoining Coleman (Stevens 1916: 126–28; see also Schmoe, 1925g: 77; Haines 1962: 48–49).

By Stevens' testimony, Sluiskin once again was perfectly at ease and thoroughly familiar with the terrain once they had reached the Nisqually River.

> Stevens speculated, however, that Sluiskin's "objections to the [Tatoosh-Paradise valley] route evidently arose from the jealousy so common with his people of further exploration of the country by the whites. As long as they keep within the limits already known and explored, they are faithful and indefatigable guides, but they invariably interpose every obstacle their ingenuity can suggest to deter the adventurous mountaineer from exposing the few last hidden recesses that remain unexplored" (1916: 128).

[It might be pointed out that Sluiskin had been shot in the hand in a northeast Oregon battle by a trooper from the Washington-Oregon militia that Hazard Stevens' father, Governor Isaac I. Stevens, had helped to raise during the 1855–56 Yakima War. Though he was marked with a bullet-shattered hand, Sluiskin's relationship with Stevens and Van Trump was decidedly positive.—Editors]

While acknowledging that Stevens' explanation of Sluiskin's behavior may be correct, Brockman advanced two alternative suggestions.

> By choosing the laborious mountain-top route to Sluiskin Falls and by attempting to lead the party back the same way, Sluiskin "may have desired to tire and discourage these white men hoping at the start to dispell [sic] their hopes of attempting what he regarded as foolhardy and impossible; [or] he may have been seeking to prolong his employment" (1934e: 4).

Still another and seemingly more logical interpretation may be advanced—i.e., ridge routes, perhaps especially when travelers are on horseback, are often less difficult than forest trails following twisting, fast-flowing mountain streams.

> Note, for example, the comment by the naturalist F.W. Schmoe: When journeying to Mount Rainier in the summer to hunt and gather berries, the "Klickitat [probably actually Yakama] followed the high divides and open summits of the secondary ridges until they came around to the open parks" of the mountain (1925g: 205).

But why did Sluiskin choose this particular summit route? Perhaps it was because of his tribal affiliation. This rests upon an assumption.

> In Stevens' recollection of Sluiskin's speech in Chinook jargon warning about the dangers of ascending Mount Rainier, Sluiskin described his grandfather as "the greatest and bravest chief of all the

> Yakima" (1916: 133). Whether dependent wholly upon this statement or supported by other evidence, Stevens flatly asserted: "Although of the blood of the...Yakimas, who occupied the country just east of the Cascades, he disdained to render allegiance to them or any tribe" (1916: 130). This Yakama identification is accepted by Schmoe (1927c: 3) and Brockman (1929b: 3, 1934e: 3–4). However, it should be noted that only one of Sluiskin's grandfathers is identified in this evidence.[7]

Nevertheless, one point is unequivocal. Stevens found Sluiskin at a village location on the Cowlitz River near present-day Packwood that clearly was in Taidnapam country. Perhaps, Sluiskin was indeed originally a Yakama, despite the fact that this was not Yakama territory. For, as already indicated, the Yakama evidently did occasionally travel west of the Cascade crest and presumably into the upper Cowlitz valley. Or perhaps, Sluiskin was a Yakama married to a Taidnapam and resident on the Cowlitz. Intermarriage between the two groups was not uncommon, as we have noted.

In my judgment, Sluiskin may well have been a Taidnapam, but identified as a Yakama from his Yakama-like speech by Stevens (or by James Longmire). Sluiskin's obviously detailed familiarity with the Tatoosh Range-Mazama Ridge trail, the Nisqually River trail down to Bear Prairie Point, and the Bear Prairie trail via Skate Creek to the Cowlitz, might imply more familiarity with the locality than a sometime Yakama visitor to Taidnapam country might have. Furthermore, the fact that one of Sluiskin's grandfathers had hunted on Mount Rainier and ascended extremely high on the slopes might be more probable for a Taidnapam-Yakama than a Yakama (Stevens, 1916: 114). With Sluiskin's Taidnapam affiliation assumed, we may now return to a discussion of the routes taken by him.

It has been demonstrated in principle that tribal limits corresponded to watershed divides, at least among groups of a Plateau orientation, as the Taidnapam are presumed to have had. In this case, the boundary between the Taidnapam and the Meshal-Nisqually to the west in the national park area likely would have been along the crest between the Nisqually and Cowlitz river systems (see Fig. 3.4). Specifically, it would have run from near the Bear Prairie vicinity (at the headwaters of Skate Creek, which drains southeastward into the Cowlitz near Packwood), northeast up mountainous terrain to the crest, then along the summits and through the western Tatoosh Range, to the Reflection Lakes area, and along Mazama Ridge. This is precisely the course followed by Sluiskin. It would have been a practical route followed by the Taidnapam up to Mount Rainier without leaving their territory.

Evidently, from Sluiskin's knowledge of the Nisqually River route, he would have known of another trail that led up this river to the Nisqually Glacier and the mountain flank in that locality. But for him to follow this might have involved moving through Meshal-Nisqually territory, which Sluiskin may quite properly have wished to avoid. In addition, it might be probable that Sluiskin did not know the locality along Tatoosh Creek and the Paradise River where Stevens had led him, for the Taidnapam had little reason to ever proceed in that direction.

If it was the resources of Mount Rainier's slopes (game and berry grounds) above the 4,500 foot level that were primarily used by native groups (as evidence presented later in this study will indicate), then the Meshal-Nisqually would have gone to the mountain parks via the Nisqually River. The Taidnapam, on the other hand, probably would have proceeded by way of the mountain route, and evidently sometimes, judging from Sluiskin's knowledge of it, via the Nisqually trail.

Hence, once in the Reflection Lakes area on the return trip, Sluiskin was committed to the mountain top trail, which he must have thought was the reasonable and practical route for returning to Bear Prairie. On the other hand, once Stevens had forced him down into the unfamiliar Tatoosh and Paradise valleys, it was not until they reached the dim upper Nisqually River trail that he was again in an area he knew well, and where he could take the lead in a competent manner.

In conclusion, the data is consistent with, and logically explained by, the assumption that Sluiskin was a Taidnapam, and that Taidnapam territory extended north to the divide between the Nisqually and Cowlitz river basins, and included the flanks of Mount Rainier immediately to the east of this line.

On the east, the Ohanapecosh River valley, between Mount Rainier and the Cascade Divide, is assigned in this survey to both the Taidnapam and the Yakama as a dual use area. This area was almost equally accessible to both groups and evidently its berry and hunting resources were exploited by both, without contest and enmity for reasons explained elsewhere. The presumed borders of the Taidnapam in this segment of their territory are indicated in Figure 3.4.

Meshal

At least from the Nisqually point of view, no separate Meshal (Mical) tribe existed. On the other hand, this group is given individual status as a tribal unit by Spier (1936: 26) and Swanton (1952: 428), both apparently following

Jacobs (Boas in Teit, 1928: 108). However, my main Nisqually informant, Billy Frank, was quite explicit regarding this matter, volunteering the following information without inquiry on the point from me:

> A village named Bišál was located at the junction of the Mashel and Nisqually rivers several miles southwest of Eatonville on top of a hill (not down in the gulch).[8] A very large spring here emerges from the sidehill. Moreover, in May, many black-mouth fish were caught with gill nets close by the village. Indian Henry, a Nisqually whose Indian name was Sů̓tɛl*ik*,[9] lived at this village and he was the chief of the band that had its headquarters here.[10] The village population was part of the Nisqually tribe, but they also spoke the Yakama language. The residents actually were more Yakama than Nisqually. Nevertheless, they were considered to be part of the Nisqually tribe. The mixture was probably attributable to the Nisqually practice of securing Yakama wives.[11] In addition, some Nisqually men bought Taidnapam women and brought them here.

Curtis did not mention the Meshal by name in his summary of western Washington groups. He did report, however, that in almost every Puget Sound group there were a few small bands that inhabited areas about the headwaters of key streams and who depended largely on the chase (Curtis, 1913: 52). Presumably the Meshal, as defined by Jacobs, are to be included among these "bands." In any event, Curtis's data does not contradict the existence of a distinct Meshal entity. It may be well, however, to summarize those views that hold that a special Meshal group must be recognized.

> Jacobs' field research led him to the view that "the tiny band of Meshal (mica′l) or upper Nisqually River people...very likely [represent] a true tribal unit of one or two villages." His Taidnapam interpreter informed him that these people were probably linguistically Kittitas (pcwa′nwapam) (1931: 95). On his 1931 diagrammatic tribal distribution map, all of Mount Rainier is assigned to the Meshal, except perhaps the northern periphery of the national park. Their territory is extended, in fact, eastward to the Cascade Divide (Jacobs, 1931: 94) (see Fig. 3.3). Likewise, in 1937 Jacobs continued to regard the Meshal as a significant tribal unit, and identified them as such (see Fig. 3.5).
>
> Following Jacobs' ethnographic findings, Ross placed the Meshal in the upper Nisqually valley: "the Mica′l, who speak a dialect closely akin to Pcwa′nwapam,...[show] that a small movement of

> Pcwa′nwapam must have occurred in recent years to the west of the Cascades" (in Teit, 1928: 108). Likewise accepting the views of Jacobs, Spier regarded the Meshal as a genuine and distinct tribe (1936: 26).
>
> From his analysis of the literature and evidently taking his cue from Jacobs, Swanton considered the "Nical" [i.e., Meshal] to be "a branch of the…Pshwanwapam [Kittitas]" on "the upper course of Nisqually River" (1952: 428).
>
> On the other hand, Marian Smith's field findings are in agreement with the views of my Nisqually informant. She reported that in the village of baca′labc, just below Eatonville on the Mashel River, which is the uppermost of the Nisqually drainage villages, Sahaptin speech was as common as Salish, or perhaps even more common. "Nevertheless, the baca′labc can only be considered as a Nisqually group" (1940: 13, 22). In fact, a relatively equal division between Salish and Sahaptin speakers prevailed in many bilingual foothill villages owing to the small western movements of Sahaptins into the area.
>
> In the Nisqually drainage, the Sahaptin influence actually even penetrated beyond baca′labc to the next village downstream (see Fig. 3.6, village no. 25) where, however, Salish was a more common language than Sahaptin. Even in village no. 24 still further downriver, Sahaptin was not wholly unknown. From this last set of data it is clear that the Meshal community was not a special phenomenon in the Nisqually system, but rather only the eastern end of a kind of Salish-to-Sahaptin continuum (Smith, 1940: 22).

Following Smith's judgment in the matter and my own informant's statements, I incline to the view that the Meshal would best be regarded as a Nisqually subgroup. Consequently, in the remainder of this report, they will only be designated as Meshal-Nisqually when it is useful to distinguish them from the other Nisqually. Before leaving this small segment of the Nisqually group, however, it is of interest to review several historical fragments, which demonstrate that the Meshal-Nisqually were familiar with the southwest corner of the national park, and hence suggests that it lay within the limits of their traditional territory.

First, the matter of Indian Henry, who has been identified by informant testimony as a Nisqually from the uppermost "Meshal" village. His name is now attached to an adjacent southwest section to Mount Rainier, identified as "Indian Henrys Hunting Ground":

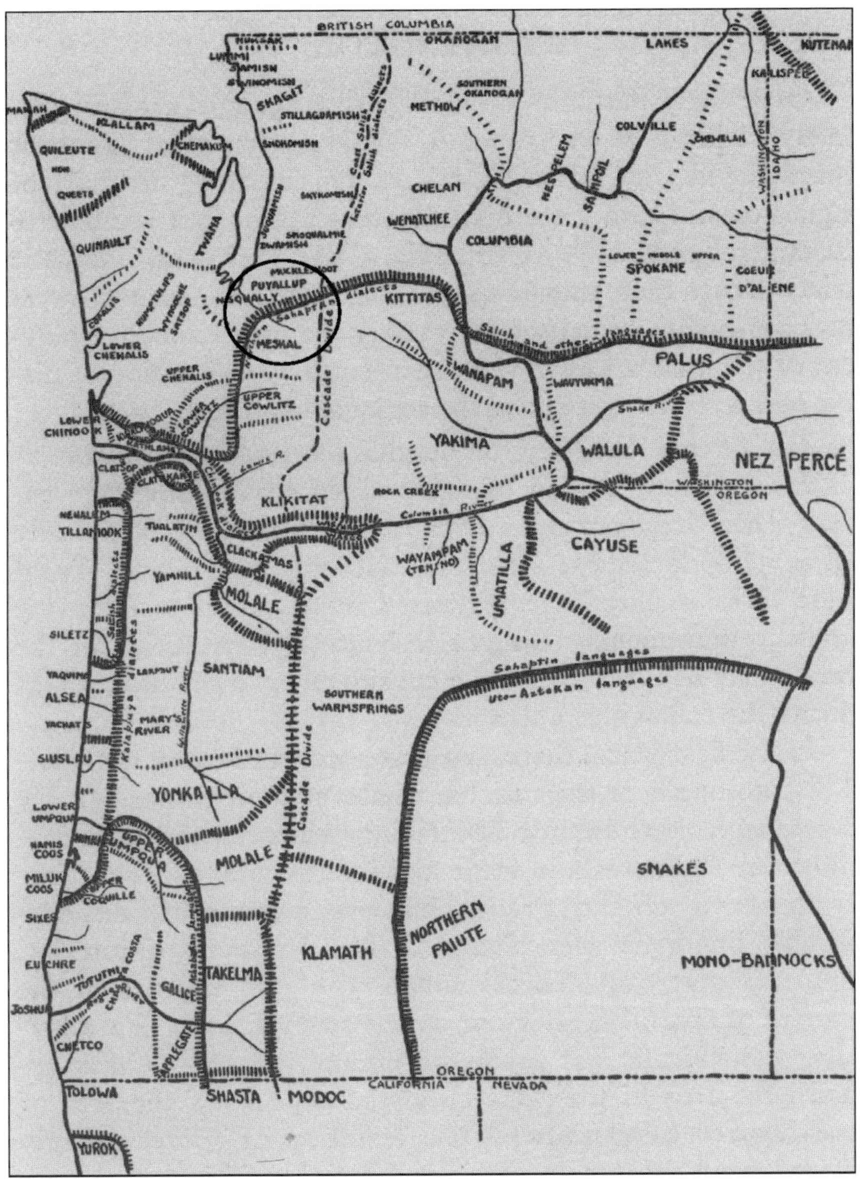

Figure 3.5. Tribal distribution in the Mount Rainier area (within circle) (after Jacobs, 1937).

According to Schmoe, this "beautiful alpine park on the southwest slope of the mountain...was, a generation ago, a favorite camping ground...of Satolick," on whom whites bestowed the

> name "Indian Henry" (1927c: 3). Edmond S. Meany, a Northwest historian with a special interest in mountaineering, also reported that Indian Henry began hunting mountain goats in this area about 1870 (1916: 310).
>
> "Satolick" is identified by Meany (1916: 310), and by Schmoe (1927c: 3; perhaps following Meany), as a Cowlitz Indian. However, my informant's statements and the known geography in terms of tribal boundaries indicate that this is in error. Upon what basis Meany and Schmoe's tribal identification rests is not indicated.

Secondly, the matter of Wapowety.

> In July 1857, an elderly guide named "Wah-pow-e-ty" (Wapowety) led Lt. A.V. Kautz's small party up to the southwest base of Mount Rainier, where the young Army officer from Fort Steilacoom accomplished the first well-documented ascent to the high slopes of Mount Rainier (Kautz, 1916: 73–93; see also Schmoe, 1927c: 3; Brockman, 1929b: 3; 1934i: 5). Their route to the mountain followed what Kautz described as "the Indian trail" up the Nisqually drainage (1916: 76). It led first to "Mishawl [clearly Mashel] Prairie," thence through dense forests to the Nisqually River at a point, according to Brockman, "a little below the present town of National," and from there along the Nisqually River again (1934c: 4). It seems quite plain that their line of march continued up the main river, as Kautz himself avers, to the Nisqually Glacier (1916: 81–82). Brockman is in agreement (1934c: 4). At one time Schmoe (1925: 52) concurred, although later he apparently plotted Kautz's course up Kautz Creek and then certainly up the ridge, known as Wapowety Cleaver, between the Kautz Glacier to the west and the Wilson Glacier on the east (1927c: 3). The route to upper Kautz Creek is said by Schmoe—though on what evidence is not indicated—to have been an old Indian trail (1927d: 1).

For present purposes, the question of whether Kautz followed Kautz Creek or the main Nisqually canyon above the junction of these two streams is not significant. The important point, of course, is that Wapowety, Kautz's guide, led the party up an Indian trail into the southwestern corner of the national park. The tribal affiliation of Wapowety thus becomes a point of interest.

Kautz identified Wapowety "as of the Nesqually tribe" (1916: 75). It might be assumed that he was a Meshal-Nisqually. Wapowety's specific subtribe affiliation is hinted at by his familiarity with the southwest section of the national park—this area falls within the Meshal-Nisqually borders as we define them. It also is suggested by the fact that Wapowety's services as a guide were secured through the aid of Chief "Leshi," whom Kautz had befriended and whom the lieutenant described as "the chief of the Nesquallies" (Kautz, 1916: 75). Leschi, according to Marian Smith, was from the Mashel River village, which we have identified as being Meshal-Nisqually (1940: 13). It would seem likely that Leschi arranged for one of his villagers to guide the explorers. In any event, Leschi informed Kautz that Wapowety knew "more about the Nesqually [River] than any other of his people," though it turned out that Wapowety "had [only] once been on the upper Nesqually when a boy, with his father, and that his knowledge of the country was very limited" (Kautz, 1916: 75, 78). It is unfortunate that Kautz failed to specify the part of the river to which he applied the term "upper."

Thirdly, Leschi himself assisted Kautz by advising him "that the valley of the Nesqually River was the best approach [to Mount Rainier from the Fort Steilacoom area] after getting above the falls" (Kautz, 1916: 75; see also Brockman, 1934c: 4). This was the line of march that Kautz followed, as specified above. Leschi himself apparently knew the route, for Kautz reports that he wished to serve as guide. One may wonder, however, if Leschi did not view this as a way to free himself from imprisonment—he was then incarcerated following the recent Puget Sound Indian war.

Even though this historical evidence may not decidedly prove a Meshal-Nisqually claim to the mountain slopes, it does demonstrate that presumed members of the Meshal-Nisqually subgroup had a familiarity with the southwest national park area, and this strongly suggests (though does not prove) that it lay within the recognized territory of this sub-group.

The Puget Sound Salishan Groups

There is a good deal of confusion in the literature as to how the Salishan Coast groups were structured. In part, this is a reflection of the cultural, political, and linguistic situation—their culture was continuous, each village or village cluster enjoyed political independence, and the speech of the Nisqually, Puyallup, and Muckleshoot was identical or very close.[12] Partly, it is a consequence of the considerable intermarrying between the groups, which was customary and of long standing. These matters already have been discussed earlier in this chapter, but more about this can be said here.

Nisqually-Puyallup Identifications

The politically autonomous Nisqually-Puyallup villages present a particularly perplexing situation. Where political bonds are lacking, special linguistic and cultural differences often have been stressed by anthropologists to define a kind of non-political "tribe." As already mentioned, in the case of the Nisqually-Puyallup, even these criteria fail. No significant dialect or cultural organization differences appear to have existed between the villages of the lower and mid Nisqually and Puyallup drainages (disregarding the Sahaptin-influenced communities of their upper courses). Nor did cultural differences set them apart from groups in other nearby river valleys. This has led to three different ethnographic treatments of the Nisqually and Puyallup peoples.[13]

(a) By some, all villages of the southern Sound region, including those on the Nisqually and Puyallup river systems, were grouped together. The Nisqually and Puyallup were, in fact, very similar in their linguistic and cultural characteristics to communities in other southern Puget Sound areas.

> Thus Marian Smith, who has given these peoples the closest ethnographic attention, noted that owing to their cultural similarity, the Nisqually and Puyallup comprise one of the four major ethnological divisions of Puget Sound (1941: 203–4, 207).
>
> Much earlier, Hale published an 1841 map assigning the "Skwale" or "Nisqually" to lower Puget Sound and up the sound's east side to just above Seattle. Their territory also is shown extending eastward nearly to the Cascade Divide, and thus including those areas in the present report as belonging to the Nisqually, Puyallup, and Muckleshoot (1846: 211–12, 196–97).
>
> Gibbs saw fundamental similarities between the Nisqually and Puyallup. In this regard, Eells noted: "Dr. Gibbs includes the Puyallups with these [Nisqually] as one tribe, and probably this was correct formerly, but they have now become separated into two tribes owing to the reservation system" (1887a: 9).

Whenever these two valley groups are coalesced together, whether with or without peoples of still other valleys, the term Nisqually often has been applied to the entire cluster. The term Nisqually thus can embrace a large segment of the peoples of the Puget Sound area (e.g., see Spier, 1936: 32). Smith, on the other hand, preferred to use the hyphenated term "Puyallup-Nisqually" for "all the Coast Salish of southern Puget Sound" (1940: xi).

Despite the above, it has been customary for most ethnographers to make some distinction between Nisqually and Puyallup "tribes"; Haeberlin and Gunther considered them so (1930: 7–9). Also, Spier felt that both Gibbs and Eells saw them as different tribes, though both observers appreciated their affinity and numerous points of resemblance (1936: 33). (But, as seen above, Eells interpreted Gibbs' view somewhat differently.) And at least during one period of her analysis, even Marian Smith for a time regarded them as distinct tribal units (1941: 203–4, 207).

As presented in the following, divisions of these two groups may be drawn according to other quite different principles based on (b) an economic/resource use basis, and (c) geographical location.

(b) Economic/resource acquisition characteristics may be employed to subdivide the Nisqually and Puyallup peoples into divisions. While the inhabitants of the two river systems otherwise were rather indistinguishable socially and culturally, those residing close to the river mouths were canoe and salt water people, while those of the middle reaches were river- and horse-oriented people—i.e., the groups on the lower reaches of the two rivers held certain resource exploitation traits in common that were different from those equally shared by the upstream groups.

This fact has led some to recognize two "tribes"—downriver "canoe" and upstream "horse" divisions. The former is sometimes assigned to the Puyallup and the latter to the Nisqually, despite the inapplicability of the terms, since representatives of both divisions occur in the two river systems.

> Thus Smith reported: "The Puyallup…[were] a salt water and river people in distinction to the horse owning Nisqually" (1940: xi).

> More specifically, Smith (1941) located the Puyallup at the mouth of the Puyallup River and oppositely across the Sound, and placed the Nisqually in the middle Nisqually and middle Puyallup drainage basins (see Fig. 3.7).

(c) In contrast, a geographical principle may govern the clustering of the separate villages into larger units. It appears that Puget Sound villagers residing in a single valley tended to have closer contacts with one another than they did with villagers in different valleys. Traveling, of course, was primarily up or down the same stream.

My Nisqually informant, Billy Frank, specifically reported, that so far as the Nisqually (sqʷəlíäbš)[14] were concerned, they had a village on either side of the mouth of the Nisqually River (sqʷəlí, referring literally to the fuzzy top of leaves above the root of carrot-like plants) and others on up the river all the way to Eatonville.

> Speaking in general terms, Smith reported that "travel was along the waterways,…upstream along the smaller water course and down-stream…. Even locations not bordering upon a beach were reached by following the water to a point opposite them and then cutting inland to save as much cross country travel as possible." And she adds: "Each village controlled, by familiarity and habitual use, the drainage…upriver from and immediately surrounding the location of its house sites and had, in addition, free access to communication by other water routes" (1940: 5).

This frequency of contact criterion, based upon geographic or more properly topographic principles, has led several ethnographers to recognize two "tribes," the Nisqually in that valley and the Puyallup in the drainage area of that name.

> In 1940, Smith saw the situation in this light. "From the geographic concept of the drainage system…[the Indians] derived their major concept of social unity. Thus, peoples living near a single drainage system were considered to be knit together by that fact if by no other" (1940: 2–4, 6, 9).

The feeling of unity that prevailed among villagers in a drainage was explicitly expressed in native toponyms. People spoke of themselves, in differentiation from other peoples, by employing a term for the larger drainage on which their village stood—i.e., with a "people of" suffix. This was true on both the Nisqually and Puyallup river systems.

> Smith concluded that "the Sound Peoples did unite [following the river drainage principle] the villages of the two river valleys, and also, some of the more scattered villages" (1940: 27–28).
>
> From his Northwest Coast experience, Kroeber corroborated the importance of the drainage principle: "The native point of view seems to be throughout that a group owns a stream with whatever flows into it from both sides" (Smith, 1940: 7, fn. 1).
>
> As early as 1877, Gibbs, too, recognized the significance of the drainage system in designation of village affiliation.
>
> A decade afterward, Eells assigned a separate "tribal" status to the Puyallup River communities, and coalesced into a separate unit those of the Nisqually River and some of the more southerly and westerly groups (1887a: 9). Thus he too was not blind to the importance of drainage location in determining village linkages to larger groupings, though, Smith contends, he erred in adding non-Nisqually groups to those of the Nisqually River proper (1940: 28).
>
> Similarly, Curtis considered the Puyallup and Nisqually to be separate tribes, ranging along the two rivers bearing their names (1913: 4, 14, 171, 174). He noted: "Prominent tribes of this [Puget Sound Salish] group were the…Nisqually, [and] Puyallup" (1913: 14). He again listed among the "Puget Sound Tribes" the Sqalắbashʾ [sqʷalæbš] (Nisqually) in the valley of the Nisqually River "from its mouth to the falls," and the Spuya′llapabshʾ [spuya′llapabš] (Puyallup), who occupied the shores of Commencement Bay and the Puyallup River valley (1913: 174).

It seems clear that Curtis here reflected the view of the coastal tribes themselves. That they (and the Klikitat, too) regarded the peoples of the two river systems as distinct population entities is demonstrated by their separate terms for the Nisqually and Puyallup (Curtis 1913: 160, 171):

Klikitat	Sqallí [sqallí]	Puyắlŭp [puyæləp]
Shoalwater Bay		Cht‘nĭsqalé [ǒtn*i*sqalé]
Quinault	Sqalíi [sqalíi]	Puyaállapsh̆ [puyaállapš]
Twana		Puyállŭpŭbsh̆ [puyálləpəbɛ̌]
Cowichan	Sqalé [sqalé]	Puyắllŭp [puyælləp]

My informants agreed with this point of view (c), as against those outlined in (a) and (b) above—i.e., the Nisqually and Puyallup should be distinguished from one another, and the proper basis for this differentiation is their river-basin affiliation. As a consequence of this, and with support in the literature, the Nisqually and Puyallup are regarded in the present study as separate groups, though closely akin in language and culture. We may now individually examine their territorial claims.

Nisqually

The reader is reminded that much informative data about the Meshal already has been presented in earlier sections of this chapter. As a segment of the Nisqually tribe, they are identified here as Meshal-Nisqually. They are the Nisqually group that was most closely associated with the Mount Rainier locality.

> According to Smith (1940: 28), Gibbs in 1877 divided the villages of the southern end of Puget Sound into three "subtribes." One of the three was "the 'equestrian' or horse Indians, including all the Nisqually River groups plus those neighboring its mouth." These are, of course, the Nisqually in the sense in which the group is conceived in this report.
>
> In 1887, Eells recognized the Nisqually as a separate tribe, considering them to be mainly composed of the Nisqually River villages, but also of settlements "about Olympia and some of the bays west of it" (1887a: 9; see also Smith, 1940: 26).
>
> Curtis identified the Nisqually as residing in the Nisqually watershed from the mouth upstream only as far as the falls. He saw them in part as equestrian: "The myriad tribes on the shores and the tributary streams of Puget sound, Hoods canal, and the water immediately northward, were quite homogenous in their habits, yet the Nisqualli, on the river of that name, found in their grassy prairies an incentive to the acquisition of horses, and, alone among the

coast Salish, they developed a culture in part equestrian, without abandoning their aboriginal acquatic pursuits" (1913: 4)

Haeberlin and Gunther stated that the "Nisqually (sqolê′abc) occupied a large territory extending from the head of the Sound to the east of Mount Rainier." Haeberlin and Gunther further held that the Nisqually shared part of the Nisqually River, which was excellent for winter fishing, with the Puyallup, and that the two tribes had joint berry picking grounds. Their map (Fig. 3.1) details the territory that they assigned to the Nisqually (1930: 7–9).

Smith interpreted Haeberlin and Gunther's statements and map to mean that they considered the Nisqually to include "all of the groups of the southern Sound," together with all of the villages in the Nisqually watershed, save for the two easternmost, which they assigned to the Puyallup (1940: 28). Smith's analysis seems correct except in one particular: Haeberlin and Gunther did not assign the two uppermost Nisqually River village areas to the Puyallup. Her definition rested upon a faulty comparison of their descriptive data and map with the locations of these two communities as her own informants gave them. On the Haeberlin and Gunther map (Fig. 3.1), the Puyallup claimed the inland territory south *to* the Nisqually River. Smith's village location map (Fig. 3.6), on the other hand, shows one of these two communities (no. 25) in a position *south* of the Nisqually River—her descriptive statement of its location is too imprecise to be helpful here (Smith, 1940: 13); hence it would presumably not have been assigned to the Puyallup by Haeberlin and Gunther. Smith considered Haeberlin and Gunther's definition of Nisqually territory inaccurate in the upper river region because their one informant from that area "confused the limited hunting territory concept and the most extended form of affiliation, that by drainage systems" (1940: 28–29).

Spier placed the Nisqually on his map (see Fig. 1.2) so as to show common Puyallup-Nisqually use of the middle Nisqually, doubtless accepting here the Haeberlin-Gunther statement mentioned above. The upper Nisqually River is assigned to the Meshal (1936: 42–43).

In 1940, Smith assigned the Nisqually River drainage to the Nisqually (sqwaleabc) from the mouth to the headwaters (1940: 12–13); see village nos. 20, 23–26 in Figure 3.6. (Coastal villages no. 21 and 22 apparently likewise were Nisqually.) She reported

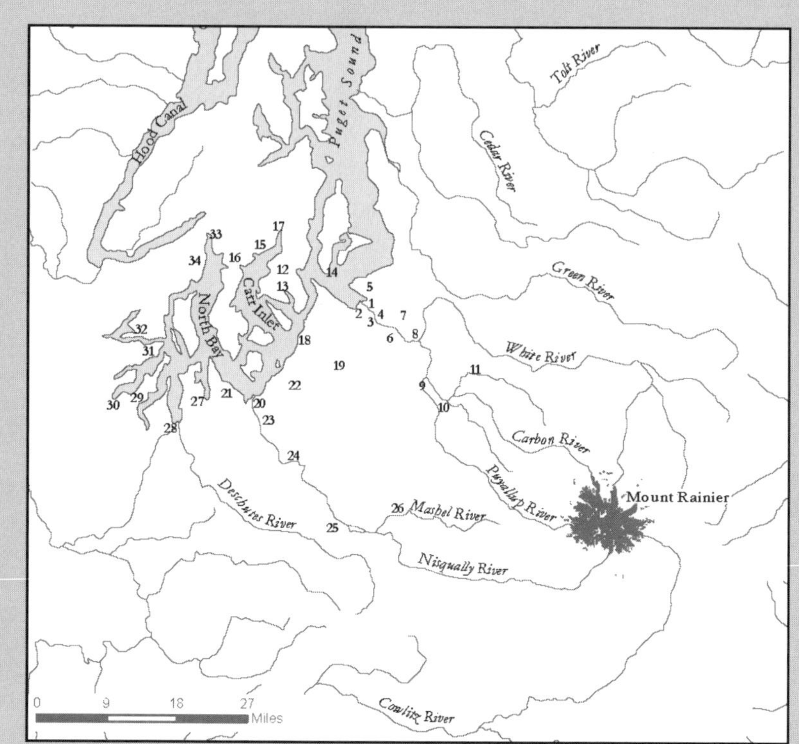

Figure 3.6. Village sites in the Puyallup and Nisqually River systems (after Marian Smith, 1940: 8).

1. *spwiyä'lαphαbc* (Gibbs: Puyallupahmish; Eells: Puyallups; Curtis: Spuyal lapabsh)[1]

Located at the mouth of the Puyallup River, now Gallaghers Gulch, the house sites at 15 Street and Pacific Avenue, Tacoma. Derived from *pwiyä'lαp*, the name of the Puyallup River from its mouth to the point at which the Carbon River flows into it.

People of this village were called "real" Puyallup.

In accord with the extended drainage system concept, the term was extended to include the three villages immediately contiguous to it and the contacts between the four (1-4) were so close that the reduplicated or plural form of the term was the one in common use and only the place names of the other three villages were employed. The name recorded by Gibbs is evidently this reduplicated form. It is this group, strictly speaking, which may be called Puyallup.

By further extension of the term, the name applied to all the villages (1-11) of the drainage of the Puyallup River. With this meaning the term was not reduplicated.

After the coming of the whites and the establishment of the reservation in the region above and around Commencement Bay, the term was still further extended to include all those peoples who took up land on the Puyallup reservation. Villages 1-20, with the probable exceptions of the *stax̣ábc* (8) and the South Prairie (11), came in to this section. These peoples, together with their spouses, whether Indians from other villages more or less distant, or whites, formed the reorganized *spwiyä'laphabc* or "Puyallup."

2. *twádɛbcab*

Located where a creek, no longer existent, emptied into Commencement Bay, the house sites at 24 Street and Pacific Avenue, Tacoma.

3. *cátcqad* ("main village": Haeberlin and Gunther: *Indians of Puget Sound,* p. 9)

Located where Clay Creek empties into the Puyallup River not far from Cushman School.

4. *kalkálaq*ᵘ

At the mouth of Wappato Creek, just above the grass lands.

5. *sháxtl'abc*

Located on Hylebos Waterway. Derived from *haxtl'*, the name of Hylebos Waterway, in which silver salmon were plentiful.

6. *tsaqwéqwabc*

Located where Clarks Creek emptied into the Puyallup River. Derived from *saqwéq*ᵘ, the name of Clarks Creek.

In addition to contacts up and down the Puyallup River this village had strong connections with that of Clover Creek (19).

7. *sq'wádabc*

Located above the Wappato Creek village, where a creek entered Wappato Creek. Derived from *q'wad*, the name of the creek, Simons Creek (?).

8. *stáx̣abc* (Curtis: Stukabsh)

Located where the Stuck River enters the Puyallup. Derived from *stax̣*, "that which has been cut through"; the name of Stuck River. This river...at one time flowed down the present Wappato Creek bed, forming a very considerable stream. It changed its course southward, however, and the village moved with it to its new junction with the Puyallup River. Mythologically this event was connected with the movement of an immense animal, whale, according to the groups near the salt water, beaver, according to more inland groups, which "cut through" the land in an effort to reach the Sound, leaving the new channel behind it.

This village had strong White River or Duwamish contacts.

9. *ts'uwádiabc*

Located on what is now the Puyallup River above the junction with the Carbon, just below the present site of the Soldier's Home. Derived from *ts'uwa"*, the name of the Puyallup River above the point at which the Carbon River flows into it. The name was said to have originated from the cry uttered by an insane woman who left her people and was later seen at various times along the banks of the stream.

This village and the one above it (10) had strong contacts with the Nisqually villages to the south of them. Both were situated on an almost treeless prairie which stretched on either side of the present town of Orting, a fact which tied them topographically to the prairie peoples of the Nisqually.

It was said that there was a log house at this village at the time of the treaty with the whites. Surprise was expressed that such direct evidence of white influence existed so early.

10. *tuwháq'hɑbc* (Gibbs: T'kawkwamish; Eells: T'kaw-kwa-mish)

Located above Orting where Vogt Creek enters the Carbon River. Derived from *tuwháq'*, the name of the Carbon River from its upper reaches to its junction with the Puyallup. The name of this village was applied by Gibbs, and after him by Eells, to all the peoples of the Upper Puyallup drainage, as opposed to the salt water groups around Commencement Bay.

11. *do'ƚíuqᵘ* (?)

Located at South Prairie below where Cole Creek enters South Prairie Creek.

This village had strong ties with Green River, and families came from Auburn every year to South Prairie Creek for salmon. There seem also to have been contacts between this group and the Snoqualmie. At the time of concentration this village moved in to the Muckleshoot reservation and its affiliations were so definitely to the north that it is considered almost outside of the scope of this inquiry.

12. *sqwɑpábc* or *sqopábc* (Gibbs: S'Homamish; Eells: S'ho-ma-mish; Curtis: Sqababsh)

People of villages 12-14. This, the main village, located at the mouth of a stream at Gig Harbor: *twáwɛlkax*. This village was said to have been founded many generations before by Puyallup from Commencement Bay. If we were to believe this tradition and to consider that the contacts with the Hylebos Waterway village were of long standing, we might suppose that the settlement was from that group. Gibbs places this people in the same group with the Sound and river Puyallup. It is also clear that there were additional contacts with the Shotlemamish.

In connection with the aboriginal importance of the Puyallup peoples, it is worth noting that they, with this Gig Harbor group, commanded the only water entrance to the entire southern section of Puget Sound.

13. *sxwlótsid*

Located at the head of Wollochet Bay.

This village was described as an overflow from Gig Harbor, the closest contacts between the two being maintained.

14. *tsugwálɛɬ*

Located at Quartermaster Harbor.

This village consisted originally of a fortification built by a single man and populated by him through wives from neighboring groups. There is reason to believe that he may have beeen a Skagit wanderer and it is certain that at least one of the village later brought in a Skagit wife. Because of his activities against the Duwamish he was in constant danger of their retaliatory measures and, consequently, when its founder became old this village moved over to Gig Harbor. This movement took place not long before the treaty.

15. *sxótlbɑbc* (Gibbs and Eells: Shotlemamish; Curtis: Shohtlbabsh)

Peoples of villages 15-17 and particularly of the village site located on Carr Inlet above the town of Minter.

16. *q'lba"lt^u*

Located at Glencove on Carr Inlet.

This village was originally peopled from the village at Minter and retained its close alliance with it.

17. *t^ulélɑq'le*

Located at the head of Burley Lagoon, Carr Inlet.

In giving village sites the informant said that he had never heard of one at this site but that is was an excellent location for a village. The term *t^uléləq'leɑbc* had been given to Arthur C. Ballard by an informant now dead and when it was repeated to him my informant said, "That's the name of the head of Carr Inlet; so there must have been people there after all." Evidently the village had united with the Minter group, or become extinct, at an early period in white occupation.

18. *tct'éləqɑbɑbc* (Gibbs: Steilakumahmish; Eells: Stulakumamish; Curtis: Stelakubabsh)

Peoples of villages 18-19 and particularly of the village site located at the present site of Steilacoom.

19. ———

There may have been two of these closely allied, so-called "Clover Creek" villages: one near Spanaway and the other at the present site of Clover Creek. If there were but one I am inclined to place it in the latter location.

This group had strong Nisqually contacts as well as those with village 6 already mentioned.

20. *elósədɑbc*

Although the name *sqwɑléabc* (Gibbs: Niskwalli or Skwallishmish; Eells: Nisqually or Squallismish; Curtis: Sqalabsh), derived from the name of the Nisqually River, was applied to all the peoples of the Nisqually drainage including McAllister Creek and, probably also the Sequalitcu River, (20-26), nevertheless there seems to have been no single village of that name. This village at the mouth of the river, contrary to the usual custom, did not bear the river name. This is undoubtedly a reflection of the fact that the *sqwɑléabc* were thought of as an up-river rather than a salt water people, the name applying more particularly to those villages than to the one at the mouth of the river, which was relatively unimportant.

21. *t^udádab*

Located at the mouth of McAllister or Medicine Creek, the spot at which the treaty with Governor Stevens was drawn up. The name is evidently derived from the word for shaman and shaman power, *t^udáb*, a fact to which informants always refer when speaking of the ill effects of white occupation.

In addition to Nisqually contacts this village had close connections with South Bay (27).

22. *sígwáletcɑbc* (Gibbs and Eells: Segwallitsu)

Located where Dupont Creek enters the Sequalitcu River.

23. *yicáxtcɑbc*

Located on Nisqually Lake at the mouth of a sizeable creek. Derived from the name of the lake, *yicáxtɑl*.

24. *yo'xwálscɑbc*

Where Muck Creek enters the Nisqually River.

Due to the fact that its site was included in the reservation and that several of its older members survived the period of early concentration, this village maintained its identity somewhat longer than most. The village site was on the flats near the river bed rather than upon the high prairie land adjoining, another fact which tended to preserve the village since white settlers on the Nisqually sought the high wheat and grazing land.

The extra-Nisqually contacts of this village were rather to the west along the southern Sound than to the northeast toward the mouth of the Puyallup River.

25. *sɑ́kwiɑbc*

Located on a hill near the junction of Clear Creek and the Nisqually River. "Perhaps the largest" Nisqually village at the time of the treaty.

26. *bɑcálɑbc*

Located on a highland below Eatonville on Mashell Creek.

This village is listed by Jacobs[2] and Spier[3] as Sahaptin. There is no doubt that Sahaptin was as common as Salish in this, as in many bilingual foothill villages, and that there have been small western movements of Sahaptins into the area.[4] Nevertheless, the *bɑcálɑbc* can only be considered as a Nisqually Group. Leschi, who fomented the "war" with the settlers in the Sound country, was of this village.

27. *t*^{u}*ts'étcaxł* (Gibbs: Nusehtsatl; Curtis: Stsichahlabsh, including "Budd's Inlet and South Bay")

Located on South Bay or Henderson Inlet, between the creek at the head and that on the south.

This village, as well as 28 and 30-32, moved in to the Nisqually reservation at the time of concentration.

28. *stɑtcásɑbc* (Gibbs: Stehtsasamish; Eells: Stehtsasamish, including "Budd's Inlet or South Bay")

Located on Budd Inlet at Tumwater, above Olympia.

29. *sqwayai'łhɑbc* (Gibbs: Skwai-aitl; Eells: Skwaiatl)

Located on Mud Bay or Eld Inlet.

The people of Mud Bay had perhaps their closest contacts with the Upper Chehalis villages immediately south of them.

30. *tɑpíqsdɑbc* (Eells and Gibbs: Sawamish)

Located on Oyster Bay or Totten Inlet, below the town of Oyster Bay. The term "Sawamish" was the only local one used by Gibbs which was not recognized immediately by my informants. The term given me derives from *tɑpíqsɛd*, the name of the inlet.

31. *sɑhéwɑbc* (Gibbs: Sahehwamish; Curtis: Sahewabsh, including Mud Bay and Oyster Bay)

Located at Arcadia. This was a large village. Since it practically commanded the outlets of Budd Inlet, Mud Bay and Oyster Bay, as well as Shelton Inlet, its name was sometimes extended to include that entire drainage and the peoples upon it, villages 27-32.

32. ———

Located on Shelton Inlet opposite the town of Shelton.

This village was small and was closely allied to its parent village at Arcadia.

33. *sqwáksdɑbc* (Gibbs: Skwawksin or Skwawksnamish; Eells: Squaksons or Skwaksnamish; Curtis: Sqaksadabsh)

Peoples of villages 33-34 and particularly those located on North Bay at the mouth of Coulter Creek.

As Gibbs pointed out, there were close contacts between these villages and those of Hood Canal. There was a well defined path across the land bridge between the mouth of Coulter Creek and Clifton on the Canal. At the time of concentration the Squakson followed this contact and moved in to the Skokomish reservation. Work with the Twana will furnish additional data on these people.

34. ———

Located at Allyn at the mouth of Mason Creek.

---

[1]These, and similar renditions of native terms which follow, appear in:
Gibbs: *Tribes of Western Washington,* pp. 178-79.
Eells: *Indians of Puget Sound,* Paper 1, p. 9.
Curtis: *North American Indian,* p. 173.
[2]Jacobs: *Sketch of Northern Sahaptin Grammar,* pp. 95-96, and *Indian Languages of Oregon and Washington,* pp. 56-57.
[3]Spier: *Tribal Distribution in Washington,* p. 26.
[4]Teit: *Middle Columbia Salish,* p. 108.

M. Smith, 1940: 9–14

that the people in the easternmost villages, however, were "thought of as an up-river rather than a salt water people." They considered the summits of the Cascade Range as marking the dividing line between their country and that of the eastern Sahaptins (1940: 24).

In 1941, when reviewing her field evidence published in 1940, she largely discarded the drainage concept of territorial boundaries, and placed the Nisqually on the Mashel River, Clear Creek, and Muck Creek and on the Nisqually River itself neighboring these three tributaries, on Nisqually Lake, on Segualiteu River, on Clover Creek, and on Clarks Creek and the neighboring Puyallup River (see Fig. 3.7).

Then, in 1949, Smith located the Nisqually in "the Nisqually River drainage" (1949: 345).

Finally, the Nisqually were assigned by Swanton, as a result of his literature survey, to "the Nisqually River above its mouth and on the middle and upper courses of Puyallup River" (1952: 429–30).

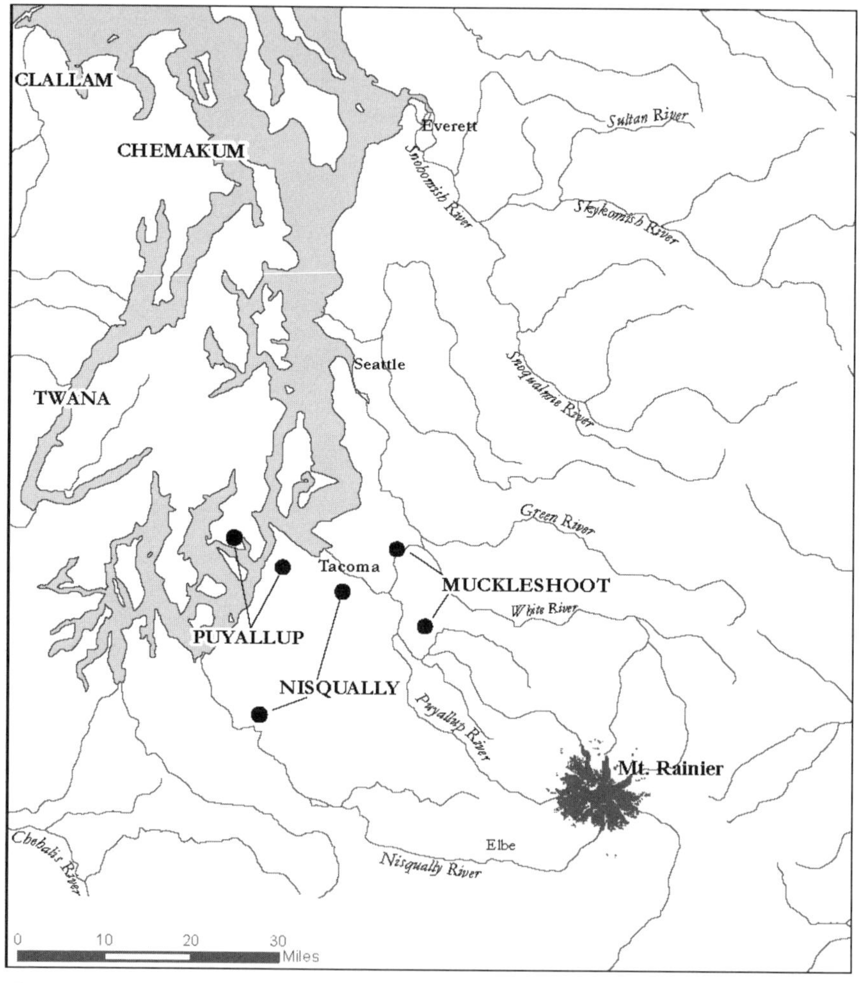

Figure 3.7. Puyallup, Nisqually, and Muckleshoot population centers (after Marian Smith, 1941).

Despite differing boundary concepts from the literature, there is ample evidence in the documentary sources to support my informants' definition of an independent Nisqually tribal entity, and hence the inclusion of them as such on my map for the Mount Rainier area (Fig. 3.4).

As to the eastern limits of the Nisqually tribe, which is the point of special interest in this study, specific data is not extensive. However, it may properly be summarized here.

Curtis placed their eastern border at "the falls," the location of which remains undetermined. [Perhaps Curtis referred to the now submerged Nisqually River falls upstream of La Grande Dam southwest of Eatonville.—Editors] Haeberlin and Gunther found that Nisqually territory extended (see Fig. 3.1), to the southeastern and perhaps eastern slopes of Mount Rainier. Spier (see Fig. 1.2) terminated the Nisqually country well to the east of the national park, but distinguished a separate Meshal group, to which all of the southwest corner of the national park is assigned. Inasmuch as the Meshal are considered in the present study as a Nisqually sub-group, this geographical area would fall into Nisqually territory. This also was confirmed by Spier's reading of the literature. To Marian Smith, not only were the easternmost villages on the Nisqually River considered as Nisqually (as likewise by Gibbs and Eells), but the river system to its source was Nisqually country. She held that the Nisqually regarded the Cascade Divide as their border with the Plateau Sahaptins.

Puyallup

In 1877, Gibbs divided the peoples of southern Puget Sound into three "sub-tribes," one of which was "the river and Sound Indians," the group in our present study termed as the Puyallup (Smith, 1940: 28). This group, in turn, was composed of three divisions, with the Puyallupahmish and the T'Kawkwamish of the Puyallup valley being the two of interest in the present context (Spier, 1936: 33–34). According to Smith, Gibbs actually assigned to the Puyallup *all* of the villages from the mouth of the Puyallup River to its headwaters (Smith, 1940: 28).

As Spier (1936: 34) noted, Eells (1887a: 9) seems to have added little additional information to Gibbs' data. However, whether following Gibbs or presenting data of his own, Eells assigned the mouth of the Puyallup River to the Puyallup proper (the spwiyä'laphabc of Smith [1940: 9], see Fig. 3.6, village no. 1), and the upper branches were assigned to the "T-kaw-kwa-mish" (which Smith identifies as tuwhá'habc [1940: 10], see Fig. 3.6, village no. 10). However, it seems to me, on the basis of its phonetic constituents alone, it might be better equated with Marian Smith's tsaqwéqwabe (village no. 6 in Fig. 3.6). In any event, Eells, like Gibbs, considered these as two of the three units forming the larger Puyallup "tribal" entity (1887a: 9).

Haeberlin and Gunther found that the Puyallup (Spuya′lupo′be) "lived along the banks of the Puyallup and White Rivers" (1930: 7–9). According to their map (Fig. 3.1), all of the northern and western slopes of Mount Rainier, and possibly those to the east and southeast as well, were considered to have been Puyallup country. These two authors also contend that the Puyallup and Nisqually jointly shared the mid and upper Nisqually River, where winter fishing was considered to be excellent, and the two tribes also jointly exploited certain berry picking grounds. However, as Smith points out, this evidently applied to just one part of the middle Nisqually River (1940: 28)—i.e., in the neighborhood of Smith's village no. 26 (Fig. 3.6) on the Mashel River.

From his survey of the literature, Spier (1936: 42–43) found that virtually the entire northern half of Mount Rainier National Park lay within Puyallup territory (see Fig. 1.2). This included the upper course of the Puyallup and the left bank of the upper White River.

According to Marian Smith (in 1940), all of the villages in the Puyallup watershed (village nos. 1–11 in Fig. 3.6) were comprised of the Puyallup. They were known as "spwiyä′laphabe, or people of the Puyallup River drainage" (1940: 9–11). The "true" Puyallup, however, were those close to the river mouth, with the term by extension being applied to the upriver communities. Some of the upriver villages, however, had strong contacts with the Nisqually to the south, or to the Muckleshoot on the Green and White rivers to the north. As with the Nisqually, Smith reported that the people of these eastern villages regarded the Cascade Divide as marking the eastern border of their territory, beyond which was the Sahaptins (1940: 24).

A year later in 1941, Smith revised her earlier treatment of the Puyallup and Nisqually, sharply redefining their tribal territories. Discarding in general the notion that a close relationship existed between Puget Sound tribal territories and drainage basins, she decided that the Puyallup were in fact an exclusively coastal group, occupying the Puyallup River only as far upstream as the mouth of Clarks Creek. The middle Puyallup River she assigned to the Nisqually, and the upper Puyallup River to the Muckleshoot. Under this definition, the Puyallup tribal area would have been far removed from the Mount Rainier area.

In 1949, Smith reconsidered the data and placed the Puyallup in "the Puyallup River drainage, especially…from Puyallup west" (1949: 345). Regarding the upper Puyallup country, she did not explicitly assign it to the Muckleshoot, thus the area appeared to be loosely designated as Puyallup by Smith.

Swanton likewise placed the Puyallup at the "mouth of the Puyallup River and the neighboring coast" (1952: 434). According to this analysis, the Puyallup could not have claimed any segment of the Mount Rainier area. However, Swanton's views were based wholly on an appraisal of the literature, and, it may be suspected, were weighted heavily in favor of Smith's revised opinion. If this is the case, Swanton's statement should not be regarded as an independent judgment.

An historical incident, too, provides a case of interest in the present context. In late summer 1833, William F. Tolmie of the Hudson's Bay Company's Nisqually House attempted an ascent onto the slopes of Mount Rainier. This was the first recorded direct approach to the mountain by a white man, and was led by a Puyallup guide (Meany, 1916: 6–12).

According to Tolmie's own words: "engaged…Nuckalkut a Poyalip (whom I took for a native of Mount Rainier) with 2 horses to be guide on the mountain after leaving the horse track" (Meany, 1916: 7). Four other natives joined the party, hoping to hunt elk and mountain goat near Mount Rainier. Under Nuckalkut's guidance, Tolmie clearly was led to the lower Puyallup River according to his own testimony, but then, from the evidence in the record, they evidently went up the Carbon River fork toward Mount Rainier.[15]

In Meany's view, the peak now bearing Tolmie's name, located in the northwest corner of the national park, is the one that Tolmie climbed in approaching Mount Rainier itself; evidently he did not proceed farther and turned back (1916: 6). This identification is at least not contradicted by Tolmie's rather general record as I read it. The significance in the present study is that Tolmie's account seems

> to validate the Puyallup claim to the northwest slopes of Mount Rainier.[16]

Together, this data seems to adequately attest to the existence of a Puyallup group in the native view, and to the placement of them throughout the full length of the Puyallup River valley. This would put the upper limits of their tribal territory well into the northwest corner of the national park (see Fig. 3.4). Haeberlin and Gunther, and Smith (in 1940), also evidently placed the eastern limit of Puyallup country along the Cascade Divide. This, however, would require coalescing the Puyallup with the Muckleshoot, which in this report are regarded as a separate tribal entities.

Muckleshoot

My informant Louis Starr said the Muckleshoot were called the Sq̓ópəbš, people who lived on the Green River, though he clearly also considered the upper White River to its sources as likewise fully within their territory.

> Spier reported that George Gibbs placed the Skopahmish "on upper Green River and the Stk'kamish (Sekamish) on White River" (Spier, 1936: 34). Spier considered these two groups to have been Muckleshoot (see Fig. 1.2), as well as other small populations mentioned by Gibbs. Also, Spier considered as Muckleshoot the Smulkamish, located on the upper White River in the *Handbook of American Indians*.
>
> Curtis likewise gave a separate tribal status to the Muckleshoot. He recorded them as the Búklsȟuhl [búklšut] (Muckleshoot) and located them in the White River and Green river valleys (1913: 18, 174).
>
> Haeberlin and Gunther aver that the "Muckleshoot (o'kElcut) lived on the White River, their territory extending from Kent east to the mountains [Cascades]" (1930: 9). On their map (Fig. 3.1), the Green River is also included in Muckleshoot country (Spier, 1936: 34).
>
> From his review of the literature, Spier concluded that the Muckleshoot should be considered a separate tribal unit, accepting the dictum of Haeberlin and Gunther on this point. To him, however, "their distinctiveness from Duwamish and Puyallup is by no means clear." On his map (see Fig. 1.2), he assigned the Muckleshoot to

the east bank of the upper White River in the extreme northeast corner of Mount Rainier National Park (1936: 34–35, 42–43).

According to Smith's view in 1940, she stated that there "seems little doubt" that the people of the Green River (known collectively as Sqwapábc) and of the White River together "represented a distinct division." With these, she included the village of do'tíuq^{u} (?) "at South Prairie below where Cole Creek enters South Prairie Creek," which is tributary to the Carbon River (1940: 11, 16). This "division," to use Smith's term, is the group designated Muckleshoot in the present study.

After reconsidering her field evidence in 1941, Smith subsequently stated her earlier position more forcefully. She considered the Muckleshoot to be a separate tribal entity—a Cascade foothills people somewhat more akin culturally to the Snuqualmi to the north than to the Nisqually-Puyallup to the south (1941: 203–4).[17] In 1941, she assigned to them the upper reaches of Wappato Creek, the Puyallup River above its confluence with the Carbon River, the latter river itself, South Prairie Creek, the White River above its union with the Green River, the latter river itself, and Susie Creek (1941: 204, 209).

In her 1949 revision, on the other hand, she regarded the Muckleshoot as the people "especially of the drainage of the White River" (1949: 344–45). The Green River is, however, left unassigned in her 1949 listing of Puget Sound group territories, being allotted neither specifically to the Muckleshoot, the Duwamish, or the Snuqualmi.

Swanton, a secondary source and hence of incidental rather than basic interest, recognized the Muckleshoot as a distinct tribal group and placed them on the "White River, their territory extending from Kent eastward to the mountains, but it seems also to have included Green River." He noted bands residing on the mid White River, the upper White River, and the upper Green River (the latter, Skopamish bands); to these groups he added Smith's "Dothliuk" at South Prairie "on South Prairie Creek, an affluent of Carbon River" (1952: 428–29).

According to my informants, Muckleshoot territory extended eastward to the "crest of the mountains," separating their country from that of the Yakama. Without doubt, they were referring to the Cascade Divide.

The documentary data quite uniformly confirms that the Green River and the upper White River systems were included in Muckleshoot territory. This agrees with my field information. The Green River basin lies well to the north of Mount Rainier, and so is of no direct concern in the present connection. The White River and its tributaries, on the other hand, drain the northeast corner of the park. My field data indicates that Muckleshoot territory extended up this river system to its sources. Hence this would counter any Yakama claim to the northeast flanks of Mount Rainier.

While necessarily shadowy, the line of demarcation between the Muckleshoot and Yakama territories in this area is placed along the Ohanapecosh-White River divide, as delineated in Figure 3.4. However, if the extreme eastern Muckleshoot village was as far west of this area as the scanty data seems to indicate, it appears unlikely that the Muckleshoot made considerable use of this territory.

Endnotes

1. Ballard identifies the "naxtce′spam" [nax̣č́íspəm] as the people "commonly called Klickitat" (1929: 147, fn. 160). Evidently he used the Klikitat designation in its widest sense as noted in the preceding discussion.
2. Here, evidently is a perplexing problem requiring field investigation. What, in fact, was the relationship between the Yakama-Kittitas and the Wenatchi? Were there two or more Wenatchi groups, some Salishan and some Sahaptin? Were the Wenatchi proper, in recent times, so deeply infiltrated by the Sahaptins that, like the Meshal, they might in fact be considered as a full Sahaptin group? Was there at one time a separate, geographically intermediate Sahaptinized Wenatchi group, between the Yakama-Kittitas and the Salishan Wenatchi? If this latter possibility is correct, has this intermediate population been absorbed by the Kittitas? Since this question, however interesting, does not relate directly to the Mount Rainier Park study, the matter was not pursued by further field inquiry.
3. These zones are not identical with Marian Smith's four "ethnic units"—i.e., salt-water, river, prairie, and inland (1940: 29–32). Her criteria are based on broad cultural and especially subsistence-economic terms; mine are in regard to attitudes concerning property and land. My "mountain zone," which is of particular relevance to the present study, would probably include Smith's "inland" group *in toto* (village nos. 9–11 in Fig. 3.6, and "certain of the White River and Green River peoples") and some of her "prairie" unit (specifically village nos. 25–26 in Fig. 3.6). It also includes the Taidnapam, who are not considered by her.

   My three-fold division is also not the same as the broad two-group arrangement recognized by the Indians themselves. Unlike Marian Smith's personal analysis, the latter appear to have seen cultural differences in terms of two extremes—a "salt-water" configuration, and an "inland" type. The first included Smith's "salt-water" and "river" groups; the latter, her "prairie" and "inland" units (Smith, 1940: 44).
4. Perhaps this also was the case with the Coast Salish to the north. When E.T. Coleman was ascending the Lummi (Nooksack) River in 1868 to climb Mount Baker, his

Lummi (Nooksak?) guides discovered, to their distress and anger, signs of Thompson River Indians poaching on their hunting grounds. The same had happened, Coleman was informed, two years previous, when a Thompson River interloper had been killed by one of the very same Lummi (Nooksak?) currently traveling with Coleman. Coleman added: "No lord in England guards his preserve more jealously; no Highland laird could be more irate against deer-stalking than was this same Indian" (1869: 803–4).

5. For another version of this tale (without the localizing data) see Brockman (1929b: 3).
6. This map is titled "Ethnographic Map of Oregon Showing the Limits of Tribes and their Affinities by Language."
7. Matthes identified Sluiskin, in passing, as a Klikitat. It may be assumed that Matthes' evidence was secondhand (1916: 221). Moreover, Matthes, like others in the past, may have confused the Klikitat with the Yakama, designating both groups by a single term as "Klickitat."
8. This village, designated bacálabc [bæšálabš] by Marian Smith, is located by her "on a highland below Eatonville on Mashell Creek" (1940: 13).
9. Rendered "Sotolick" by Van Trump (Meany, 1916: 310), and "Satolick" by Schmoe (1927c: 3).
10. Billy Frank himself saw Indian Henry between 1880 and 1890. He was, Frank reported, a fine hunter and wealthy man, and, owing to his ability to supply them with food, he had four or five wives.
11. Perhaps Smith saw this intermarrying as including both sexes, for she made this general statement: "both men and women from Sahaptin groups married into and took up residence in Sound villages" (1940: 23). Only Salish Sound women, on the other hand, went east of the Cascades to live among Sahaptins.
12. Smith makes these same cultural and political points (1941: 197, 205).
13. In actual fact, still other treatments are theoretically possible. For, as Smith remarks: "the Puget Sound villages formed a continuous series criss-crossed by *many* lines of conflicting affiliation according to any one of which different villages may be grouped together as 'tribes'" (1940: 23; italics mine).
14. In 1941 Smith agreed that this term was applied "to the people of all the villages of the Nisqually River," though in her reformulation in that year she chose to emphasize group linkages based on cultural criteria (1941: 198).
15. One may wonder why Tolmie was not led all the way up the Puyallup River proper, instead of branching off to the Carbon River valley as appears to have been the case. An east-west variant of the trails across the Cascades through Naches Pass followed the Carbon River, and, quite possibly, Tolmie's Puyallup guide was influenced by this, and chose to continue along that route. In addition, though modern maps consider the Carbon River to be a branch of the Puyallup River, different proportional runoff rates might make the relationship seem the reverse at certain times of the year. In May 1841, for example, Lt. Robert Johnson of the U.S. Exploring Expedition reported that the "Upthascap [the Carbon and its branch South Prairie Creek] is a much wider stream than the Puyallup" (Meany 1916: 17, fn. 1).
16. Historian Aubrey L. Haines (1962: 7) interpreted Tolmie's directional information as indicating they proceeded up the Mowich River, rather than the Carbon River, and that Tolmie ascended the ridges in the Mount Pleasant vicinity. In any case, the headwaters of these two streams are tributaries of the Puyallup River and were in territory claimed by the Puyallup tribe.
17. I secured some incidental evidence that tends to support this view of a closer social, if not cultural, relationship to the Snuqualmi.

4

Village Sites and Structures

No evidence was secured from my informants indicating that permanent or semi-permanent village sites were located within the national park boundaries, although several Taidnapam villages were situated nearby (see *Taidnapam* below). The literature search confirmed these findings.

> F.W. Schmoe, a Mount Rainier National Park naturalist, who possessed an intimate knowledge of the area through years of tramping its mountain slopes and river valleys, reported that he "never found evidence of permanent camps within what is now the...Park, unless a stone pestle used for grinding dried berries, seeds, or roots, which was found years ago near the [Nisqually] Park Entrance can be interpreted as such" (1926d: 2).
>
> In 1929, acting park naturalist C. Frank Brockman made the same point: "Mt. Rainier...gives little evidence of any permanent residence on the part of the tribes that roamed about this country" (1929b: 3).
>
> The following year, park ranger L.G. Richard repeated this opinion: "No Indians are known to have lived permanently in the Park" (1930c: 7).

Perhaps Brockman and Richards were merely restating Schmoe's report quoted above, but their comments at least suggest that no data came to light in the period up to 1929–30 to alter the view of the park staff in this matter.

Sites

Yakama

My Yakama informants agreed that the Yakama did not have settlements or band-focused residence sites within the national park area. Also, none of the informants could provide a clear statement regarding the locations of the villages closest to the national park borders. However, I was informed that one not-too-distant village was located southeast on the Tieton River (T. 14 N., R. 13 E.) in the Rimrock vicinity (Yakama: miáwax̣, miyáwax̣; Coyote's son, according to a myth). It was in an area where quantities of wild carrots (Yakama: sawítk) and other roots were dug and dried, and where salmon were caught and likewise dried. According to my informants, wild carrots are edible until after blooming in mid summer, when they become spongy. Thus, the roots had to be secured before early July. Pit house depressions are still visible at the Rimrock site. White Pass would have been about 14 miles by trail west of this village. This information from my Yakama informants checked neatly with Ray's data.

> According to Ray's field findings, the highest settlement on the Tieton River was miya′wax, a permanent village at Rimrock (see Fig. 3.2, site no. 23 on the Tieton R.). It was an important center for hunting, fishing, and berry gathering (1936: 119, 144–48).

To the north of the Rimrock area, my informants reported that an old camping site was located at Bumping Lake on the Bumping River, a tributary of the Naches River. This site is situated about seven miles down the Bumping Creek trail from Carlton Pass (see Fig. 1.1), and only several miles east of the park boundary on the Cascade Divide.

Ray did not record the existence of this site on the Bumping River (1936: 144–48). However, the data reviewed by Spier (1936: 16), derived from James Moony and Edward S. Curtis, did reveal the presence of the Naĥchísh-hlama on the Naches River, which checks with my findings. As already noted in chapter 3 of the present study, Spier regarded these people as a Yakama band. Consequently, one may wonder why Ray recorded no settlement on the upper Naches River tributary during his exhaustive investigation of Plateau village locations (see Fig. 3.2). Could it be that he had asked his informants to identify "Yakama" villages, but the latter, like my informants, considered the Naches as a separate tribal unit? Could Ray have failed to realize this, and thus there is a gap in his documentation?

In any case, it may be of some interest that Ray recorded sites on other Naches River tributaries, located to the south of the Bumping River. He identified, for example, the previously mentioned Rimrock site (see Fig. 3.2). Further south, on Cowiche Creek, Ray located a small permanent village called tautunu′k, situated near important hunting territory at the extreme head of the creek. It stood perhaps 18 miles in a direct line from White Pass, and about 19 miles from Tieton Pass (1936: 119, 144–48). In his compilation of the published data, Spier also speaks of the Tkaíwaichash-hlama band on Cowiche Creek (1936: 16).

On Ahtanum Creek, a Yakima River tributary, the highest village was situated on the south fork of that stream and termed ts'a'pas by Ray (1936: 119, 144–48). And, on the upper course of Toppenish Creek, the village closest to Mount Rainier was tsumkwi'' "at the head of Simcoe creek near Saddleback ridge." Being off to the south, however, the latter two villages were somewhat closer to Mount Adams than Mount Rainier. This might suggest that the inhabitants in ordinary years possibly might have preferred visiting the Mount Adams area when attracted to high elevation localities.

Taidnapam

According to my informants, the Taidnapam villages of interest were located on the Upper Cowlitz drainage, just south of the national park. The highest settlement on the Cowlitz was in the vicinity of where the Clear Fork and Muddy Fork enter the Ohanapecosh River, forming the Cowlitz proper. This village stood about 5-1/2 miles south of today's Ohanapecosh Visitor Center; it was termed ləkalwít by Mary Kiona, and lakálwit by George Satanus. Here, there was a salmon fishery where the catch was dried; huckleberries were to be found in the mountains; goats, deer, and bear were hunted nearby.

About five miles downriver, the next village čawáčas, stood where Packwood is now located. And approximately three miles below Packwood was qwáqwatam, where Johnson Creek meets the Cowlitz. The next downstream village from there was called temx̣ɛ́x̣.

> Without doubt, Hazard Stevens visited the village site at present-day Packwood during his August 1870 venture to Mount Rainier. As noted in chapter 3, Stevens journeyed from the Nisqually River to the Cowlitz via the Bear Prairie-Skate Creek trail—this canyon forming "a low pass between the Nisqually and Cowlitz rivers." At that time, Stevens and his guide, James Longmire, anticipated encountering the "band of Indians who usually made their headquarters at this point, and among whom…[I] hoped to find some hunter familiar with the mountains who might guide…[my party] to the base of Takhoma." The Indian camp was deserted but for Sluiskin's family, residing in "a rude shelter formed of a few skins thrown over a frame work of poles" (1916: 106–7). This location cannot be any other than my informants' Packwood site.

Nisqually

My Nisqually sources stated that no traditional Nisqually settlement sites lay within the national park boundaries. Specifically, Billy Frank asserted that the upriver-most village in the Nisqually drainage was located near Eatonville. He further remarked that Marian Smith's village list was complete and the settlements accurately located (Smith, 1940: 10, 13). Smith likewise placed the highest village in the Nisqually River drainage "on a highland below Eatonville" on the Mashel River (see Fig. 3.6, village no. 26). This location is approximately 17 miles directly over the mountains from the western edge of the national park.

> It seems probable that Hazard Stevens passed through this village site in August 1870 on the way eastward. In brief, after leaving the south end of Mashel Prairie, about one mile below the mouth of the Mashel River, he noted: "For eight miles the trail led through thick woods [up the Mashel valley], and then, after crossing a wide 'burn' [passed] a number of deserted Indian wigwams [i.e., the Eatonville village site]."

However, my search of the literature (including the Stevens' account) indicates that there was another Nisqually habitation site further up the Nisqually River.

> At the Eatonville site, "where another trail from the Nisqually plains [La Grande area] joined ours," the Stevens party took the latter route and "descended a gradual slope, transversed a swampy thicket and another mile of heavy timber, and debouched on the Mishell [sic] River." Crossing the Mashel, they next ascended a high, steep hill and traveled south "over high rolling ground" for about 12 miles to the Nisqually River. This locality is at, or close to, Elbe, where Stevens reported they camped "near an old ruined log-hut; the former residence of a once famed Indian medicine man" (1916: 103–5).

The following day, the party ascended the Nisqually River for "20 miles" to the mouth of Copper Creek, about two miles west of today's Nisqually park entrance. My locality identifications suit Stevens' data and the topography as he describes it. It is clear, though, that Stevens overstated distances; for instance, he placed Goat Creek 2 miles from Copper Creek, when in fact it is much closer, at 1 mile. His recorded mileage, considered as a set of ratios, should be roughly corrected (shortened) as follows: 8 + 1 (?) = 5-1/2; 1/2 (?) + 1 = 3/4; 12 = 8-1/2; and 20 = 12.

Haeberlin and Gunther also identified a Nisqually habitation site at Elbe on the Nisqually River (1930: 9). If accurate, this indicates that a Nisqually village stood about 13-1/2 miles west of the southwest corner of Mount Rainier National Park.

Stevens made no other mention of Nisqually settlements, though he traveled along the full length of the Nisqually River valley from the Elbe vicinity to the Paradise River in the national park (1916: 104–30).

Puyallup

No informant data relating to Puyallup settlements was secured by me for the reasons noted in chapter 1. The literature data, though meager, placed the easternmost Puyallup villages well outside of the Mount Rainier National Park boundaries.

> According to Marian Smith, the village of ts'uwádiabc stood furthest upstream on the Puyallup River (see Fig. 3.6). It was situated above the junction of the Puyallup and Carbon rivers, and maintained strong contacts with the Nisqually villages to the south (1940: 10).

This settlement, the closest on the Puyallup River to Mount Rainier, lay about 23 miles downstream from the western national park limits. It appears to have been the village seen, in a much reduced form, by Lt. Robert Johnson on May 21, 1841, while on his eastward traverse of the Cascade Range.

> "[The Johnson party] encamped at the junction of the Puyallup with the Upthascap [identified by Edmund S. Meany as the Carbon River (1916: 16, fn. 2)]. Near by was a hut...remarkably well made [of planks]." It was inhabited by two elderly Indians and two boys, "who were waiting here for the arrival of those employed in the salmon-fishery." On the 22nd, they observed a small fish-weir a short distance up the Carbon from this locality (Wilkes 1916: 16–17). Presumably the village inhabitants tended this trap.

On the Carbon River, Marian Smith placed the extreme upriver village of tuwháq'habc at just "above Orting where Vogt [i.e., Voight] Creek enters the Carbon River" (1940: 10–11). The western national park border is 17-1/2 miles up the Carbon River from this site.

Haeberlin and Gunther only mentioned Puyallup settlements close to Puget Sound (1930: 9). Swanton, in his compilation of data from published sources, did not add any information in regard to Smith's village listings (1952: 429–30).

Muckleshoot

I did not obtain a list of Muckleshoot villages during my informant research. However, Marian Smith's listing did not record any villages on the White River east of Boise Creek, in the modern-day Buckley-Enumclaw vicinity. This locality, of course, is located in the Puget Sound lowland and many miles from Mount Rainier National Park (1940: 17).

Structures

Only temporary camps, used by gathering and hunting parties, were established and occupied within the national park area. During the informant interviews, no specific inquiry was directed in regard to the specific architectural characteristics of dwellings utilized in the national park.

In the literature, however, Teit described the summer-time hunting, root digging, and berrying lodges of the Wenatchi, which appears pertinent to the present study.

> Temporary structures were "of two common shapes, the oblong or lean-to, and the conical. The latter is said to have been most used. The former was in large measure merely a shelter at fishing and gathering places in fair weather. Small lean-tos were often used as temporary lodges on journeys, as they required fewer poles, fewer mats, and any kind of poles would do. In windy places extra poles were laid on top of the lodge-mats, and steadied at the butt end with stones. This accounts for the circles of stones on tent-sites" (1928: 114).

For the Yakama, too, temporary shelters were presumably of the lean-to and mobile, tule-mat tipi types.

> Curtis described the Yakama summer shelter as a conical framework of poles covered with a single layer of matting. The bed consisted of dry grass spread on the ground, with woven rush mats over the grass; covers could be rabbit-skin blankets (1911: 5).

Haeberlin and Gunther have described the temporary summer dwellings of the Nisqually, which may be regarded as representative for the Puget Sound groups:

> "The Nisqually summer house was either tipi shaped or square. The tipis had a frame of poles tied together at the top and covered with mats which ran horizontally around the structure. The square house had a gabled roof or was a lean-to with a single pitch roof. This frame was also covered with mats and a loose mat at the front served as a door. The fire was always outside. The Nisqually also built temporary houses of brush when camping in the mountains. These were like the square houses and were covered with maple, alder or fir boughs" (1930: 18).

The literature search for the present study also revealed a brief description of a Taidnapam shelter in the national park vicinity—i.e., Sluiskin's aforementioned summertime dwelling in the Packwood area that Hazard Stevens visited in August 1870. Stevens described it as "a rude shelter formed of a few skins thrown over a framework of poles." A half-dressed deerskin was spread on the ground inside for sitting on, and the fire was in front of the shelter (1916: 108–30).

Two additional categories of "structures" mentioned by my informants were fashioned in the national park area. These included drying racks and steaming pits for preparing berries and meat (which will be described in chapter 5), and the sweat lodge.

"Sweating," according to the Yakama informants, had to be practiced for cleansing and purifying preliminarily to hunting. Some sweat lodges had only enough room for a single person, while others were large enough for three or four people. Hot rocks were rolled or carried into a sweat lodge, then water was sprinkled on them to generate steam. When an occupant's skin was thoroughly saturated by the hot mist, dirt and grease were rubbed off the skin. The sweating was followed by a plunge into a nearby stream. Sometimes, this sequence—sweating, and then a cold plunge—was repeated two or more times. Following this, hunters bathed themselves with water in which fir boughs had been boiled, and then rubbed themselves with sweet-smelling leaves. Then, it was claimed, hunters, having no human scent, could closely approach a deer.

> According to Marian Smith, the Puyallup and Nisqually, too, thought it necessary to sweat before hunting, gambling, or power quests. These groups constructed two types of sweathouses, but evidently only one was used in the mountains. It was hemispherical in shape and just large enough for one person. Its frame consisted of vine maple limbs stuck in the ground and tied together at the top; then it was covered with evergreen boughs. Inside the small structure, a hole was dug off to one side to receive the stones, and the loose earth was put around the base of the lodge. The floor was covered with cedar boughs. The stones were heated by a bark fire and were sprinkled with water to generate steam. The sweat bath was followed "by an immediate plunge into cold water" (1940: 121).

5

Economic and other Uses

All of my informants agreed that their individual tribal groups economically utilized parts of Mount Rainier National Park, but this use was exclusively for gathering and hunting in the latter part of summer.

Testimony to this same general point—that Indians sought game and plant foods in the national park area, but did not maintain any permanent or even seasonal abodes of any duration—likewise occurs in the documentary sources. Some statements regarding Indian parties, however, are so general that it cannot be determined whether Plateau or Coastal groups are being referred to. The following comments by F.W. Schmoe, a park naturalist in the 1920s, are a case in point.

> Schmoe noted no evidence for any permanent camps within the park area, but added "there is no question but that the Indians made summer pilgrimages into the high country to hunt and to gather wild berries" (1926d: 2; see also 1925g: 80; Brockman, 1929b: 3). Also commenting in 1926, Schmoe observed that "local Indians" still were coming "each season into the open parks and gather[ing] the years supply of berries. Several varieties of huckleberries…[were] abundant in the region, and these…[were dried] for the winters food supply" (1926f: 3; see also 1925g: 82–83).
>
> In that same year, Schmoe further noted in *Mount Rainier Nature Notes* the presence of contemporary "local Indians…[who] started [in late July or early August] their annual migration to the alpine berry fields to gather the ripening blueberries" (August 4, 1926: 2).
>
> Charles Landes, another contributor to *Mount Rainier Nature Notes*, provided evidence on the same point (1925a: 1).

Plateau Tribes

On the other hand, a number of statements in the literature do clearly identify specific groups in the national park area.

> Regarding the Yakama, Curtis reported that each band in midsummer moved into the mountains to gather berries. The Mount Rainier and Mount Adams areas were the objective of "numberless little parties" of Yakama. The berries were picked, dried, and packed in bags for winter consumption, and then brought back to the valley villages as autumn approached and late fishing began on the lowland rivers (1911: 4, 6).[1]

Though designated as "Klickitat" below, G.F. Allen probably was actually referring to the Yakama (i.e., people "from the sagebrush plains") in the following explicit statement.

> "The old burns in the middle altitudes of the Park occupy regions once frequented by the Klickitat Indians. Every summer parties of hunters and berry pickers from the sagebrush plains crossed the Cascades with their horses. They followed the high divides and open summits of the secondary ridges until they came around to the open parks about Mount Rainier where they turned their horses out to graze and made their summer camp. The women picked huckleberries and the men hunted deer and goats. They made great fires to dry their berries and kindled smudges to protect their horses from flies. It was also their custom to systematically set out fires as they returned" (1916: 5–6; quoted by Schmoe, 1925g: 205).
>
> Schmoe adds, but without recording the basis for his tribal identifications, that the Yakama and Klikitat "came into the high valleys[2] [of the national park] each summer, the women to gather berries, and the men to hunt the goat, deer, elk, and bear that abounded, but never to make homes" (1926e: 2–3).

Puget Sound Tribes

C. Frank Brockman, a Mount Rainier park naturalist, presumably was repeating from other sources when he wrote:

> "Indian Henry, otherwise Satulick, used to visit the region [the southwest part of Mount Rainier National Park] in company with other Indians to hunt and pick huckleberries in order to provide for the coming winter" (1929g: 3).

Len Longmire provided a further statement attesting to this same point. As a youngster in 1888, Len helped his father, Elcain Longmire, establish a homestead at what is now Longmire in the southwest part of the park. (Len's grandfather, James Longmire, had discovered the mineral springs here in 1883, and had established his own homestead in that same year [see Brockman, 1933d: 9].) As an informant to ranger-naturalist Alton A. Lindsey, Len Longmire stated:

> "Indian Henry was a very wise Indian.... His real name sounded like 'Sotulie'.... Indian Henry was a chief of the Klickitats and a mighty good one too.... He led his tribe...[to the large 'park' north of Satulick Point known as Indian Henrys Hunting Ground] every year for their summer camping grounds; the men hunted game while the women picked huckleberries. Satulick point was named for Indian Henry" (1933: 4)
>
> According to Schmoe, Puget Sound Indians, including the Puyallup, Nisqually, and "Cowlitz from the Columbia River basin to the south [probably the Taidnapam]" likewise occasionally "wandered into the [national park's] high valleys to gather berries, and to dig roots" (1925g: 79–80; 1926e: 2–3).

So far as my informants were aware, the national park area was visited for hunting and gathering purposes only, and during the late summer season. However, Billy Frank, a Nisqually, admitted to the possibility that in earlier times members of his tribe may have journeyed to this area at other times of the year. If such had been the case, however, he had never been informed of the fact.

This data and other sources appearing later in this chapter uniformly recognize the utilization of berry and game resources in the park. However, it is of interest that two early literature sources mention native reverence toward, and even actual fear of, Mount Rainier. My informants mentioned no such concern, but then they were not specifically queried on this point either. The two documentary references are those of Lt. Kautz and Hazard Stevens.

> Kautz, who in 1857 nearly scaled Mount Rainier, reported that the "Indians were very superstitious and afraid of it" (1916: 75).
>
> Stevens noted: "The superstitious fears and traditions of the Indians, as well as the dangers of the ascent, had prevented their attempting to reach the summit" (1916: 96; see also Brockman, 1929b: 3, 1930a: 4, 1931b: 2, 1934e: 11; Richards, 1930c: 7). Stevens' guide, Sluiskin, described the mountain as "inhabited by an evil spirit, who dwelt in a fiery lake on its summit. No human being could ascend it or even attempt its ascent, and survive." Sluiskin further contended that his own grandfather, "a great chief and warrior, and a mighty hunter, had ascended part way up the mountain, and had encountered some of these dangers." Sluiskins's earnest warning, and later his astonishment at Steven's successful return from the summit, convinced Stevens that Sluiskin was expressing a genuine, traditional fear of the peak (1916: 114–15, 124).

Whether or not related to this Indian concern, enough of the internal heat of the volcano has persisted to produce numerous steam jets in the summit craters. Moreover, the mountain "is known to have been active at intervals during the last century, and actual record exists of slight eruptions in 1843, 1854, 1858, and 1870" (Matthes: 1916: 205–6). Matthes noted that "Indian legends mention a great cataclysmal outburst at an earlier period."

These two seemingly contradictory sets of data—one testifying to a hunting-collecting utilization on the higher slopes of the mountain, and the other to a timorous avoidance of these slopes—may possibly be brought into harmony by assuming, reasonably enough, that the latter applied only to the areas above the permanent snowline and to the summit crater itself.

Food Collecting

Huckleberries and Blueberries

According to my informants, the most important food resources were huckleberries (Yakama: wiúwno·, wiwúno; Taidnapam: atiť),[3] which grew to large size in the national park area, and blueberries (Yakama: ililmúq, alilmíkʷ), which were especially abundant there. According to my Muckleshoot informants, huckleberries formerly were firmer than now, and grew in both high and low bush varieties, with the low type tasting "a little like bananas."

Since, according to my informants, berry gathering was the primary attraction of the park, the locations of the berry grounds are of special interest, and archaeological surveys might be most appropriately concentrated in those areas. One way to approach this is by looking at the purely botanical data and thus identify the types of huckleberries and blueberries that exist within the national park, and to locate where they occur. Inasmuch as huckleberries and blueberries are not consistently differentiated in popular parlance and given that they belong to the same botanical genus, they are referred to here by the term "huckleberry" in the commentary throughout the remainder of this section.

According to G.N. Jones, huckleberries are typical shrubs in three of the four life zones recognized for the Mount Rainier area (see Life Zones in chapter 1). Only the Arctic-Alpine zone, extending upward from approximately 6,000 feet in elevation, had none of these shrubs.

Both Jones (1938: 10, 131–32) and C. Frank Brockman (1947: 127–28; 1934h: 10) present lists of these plants—their categorizations are identical except that *Vaccinium occidentale* is given only by Brockman, and *V. membranaceum* is placed by Jones exclusively in the Canadian Zone, as also *V. parvifolium* in the Humid-Transition Zone. Figure 5.1 represents a compilation of their two sets of data, with a few additional notes from Piper (1916: 168–69), Schmoe (1925g: 158, 162–64), and Hoversen (1936: 82–86) as indicated.[4]

Two notes of interest may be appended to the Figure 5.1 list:

> (a) The data presented for *V. parvifolium* checks in detail with the information on this variety provided by F.A. Warren (1926: 2).
>
> (b) Piper, Landes, Schmoe, and Hoverson also mention a *V. macrophyllum*, a scientific name not included in Figure 5.1.

The first of these authors (Piper, 1916: 255, 268) describes *V. macrophyllum* as "the most valuable of all the native huckleberries…nearly black, not glaucous berries….Plentiful at 3,000 to 4,000 feet altitude."

Landes (1925a: 1) identifies it as large, wine-colored or nearly black, and without bloom, and reports that it "is preferred [by the Indians] because of its superior sweetness and keeping qualities."

Schmoe (1925g: 162–63; following Piper) adds that these high-bush blueberries or blue huckleberries yield berries that are fine-flavored and often the size of small grapes.

Figure 5.1

Life Zone	Species Name	Common Name	Miscellaneous Notes
Humid-Transitional Zone	*Vaccinium parvifolium*	red huckleberry; red whortleberry	Very common in forests; berries large, bright red, acid; ripen in August and September; fruit abundant.
	V. ovatum	evergreen huckleberry; box blueberry	Low bush; common in moist woods (Jones); not common (Brockman); berries black.
Canadian Zone	*V. parvifolium* (see description above)		Very common in lower Canadian Zone; grows best in the national park at elevations about 3,500 feet.
	V. ovalifolium	blue huckleberry; ovalleaf whortleberry; low-bush blueberry	Perhaps most common blueberry in the national park. In burns and open coniferous forests; often occurs with black huckleberries. In sf. with *V. macrophyllum* (v.i.); bush lower; berries pendant and usually slightly smaller (Schmoe, 1925g: 163). Berries: black (Brockman); glaucous black, not nearly so sweet as those of *V. macrophyllum* (Piper, 1916: 268); much lighter than *V. marcrophyllum* owing to covering of light bloom (Schmoe, 1925g: 163). Fruit abundant and furnish much of the late-season food for bear and grouse (Schmoe, 1925g: 163).
	V. membranaceum	black huckleberry; big whortleberry	Common in upper Canadian Zone; abundant in coniferous forests; berry large, black, or dark wine-colored; delicious.
	V. occidentale	westernhog blueberry	Berries black.
	V. scoparium (V. myrtillus microphyllum [Piper, 1916: 268])	grouseberry; grouse whortleberry	On rocky slopes and ridges, dry open woods, or edges of meadows or thickets. From 4,000' upwards (Piper, 1916: 268); abundant between 2,000' and 4,000' (Hoverson, 1936: 82). Low, broom-like; berries small; red or wine-colored.
Hudsonian Zone	*V. scoparium* (see description above)		Common in lower Hudsonian Zone; up to 5,000' elevation (Piper, 1916: 268).
	V. membranaceum (see description above)		Common in lower Hudsonian Zone.
	V. deliciosum	mountain huckleberry; delicious blueberry; bilberry; dwarfed huckleberry	Low bush; common in sub-alpine meadows from 4,500' to 5,500' elevation; berries dark blue or black; sweet, ripen in late August. (Schmoe, 1925g: 158.)

Hoverson describes it as a high-bush huckleberry, highly prized by the Indians for its taste (1936: 82–86).

Evidently, these four authors are referring to the same species. Though *V. macrophyllum* cannot certainly be correlated with a botanical identification in Figure 5.1, it would seem to be either *V. membranaceum* or *V. occidentale*, since Piper (1916: 268–69) and Schmoe (1925g: 158, 162–63) also list both *V. ovalifolium* and *V. deliciosum*, apparently the other two possible identifications, as distinct species in their *Vaccinium* listing.

On the basis of the details provided in Figure 5.1, an identification with *V. membranaceum* seems most probable, and is assumed to be the correct one. This seems to be confirmed by Hoverson, who lists both *V. macrophyllum* and *V. occidentale*, but not *V. membranaceum*, as Mount Rainier species (1936: 83). To this same point is Hoverson's note that *V. occidentale* is not much found on Mount Rainier.

Comparing *Vaccinium ovalifolium*, *V. deliciosum*, and his *V. macrophyllum* [*membranaceum*?], Schmoe notes that all are fine-flavored, but possess slightly different tastes (1925g: 162–63). This is of interest since it confirms my informant's observation that berries with different flavors grew on the mountainsides.

Next comes the question regarding which of the huckleberry varieties were most sought after by native groups—

The red huckleberry (evidently *V. parvifolium*) seemingly can be eliminated. Though common and bearing single berries of an intense red, in the estimation of Schmoe it was not "especially desirable for food" (1923c: 1).

On the other hand, evidence suggests that *V. ovalifolium*, *V. membranaceum*, and *V. deliciosum* were all highly favored. *V. membranaceum* in particular is described as having been prized. The data for *V. deliciosum*, however, is somewhat conflicting:

> While praising its flavor, Schmoe stated: "The dwarfed blueberries [*V. deliciosum*]...are abundant in the high meadows, but the berries grow so close to the ground, the bushes are so small, and they ripen so late in the season, that they play little part in the economic life of either the bears or the Indians. In the lower park lands such as those found about Reflection Lake, Lake Louise, and Mountain Meadows below Mowich Lake and the burned-over areas throughout the national park, two other varieties of blueberries

> [*V. ovalifolium* and his *V. macrophyllum*] grow in great profusion" (1925g: 162). Indian gathering parties, it is implied, actively sought these latter varieties.
>
> On the other hand, Hoverson describes *V. deliciosum* as being abundant in Indian Henrys Hunting Ground (1936: 84). He notes that its sugar content is high, and observed that it was a variety which, even in the mid-1930s, was gathered in quantity by the Indians and bears because the berry is large and low to the ground.

Thus, this one explicit characteristic of *V. deliciosum* that Schmoe regarded as disadvantageous—i.e., its closeness to the ground—Hoverson found to be in its favor.

P.M. Fogg (1925: 1) claims that three types of blueberries, all excellent and edible, exist in the national park:

> (a) bush 2–3' high; berry large, almost black, rises erect from the plant.
> (b) bush 1' high or less; berry large, dark blue, pendant.
> (c) bush very low (inches only); berry small and blue.

The first (a) may probably be identified as *V. membranaceum*; (b) as *V. ovalifolium*; and (c) as *V. deliciosum*. This categorization by Fogg obviously is deficient as an exhaustive listing of berry types, nonetheless it appears to be a practical guide to the useful and edible berries in Mount Rainier National Park.

Both Schmoe and Fogg describe three kinds of berries as being especially attractive as food. Moreover, they apparently refer to the same three species. My informants likewise mentioned three distinct types collected by berrying parties. These match the characteristics of *V. ovalifolium*, *V. membranaceum*, and *V. deliciosum* in Figure 5.1—the Indian "blueberry" being equated tentatively with *V. ovalifolium*, the "high-bush huckleberry" with *V. membranaceum*, and the "low-bush huckleberry" with *V. deliciosum*. In this connection, it is reassuring that Kitchin (1939: 124) and Brockman (1930g: 3) also identified the "low-bush huckleberry" with *V. deliciosum*.

In any event, both Landes (1925a: 1) and Schmoe (1925g: 162) provide data to underscore the assumption that these were the three species sought by the Indians, whether or not the *V. ovalifolium* and *V. deliciosum* identifications are sorted out correctly with the types mentioned by my informants.

The botanical data does not provide specific details about the abundance of berries in the different life zones, nor generally of the quantity of one variety as compared to others. However, ranger-naturalist Scheffer noted that anywhere "alpine firs withdraw to open up a meadow, this plant [the huckleberry] will find its place and set about to form a sturdy mass of growth" (1933: 6). [Alpine and sub-alpine fir are alternative names for *Abies lasiocarpa* common to the sub-alpine (Hudsonian) zone in Mount Rainier National Park.—Editors]

Alpine firs are characteristic of the Hudsonian Zone. Hence, Scheffer's statement explicitly indicates that a high frequency of at least some varieties of huckleberries thrived at these higher elevations. Assuming the accuracy of the identification of *V. ovalifolium*, *V. membranaceum*, and *V. deliciosum* as the three species customarily gathered, the higher elevations of the national park, specifically in the Canadian Zone and middle altitudes of the Hudsonian Zone, seem clearly to have been the areas most visited for berry collection. Therefore, it may be concluded that the main berrying areas extended from approximately 3,000 feet in elevation, or slightly higher, to about 5,500 feet, or the upper limits of the parks.

We may now turn to the published ethnographic and ethnohistorical information supporting my informant data that huckleberries and blueberries were traditionally gathered on the slopes of Mount Rainier. Some relevant observations in the published record do not specify the Indian groups involved. The following are four cases in point, mostly focusing on contemporary use in the 1920s.

> Schmoe in 1925 noted that great quantities of blueberries "are picked by Indians who come into the national park late each August to secure their year's supply of blueberries" (1925g: 162).
>
> According to Hoverson, the Indians gathered huckleberries for winter use (1936: 82–86). Even in the pre-contact period, aboriginal tribes "for miles around" knew well the berry areas within today's national park. Trails led to these grounds from both east and west. Each fall, parties from the different tribes made the trip to their favorite sites, where they not only gathered and dried the berries for winter storage, but also hunted with good success.
>
> On August 4, 1926, Schmoe noted that "the local Indians have started their annual migration to the alpine berry fields"; the groups are not named (1926l: 1–2).

> Finally, in 1929, Robert Anderson found "a band of Indians picking huckleberries in the manner of their forefathers who ventured upon Rainier's slopes each year about that time in search of these berries and to hunt. Now, of course, their activities are limited to picking berries" (1929: 4). This was evidently on the northwest slope of Indian Henrys Hunting Ground, on the trail from Tahoma Creek. The date of this encounter is uncertain, but it appears to have been in September.

In addition to the above, Schmoe mentions Indian berry gathering in similarly general terms in three other sources (1926d: 2; 1926f: 3; 1926l: 2).

In contrast, the following two references imply the identity of specific tribes within the national park.

> Curtis supports the contention of my informants that the Yakama were accustomed to securing huckleberries in the national park area. He reported: "Of fruits the huckleberry was the most important. Quantities were gathered [i.e., by the Yakama] on the slopes of the Cascades, particularly at Mount Adams and Mount Rainier" (1911: 6)
>
> Without identifying the group involved, Landes noted in mid-August 1925: "Huckleberry time as usual was heralded by the arrival of parties of Indians who came to the mountain each year to get a supply of the delicious fruit. The Indians usually camp on this [southwest] side of the mountain either up the Kautz a few miles from the road or at Rocksecker [Ricksecker] Point, where the large wine-colored or nearly black variety, without bloom, (*Vaccinium macrophyllum*) grows in great abundance in the burned over land. This variety is preferred because of its superior sweetness and keeping qualities. This annual pilgrimage of the Indians has lost much of its picturesqueness. A few years ago they arrived on horseback in gaily colored attire.... Before the time of the white man Indians came to the Park for berries" (1925a: 1). Since both areas mentioned in the latter account lie in the upper Nisqually drainage, it might be supposed—though without definite proof—that members of the Nisqually tribe were involved.

My informants could not describe the specific locations of any berry grounds used by Indian parties. The reasons for this are mentioned in chapter 1 (see Ethnographic Field Findings). Notably, the Indian berrying excursions that continued up into the 1920s were soon after halted by NPS decree. Few Northwest Indians visited the park after that time, memories faded, and locational descriptions were not passed along to the younger generation. Also, as one Yakama informant phrased it, "where my family used to gather berries is now all grown up," with the result that to recognize the area, if its general vicinity were visited, would be difficult at best. It was noted that it took two or three days by horseback from Yakama country to reach the Mount Rainier berry grounds.

However, references in the literature delineate areas in the southern and northwestern parts of the national park where huckleberries grow in particular abundance—or at least did so in the recent past. This list certainly is not exhaustive, having been compiled with some happenstance during the literature review:

> (1) The northwestern slope of Indian Henrys Hunting Ground (Anderson, 1929: 4).
>
> (2) The open ridge in the southern part of Indian Henrys Hunting Ground south of Mount Ararat, an area "scarred by a great burn." The Kautz trail, from Kautz Creek north to the base of Mount Ararat, passes through this burn, which "changed a great forest into open barren lands covered only with huckleberry" (Landes, 1924b: 3). This evidently is where Landes saw Indians camped in August 1925 (1925a: 1). And, it evidently is the same berrying ground, or at least another very close by, described by Anderson in 1929: "a band of Indians [were] picking huckleberries [on Indian Henrys Hunting Ground] in the manner of their forefathers" (1929: 4).
>
> (3) An unbroken four-mile patch along Rampart Ridge, between Kautz Creek and the Nisqually River. Here grew the "*deliciosum*," said to be the best of all huckleberries. This fine, large berrying ground was well visited by black bears (Writers' Program, 1941: 598).
>
> (4) The hills along the Nisqually Glacier canyon. Here, in 1928, were "great patches" of huckleberries (Brockman, 1928b: 4).
>
> (5) Ricksecker Point, on the upper Nisqually River. Indians berried here in August 1925 (Landes, 1925a: 1).

(6) Paradise Valley on the upper Paradise River, specifically in the burn known as the "silver forest," between Glacier Bridge and Narada Falls. This location offered blueberries and red huckleberries in profusion, at least in the mid-1920s. Long "a mecca for [Indian] berrypickers" (Schmoe, 1924b: 1; Brockman, 1928a: 3).

(7) From the Reflection Lakes and on down Stevens Canyon to, and including, the Nickel Creek Burn. Here were acres of huckleberry bushes, according to Kitchin (1939: 116). Other observers describe the following areas within this strip more precisely:

(a) Blue huckleberries were found around the southern end of the Reflection Lakes between Mazama Ridge and the Tatoosh Range (Writers' Program, 1941: 594). In the parks about Reflection Lakes, *V. ovalifolium* and *V. macrophyllum* [*membranaceum*?] grew in great profusion (Schmoe, 1925g: 162).

(b) Blue huckleberries grew in the immediate vicinity of Lake Louise, just east of the Reflection Lakes, and in the high saddle between Mazama Ridge and the Tatoosh Range. Here, the tall bushes drooped "with fruit in the late summer." Bear and deer were in the forests of this vicinity (Writers' Program, 1941: 594). Schmoe also identified the slope above Lake Louise as a berry area (1925g: 162; 1926n: 2; 1928b: 4).

(c) In 1927, Jones found the first ripe huckleberries of the season on Stevens Ridge, at an elevation of approximately 5,000 feet (1927: 3).

(8) At Mountain Meadows, below Mowich Lake. Here huckleberries grew in great profusion (Schmoe, 1925g: 162).

(9) Sunset Park, where the huckleberries were sufficiently abundant to attract sooty grouse, band-tailed pigeons, and other birds by the hundreds. It was low-bush huckleberries, "*V. celiciosum*" [sic], that attracted the birds (Kitchin, 1939: 92, 124).

The first six of these areas (1–6) seem clearly to be in Nisqually country, as defined in the present study. Areas (7a) and (7b) lie on the border between Nisqually and Taidnapam territories, while (7c) is in Taidnapam country. To the northwest, (8) and (9) fall within Puyallup boundaries. As already noted, my informants did not specify the locations of berry grounds. However, the literature points to the use of at least some of these areas as gathering areas. Furthermore, most, if not all, of these localities are in the proper altitudinal zone and possess the biotic characteristics apparently favored as berry collecting localities.

Huckleberries thrive best in burned-over open areas. Landes, for example, stated explicitly that huckleberries "are at their best in the open burns as...[they] grow best in these regions" (1925a: 1).

Possibly, efforts were made traditionally to increase the Mount Rainier huckleberry yields by intentionally burning the slopes, though none of my informants alluded to the practice. At any rate, several statements in the literature suggest it.

> In 1900, Plummer was among the first to make a statement in this regard: "Indians...start fires on the slopes and summits [of the national park area] for the purpose of promoting the growth of huckleberries, blackberries, and raspberries, and also to drive game" (1900: 135).
>
> In 1925, Landes reported: "Before the time of the white man Indians came to the national park for berries and it is thought that many of the burned areas of the park were originally burned over by the Indians to increase the distribution and yield of the huckleberry" (1925a: 1).
>
> Schmoe writes: "It is likely the Indians set many of the fires that have occurred in the area now included in the national park for the express purpose of increasing the crop of blueberries" (1925g: 162).
>
> Allen (1916: 5–6) reported at greater length: "The old burns in the middle altitudes of the national park occupy regions once frequented by the Klickitat Indians [probably Yakama]. Every summer parties of hunters and berry pickers from the sagebrush plains crossed the Cascades with their horses.... It was also their custom to systematically set out fires as they returned. Burning made the country better for the Indians. The fires kept down the brush and made it more accessible. Deer could be more easily seen and tracked and the huckleberry patches spread more widely over the hills" (quoted by Schmoe, 1925g: 205). A similar view is expressed in the 1941 *Washington* handbook of the WPA Writers' Program, which,

however, may well be based on the Landes or Schmoe accounts, since it presents precisely the same information (1941: 594).

Allen (1916: 5) lists the following large, ancient burned-over areas between the sub-alpine zone and the river valleys. By 1925, Schmoe noted that these localities had been partially reclaimed by reforestation (1925g: 204–5):

(1) The Muddy Fork burn was the most extensive of all (about 20 square miles in the national park), resulting in hillsides covered with huckleberry bushes. From west to east, the burned area extended from the Reflection Lakes locality to Ohanapecosh Hot Springs. From north to south, it extended from near Mount Rainier's glacial snouts and almost to the main stem of the Cowlitz River south of the park. This fire occurred many years before the coming of whites.

(2) The ridge country between Huckleberry Creek and the White River.

(3) The ridge below Indian Henrys Hunting Ground between Tahoma Creek and Kautz Creek.

These burns are of especial interest since, according to Allen, reforestation at these higher elevations is extremely slow (1916: 5). From his period of observation—1886 to 1916—there had been little apparent change in the vegetation of these alpine burns. Indeed, more than a century is required, Allen contends, for trees to return growing at these heights, though at lower elevations the forest recovery is more rapid. My informants did not make mention of burned-over areas as favorite berrying spots. Nevertheless, on the basis of the above data, it would seem appropriate during any reconnaissance for archaeological sites to examine burn areas located at the proper elevations. [Note that in the 90 years since G.F. Allen recorded these remarks, many, though not all, of the huckleberry-rich burned areas in the park have become substantially reforested. It is reasonable to assume that the huckleberry fields on Mount Rainier are not as productive as they were in the late 1800s and early 1900s.—Editors]

A comparison of the information from my informants, the literature research, and the botanical data strengthen the notion that higher elevation berries were collected, rather than those growing lower down. In coming to this conclusion, three questions were explored:

> (a) When was the berrying season as indicated by my informants and the literature research?
>
> (b) What are the normal ripening periods for the various species of berries?
>
> (c) What does a comparison of the Indian berrying season and the ripening periods reveal in regard to the locations (elevations) of the berrying grounds?

As to the timing of the berrying season, my informants were entirely explicit on this point. To harvest huckleberries and blueberries, small groups visited the mountain meadows during late August and early September. Camps were made for a week or two, while the women picked and dried berries. A number of statements in the literature generally confirm the seasonal timing of these mountain visits as presented by my informants.

> The Yakama, Curtis reported, journeyed to Mount Rainier in midsummer to gather berries (1911: 4, 6). As autumn approached, they returned to the east of the Cascades to their villages to fish.
>
> The "klickitat"—evidently the Yakama are meant—are said by Schmoe to have once frequented the national park area "every summer" (1925g: 205).
>
> Additional "summertime" confirmation is provided by Schmoe (1926d: 2; 1926e: 2–3) and Longmire (in Lindsey, 1933: 4).
>
> Schmoe reported in 1926 that the annual berrying pilgrimage to Mount Rainier began in late July or very early August (1926l: 2).

The botanical data did not explicitly specify the normal ripening periods of the various species of berries in the park. Clearly, however, the ripening times for huckleberries growing at different elevations vary to some degree. A statement suggesting this was made by Schmoe on July 16, 1923, when he noted that wild blueberries "will soon be ripening in the low valley and are not yet through blooming in the Alpine meadows" (1923a: 1). When compared with the time for berry gathering as indicated by my informants, this indicates that it was the berries growing at higher elevations that drew Indians to the mountains. The literature references to the Indian collecting season suggest this same conclusion.

On August 14, 1923, for example, Schmoe noted: "The most common berry in the park is the blue berry or blue huckleberry. There are two species very similar, one called the high bush and the other low bush blueberries. These berries are ripe now" (1923b: 1).

On August 18, 1925, Fogg recorded that blueberries were ripe on the sunny slopes (1925: 1). In the same year, Landes noted: "the crop [of huckleberries] has ripened earlier than usual and are hanging heavy and ripe on bushes" (1925a: 1).

In 1926, Schmoe reported that the season was especially advanced (1926l: 2). Blueberries were ripe by August 4, and the Indians had started their berry gathering.

In 1930, on the other hand, huckleberries began ripening about August 15 (Brockman, 1930f: 3), and still bore fruit in early September. According to Brockman under a September 1, 1930, date: "Huckleberries are ripe. Great, luscious blue-black berries are found in large quantities on the low-bush huckleberry. So…we discover why this species bears the botanical name of delicosium [sic]. 'Delicosium'—delicious indeed!" (1930g: 3).

The data may be summarized as thus:

August 14, 1923. Berries ripe.
August 18, 1925. Berries ripe; ripened earlier than usual.
August 4, 1926. Berries ripe; season especially advanced.
August 15, 1930. Berries began to ripen; still ripe in early September.

From this information, it may be concluded that annual variations in the ripening seasons are not very significant. It would also appear that the normal season for traditional berry gathering extended from about August 15 into September. This agrees well with Brockman's general statement, when speaking of "the abundant huckleberries that ripen during the late summer and early fall" (1933a: 7).

It also conforms to my informants' statements that late summer was the season of berry collecting on the high hillsides. It is consistent with the documentary record noting, in the historical period, that Indians sometimes began journeying to the mountain slopes to secure the berry harvest soon after the start of August. In sum, this data, considered as a whole, seems to confirm the conclusion that Indian parties sought berries at the higher rather than lower elevations. Two additional lines of evidence support this opinion.

First, mention is made in the literature of mountain parks as favorite objectives of Indian berry gatherers.

> It is in this context when Schmoe speaks of the "open parks" about Mount Rainier (1925g: 205; 1926f: 3), of "alpine berry fields" (1926l: 2), and of "the high valleys" of the national park (1926e: 2–3). This same author reports the importance of the "park lands such as those found about Reflection Lake[s], Lake Louise, and Mountain Meadows" (1925g: 162).
>
> Brockman (1929g: 3), Longmire (Lindsey, 1933: 4), and Hoverson (1936: 82–83) indicate that the park known as Indian Henrys Hunting Ground was a well-known berry area.
>
> [These parklands are characteristic of the Hudsonian, or subalpine, life zone.—Editors]

Secondly, mountain goat hunting was a common pursuit of the men while the women gathered berries. Since these animals frequent the loftier mountain crags, especially in summer, this suggests that the summer berrying camps were pitched at the higher, or at least the middle, elevation huckleberry grounds. Their length of stay presumably varied from year to year, though again my informants did not discuss the matter. The data, however, indicates that berries were more plentiful in some years than in others, which may have affected the length of visits.

> In general terms, according to Schmoe, the annual huckleberry harvest was vast in quantity. Referring specifically to *V. ovalifolium*, *V. deliciosum*, and *V. macrophyllum* [*membranaceum*?], Schmoe noted: "Each year tons of blueberries ripen in the meadows and old burns and go to waste. Other tons are eagerly devoured by the bears and grouse or are picked by Indians" (1925g: 162).

Other data, though, makes it clear that from year to year huckleberries do vary substantially in relative abundance.

> The year 1923, according to Schmoe, showed "every prospect of another heavy crop of wild blue berries" (1923a: 1).

> On the other hand, in 1924, the same author reported a scarcity in the national park (1924g: 3).
>
> But in 1925, Fogg noted that every "sunny slope teems with the delicious fruit" (1925: 1). Also in 1925, Landes observed "an abundant crop of huckleberries this year. All varieties, high bush and low bush, blue and black and red; those found in the wood and in the sub-alpine region—all are plentiful" (1925a: 1).

Finally, all of the evidence seems to indicate that the berry resources were not exploited by "large" parties in one location. My informants provided explicit testimony to this fact—"small" groups were involved in gathering berries on the mountain slopes. Curtis seems to agree. He described the Yakama berrying visitors to Mount Rainier in terms of "numberless little parties" (1911: 4, 6).

All other documentary sources referring to the berrying groups confirm this assumption. The data points to the conclusion that the berrying-and-hunting camps were small, temporary affairs. Thus, it can be expected that the archaeological evidence that might be found at these sites will be consistent with these characteristics.

As the berries were picked, my informants said, they were collected in hard, coiled, root baskets.

> Curtis described the Yakama containers as follows: Berries were gathered in baskets with flat bottoms and flaring sides, and with capacities varying from about 2 to 4 gallons. They were of coiled cedar roots, stitched together with outer shreds of the roots, and bore imbricated ornamentation of bear grass either left white in its natural state or dyed black by immersion in blue clay or yellow by being boiled in water with certain berries (1911: 5).
>
> In 1925, park naturalist Schmoe observed that "the women still… use some very remarkable baskets made by their mothers from the local Squaw grass" (1925g: 82–82). [Schmoe is probably referring to bear grass (*Xerophyllum tenax*).—Editors]

The Taidnapam, Nisqually, Puyallup, and Muckleshoot dried berries on mat-covered racks. My Nisqually informants said these mats were made of split cedar roots and female cattails[5] woven with cedar bark. Those of the Muckleshoot were 4 feet wide, and fashioned of split cedar woven with inner cedar bark, since cedar is resistant to rot. The mats were rolled up at the close of the berry season and hidden for use in the following year. Two small fires were built under the mat racks, each close to the end of the structure. (Among the Nisqually in recent years, the berries are covered with cheesecloth to keep flies away.) This data was supported in detail by several accounts in the ethnographic literature.

> In broad descriptive terms for the Coast Salish, Curtis reported that huckleberries of several varieties were gathered in enormous quantities. A large part of the crop was dried for winter food. Commonly, the berries were spread over a mat stretched between Y-stakes and a small fire was kept burning beneath to aid the drying action of the sun (1913: 57–58).
>
> Regarding the Puget Sound peoples, Haeberlin and Gunther noted: "Often…[berries] were dried over the fire, spread on cedar bark" (1930: 22).
>
> Marian Smith reported: "Long trips were made by inland [Puyallup and Nisqually] groups and sometimes by salt water peoples to obtain the mountain huckleberry which grew in the foothills and on up into the mountains." The berries were dried on racks covered with "a plaited screen of cedar bark strips and built about four feet from the ground." Fires were ignited beneath the racks, and the dried berries were stored in baskets (1940: 247–48).

My Yakama informants, on the other hand, said they did not use racks of this type. Rather, they raised a long mound of earth, covered one side of it with mats upon which the berries were spread, and built small fires before them. Some Yakama women secured as much as 50 pounds of the dried berries, which became raisin-like, but when later boiled expanded in size. The use of drying fires by the Plateau visitors was noted by Allen, who reported that they "made great fires to dry their berries" (1916: 5–6; also see Schmoe, 1925g: 205).

The Muckleshoot, my informants reported, poured the dried berries into a basket, shook them down, added more, shook them down again, and so on until the basket was well filled. The baskets then were covered with small boughs and stored in the shade. The Yakama, according to Curtis, packed the dried berries in bags for transportation back to their winter villages (1911: 4, 6).

Under favorable conditions, some evidence of these traditional activities might yet be preserved in archaeological sites. On the basis of the available data, it would be expected that the Yakama drying mounds were limited to the eastern side of the national park. [In recent years, Yakama-style mounded huckleberry drying features have been identified and excavated in the Mount Adams area of the Gifford Pinchot National Forest, south of Mount Rainier. Such features have yet to be identified in Mount Rainier National Park, but likely will eventually be found here as well.—Editors]

Other Plant Foods

The literature suggests the possibility that other plant foods also were obtained by Indian groups while in the national park area. It is likely that if other plant resources were utilized, they were secured in relatively lesser quantities and as by-products of visits for huckleberries and other gathered and hunted resources. My informants mentioned none when questioned about subsidiary reasons for journeying to the Mount Rainier area.

In the literature, only Schmoe mentioned the acquisition of "roots."

> Schmoe, quoted earlier in this chapter, noted that the Puget Sound Indians, including the Puyallup, Nisqually, and "Cowlitz from the Columbia River basin to the south [Taidnapam?] wandered into the high valleys" of the national park to dig roots as well as to gather berries (1926e: 2–3). (In another version of this general statement, Schmoe identified the roots secured in the "high valleys" as "camas" [1925g: 80]. This identification seems almost certainly in error, as camas thrives in wet, lowland, prairie country.)

Two other possibly utilized plant foods also are noted in the documentary sources.

> Flett, in a discussion of the national park's flora, reported that the tuberous root of *Claytonia lanceolata* was a native food. It is common on dry grassy slopes in the Hudsonian Zone (1916: 43). While Flett did not explicitly state that these roots were gathered on hillsides within the national park, this seems implied at least as a possibility.
>
> White-Bark Pine (*Pinus albicaulis*), which grows on high windswept ridges and summits, yield edible nuts from its cones. Schmoe stated: "They ripen early in September and produce chocolate-brown seeds a little larger than a grain of corn. These are edible and

> are much relished by the Klickitat [i.e., Yakama] and Cowlitz [Taidnapam?] Indians, who go to considerable pains to secure them" (1925g: 221–22).

In addition, other plants known to have been gathered as food resources elsewhere in the Pacific Northwest grow on the mountain slopes. The salmonberry and the thistle *Cirsium edule* are examples, and the list easily could be extended.[6] But little in the literature indicates that Indian visitors to the national park specifically obtained them.

Hunting

Historical references suggest that while women gathered berries in the national park, the men, individually or in groups of two or three, went out hunting in the forests and on the nearby ridges. Some general references in the literature to hunting are presented here:

> According to Schmoe, Indians (tribal affiliation unspecified) made summer pilgrimages into the high country of the national park to hunt as well as to gather berries (1926d: 2).
>
> Hoverson reported that parties of Indians, including in the precontact period, frequented the slopes of Mount Rainier to berry and hunt (1936: 82–86). They came from both east and west, along trails up onto the mountain slopes. While berrying activities were underway, the men procured a good share of their winter's meat supply. Animals also were attracted by the abundant berries, which they needed to carry them through hibernation or the rigors of winter.
>
> Indian Henry (Satulick), accompanied by other Indians, visited Indian Henrys Hunting Ground in the park's southwest corner every summer to hunt and berry (Brockman, 1929g: 3; Longmire in Lindsey, 1933: 4).

As mentioned earlier in this chapter, my informants stated that berrying was the primary economic activity, at least in the Mount Rainier area, whereas hunting was secondary.

> Curtis suggested that his Yakama informants likewise thought of hunting as subordinate to berry gathering (1911: 6).

> Marian Smith, however, remarked in regard to the Puyallup and Nisqually: "if a man had success in hunting elk, a pursuit which took him back into the mountains, his family group shifted to a camp near the scene of his operations and his wife busied herself in picking mountain huckleberries rather than the swamp variety" (1940: 140).

It appears, however, that hunters, alone or in groups, sometimes visited the national park area, unaccompanied by women.

> For instance, the five Nisqually and Puyallup companions that guided Dr. William Fraser Tolmie to Mount Rainier in 1833 appeared to do so more for an opportunity to hunt elk, deer, and mountain goat, than payment for their services in ammunition and blankets (Haines, 1962: 4).
>
> Sluiskin informed Hazard Stevens in 1870 that his grandfather had been a great chief and warrior, and "a mighty hunter," while implying that he had hunted on the flanks of Mount Rainier (1916: 114–15).
>
> In the fall of 1886, A.L. Brown accompanied about 30 Yakama men in a six-week hunting excursion through Packwood Pass, up the Ohanapecosh River, and onto the Cowlitz Divide. As hunting proved unsuccessful, Brown and seven or eight Yakama, mostly in moccasins and with a few hastily crafted alpenstocks, attempted to climb Mount Rainier via the Ingraham Glacier. They ascended mountain goat tracks to the Cathedral Rocks-Gibraltar Rock vicinity before turning back after a night on the mountain (Brockman 1934i: 5; Haines 1962: 81–82). Haines also noted that the Yakama "had always considered the country over to and including the eastern slope of Mount Rainier as peculiarly their own."

Columbia Black-tail Deer (*Odocoileus hemionus columbianus*)

Known to the Yakama as yamáš and to the Muckleshoot as sqéiGwəc,[7] deer was the primary game sought by all tribal groups. Deer were stalked with bow and arrow, the Yakama reported, and were not driven over cliffs or pursued with dogs. The Muckleshoot particularly favored the West Fork of the White River for deer hunting; the headwaters of this stream lie within the northern borders of the national park.

> Indians from east of the Cascades are said by Allen to have hunted deer near Mount Rainier, while the women picked huckleberries (1916: 5–6; see also Schmoe, 1925g: 79–80; 1925g: 205).
>
> Schmoe reported, without specifying the source of his information, that deer were among the animals sought by the Yakama and Klikitat when they came into the high valleys of the national park each summer to hunt and berry (1926e: 2–3).
>
> Tolmie's diary underscored the importance of Mount Rainier's northwestern slopes as a hunting ground for deer and elk. During his 1833 excursion, Tolmie wrote the following about his companions: "The Indians are all in great hopes of killing elk and chevriel [deer]... It is in a great measure the expectation of finding game that urges them to undertake the journey" (Meany, 1916: 7; see also Haines, 1962: 3–8). The mixed Puyallup-Nisqually group clearly were aware of the hunting potential of what is now the Tolmie Peak sector in late summer and early fall season. Tolmie's main guide was Puyallup, and evidence suggests that the area was thought of as Puyallup country.

In May 1930, Brockman reported that deer were "common throughout the lower elevations of the Park" (1930c: 6). In the traditional period, too, deer evidently were widely dispersed around Mount Rainier.

> They were found "generally distributed around the mountain, in the meadows and timber up to 6,000 feet elevation" (Schmoe, 1925g: 235).
>
> Deer "were numerous almost everywhere in the wood" (Schmoe, 1924h: 5; Brockman, 1929c: 4).

Black-tailed deer are abundant in the Humid-Transitional Zone and common in the Canadian Zone, according to Dalquest (1948: 45, 399–403). As described by this author, these zones clearly apply to Mount Rainier National Park. Nevertheless, there appears to be two ways in which this general distribution was modified to some degree.

> (a) Deer seem to have been rather more numerous in certain areas than in others. They were especially abundant along the Cowlitz Divide, in Sunset Park, and around Indian Henrys Hunting ground (Schmoe, 1924h: 5; Sedergren, 1933: 9). Every summer, according

to Meany, deer were numerous in Grand Park (1916: 309–10). In 1928, Brockman reported them as particularly abundant on Mazama Ridge (1928d: 4). Their chief winter range in the national park's southwest sector was around the mouth of Tahoma Creek (Schmoe, 1924a: 1).

(b) In wintertime, black-tailed deer, like elk, "migrate from the sub-alpine meadows to below the snowline, which...often means beyond the boundaries of the Park" (Brockman, 1930b: 5). According to Dalquest, they descend to the denser Douglas fir and hemlock forests (i.e., into the Humid-Transitional Zone below about 3,000 feet) (1948: 401). Discussing this phenomenon in general, McCullough notes that the migration of these animals from their high mountainous summer ranges to protected valleys for the winter is often spectacular: "thousands of deer may move over long distances in a matter of several days" (1964: 249). These mass movements are usually associated with severe snowstorms in the fall. On the other hand, fall migrations sometimes take the form of gradual, almost imperceptible, drifting of deer from the high elevations before the first autumn storms. However, in very mild winters, such as in 1933–34, they continued to range high up in the national park. That winter, a greater part of the deer population that had summered in the park wintered there also (Brockman, 1934b: 9). In late summer, particularly August, deer sought "the higher meadowlands [4,000 to 6,000 feet] where the herbage is more tender" (Landes, 1925b: 2). Deer even "go to timber-line and above but seldom if ever much above eight thousand feet" (Schmoe, 1927f: 3).

The final statement above is of particular relevance to the present study, inasmuch as it identifies where deer were found during the season when, according to the evidence, traditional berrying-hunting parties were accustomed to visiting the Mount Rainier area. Undoubtedly, deer varied somewhat in numbers from year to year in the national park.

This is suggested by Richards' observation in 1930 that the "deer are sleek this summer—and plentiful. A mild winter made life easy for them and the woods are full of them" (1930c: 6).

In 1924, Schmoe estimated the park's deer population was 350 animals, and in 1925, at between 300 and 400 (1924i: 5, 1926a: 3).

Some fluctuation is again indicated by Landes in August 1925 when reporting that they were "more abundant than usual in the meadows and park-lands at altitudes of from four to six thousand feet" (1925b: 2).

Elk (*Cervus camedensis*)

When bugling and whistling during the autumn breeding season, elk (Yakama: nc̓í winat; Taidnapam: wínat; Nisqually: Baiyɛc, which also glosses as 'meat in general')[8] were hunted by the Yakama, Taidnapam, and Nisqually, although this was reported not to have been the case with the Muckleshoot.

> Without providing the source of his information, Schmoe mentioned that elk were among the animals hunted by the Yakama and Klikitat when berrying-hunting parties came each summer to Mount Rainier's slopes (1925g: 79–80; 1926e: 2–3).
>
> The Nisqually case for hunting elk is supported by a traditional story involving Mount Rainier that was included in Theodore Winthrop's noted 1862 travel account, *The Canoe and the Saddle*. The author heard the tale in 1853 while at Fort Nisqually. It was told by an "ancient of the Squallyamish," who claimed it recounted an episode in the life of his own grandfather, who once lived where the fort then stood. The protagonist in the narrative was a great hunter, especially of elk (Meaney, 1916: 41–57)."Elk...were every way identified with his life; and he hunted them...*though the forests on the flanks of Tacoma*.... And [hunted] near the snows...of *late summer* [ital. mine]" (Winthrop quoted in Meaney, 1916: 42–44).

The native elk, according to my informants, were different from the present-day introduced ones. The taxonomic identities of the "native" and "introduced" animals are not wholly clear, the available data being too meager and imprecise to settle the matter. Unfortunately, this problem was not recognized during my period of field research. Thus, crucial questions in regard to identification were not asked of my informants. It would appear, however, that the native form was the Olympic elk (*Cervus canadensis roosevelti*; also termed *C. c. occidentalis*).

> According Schmoe, the "lower slopes of...[Mount Rainier] were formerly within the range of the western or Olympic elk.... These

> bands of elk were practically wiped out some years ago by persistent hunting" (1924a: 2).
>
> Schmoe also put the situation as thus: "At one time elk ranged through the forests and parklands of the reservation [Mount Rainier National Park] in large numbers. Before the national park was established they were almost exterminated by hunting but recently they are reappearing in small bands" (1925g: 236). In comparison with Rocky Mountain elk, the Olympic variety is slightly larger and is a browse-feeding animal rather than a grazer.
>
> Similarly, Dalquest asserted that the range of the Olympic elk extended from the coast to the Cascades, and perhaps even into the eastern Cascades (1948: 391–94).
>
> In reestablishing the native herds, Schmoe reported that Olympic elk were brought into the national park during the 1920s, and these efforts were successful (1924a: 2; 1924h: 5; 1924i: 5; 1924j: 3; 1925bb: 1; 1925bbb: 3; see also Brockman, 1932d: 8; 1934f: 10).

What, then, can my informants have meant when saying that modern elk were different? Apparently, it must be assumed that the reintroduction of Olympic elk finally failed; and Rocky Mountain elk (*Cervus canadensis elscai*) replaced the original herds. Dalquest appears to lend possible support to this interpretation: "Introduced in the eastern Cascades,...the Rocky Mountain elk thrived and increased on what was probably once the peripheral range of the coastal elk" (1948: 391). Perhaps, when spreading westward over the Cascade Divide, they replaced Olympic elk in Mount Rainier National Park, or they were actually introduced into the national park as well, and there became established. It would appear that only this assumption could explain my informants' information.

Olympic elk, according to Dalquest, were abundant in the Humid-Transitional and Canadian zones, but rare in the Hudsonian Zone (1948: 45). More meaningful in the present context is Dalquest's statement that they ascend "to the open meadows of the Hudsonian Life-zone in the early summer," and return to the lower dense forests of the Humid-Transitional and lower Canadian zones with the winter snows (1948: 393). Brockman confirms this by noting that elk leave the sub-alpine meadows in winter and migrate down slope to below the snowline (1930b: 5). In conclusion, in the August-September huckleberry season, Olympic elk were within easy reach of hunters from the traditional gathering parties.

Bear (*Ursus americanus*)

Black bear (Yakama: anáxʷi, anahúi; Muckleshoot: ščə́twit)[9] were hunted if chanced upon in the berry patches, though many Muckleshoot regarded their meat as too strong owing to the fatty condition of the animals at that season, and at least some Yakama avoided killing them because of guardian spirit restrictions. Schmoe, without giving the source of his information, reported that bear were one of the animals hunted each summer by the Yakama and Klikitat when on berrying-hunting excursions (1925g: 79–80; 1926e: 2–3).

Evidently, bear were rather widely distributed throughout the forests in the park. They were abundant, Dalquest observed, in the Humid-Transitional, Canadian, and Hudsonian zones, which places them at the lowest elevations of the national park and upward to approximately 6,000 feet elevation or slightly higher (1948: 41).

> Unlike mountain goat, black bear according to Schmoe appeared to be "rather uniformly distributed over the entire Park below timberline." They were, he reports, probably most numerous in the Nisqually watershed (1924h: 5; see also 1925g: 238).
>
> In 1928, doubtless speaking only of the Nisqually area, Brockman noted that "bear seem to be particularly abundant" on Mazama Ridge, just east of the Paradise Valley (1928d: 4).

Such was the case, at any rate, in the Nisqually area in the 1920s. Presumably, this reflects the earlier and customary environmental adaptation of this animal. In the mid-1920s, they also were common in the northern sector of the national park. Bear were plentiful, for instance, in the Yakima Park and Huckleberry Creek areas as well as in more remote localities (Trolson, 1926: 4).

There seems, however, to be some evidence of variations in numbers from year to year, a situation expected on ecological grounds. In 1930, Brockman wrote: "The woods are full of…[bears]. They seem to be more numerous than ever before" (1930d: 6; see also 1930e: 6).

However, during the huckleberry season they congregated in the berry patches.

> Schmoe observed, for example: "There is every prospect of another heavy crop of wild blue berries this year…. This means a

> good season for the bears" (1923a: 1; see also 1923b: 1, 1925d: 2; 1925g: 162; Brockman, 1928f: 4; 1932c: 3; 1933e: 7). And, bears were particularly "abundant in the open meadows and park like regions during huckleberry time" (Schmoe, 1925g: 238).
>
> These naturalists' observations are in agreement with the general statements of Dalquest: "The principal food of the black bear in Washington is berries," the huckleberry being particularly favored. Furthermore, in the mountains bears hibernate "with the first snows or, if the snows are late, when the huckleberries are gone" (1948: 173–74). This seems clearly to mean that bears were available to hunters on the mountainsides during the berry gathering season.

In late August or early September 1926, seven bears, all berrying, were seen on the slope above Lake Louise (Schmoe, 1926n: 2). In 1924, the national park staff estimated a black bear population of 200 animals (Schmoe, 1924i: 5); and, in 1925, at between 200 and 300 (Schmoe, 1925a: 2).

Mountain Goat (*Oreamnos americanus americanus*)

Though regarded as being extremely difficult to hunt, mountain goat (Yakama: wáu; Nisqually: sx̣ʷíƛ̓i; Muckleshoot: sxʷíƛ̓ai)[10] were sought by at least the Nisqually, Muckleshoot, Yakama, and Taidnapam.

> Allen reported that the "Klikitat" [probably the Yakama] hunted mountain goat on the flanks of Mount Rainier while the women gathered huckleberries (1916: 5–6; see also Schmoe, 1925g: 79–80, 205).
>
> In 1926, Schmoe wrote that mountain goat were hunted by both the Yakama and Klikitat each summer when they journeyed to Mount Rainier to hunt and collect berries (1926e: 2–3).
>
> In 1870, Hazard Stevens had noted that Sluiskin "frequently hunted the mountain sheep upon the snow-fields of Takhoma" (1916: 108). Evidently in his statements, Stevens meant mountain goat when he wrote "mountain sheep." Sluiskin himself, as translated, reported that he had "often hunted the mountain goat" on Mount Rainier's snowfields (1916: 134). Stevens further explained: "Even Sluiskin, a skillful hunter and accustomed to the pursuit of this animal [mountain goat] for years, failed to kill one, notwithstanding he hunted assiduously during our entire stay upon the

> mountain, three days [i.e., while Stevens and Van Trump climbed Mount Rainier]. Sluiskin was greatly chagrined at his failure, and promised to bring each of us a sheep-skin the following summer, a promise which he faithfully fulfilled" (1916: 124–25). Sluiskin is identified by Stevens as a Taidnapam-Yakama, which makes it probable that the Taidnapam pursued mountain goat, as well the Nisqually and Muckleshoot.

Mountain goat inhabited open belts around the mountain above timberline (Schmoe, 1924d: 3). According to Dalquest, without specific reference to Mount Rainier, they occurred in the Arctic-Alpine and Hudsonian zones, and descended to the Canadian Zone if there were extensive, open, rocky areas in the latter zone (1948: 45, 407).

> Richards put the matter thusly: when the weather is fair, they are found high up on the mountain-side among the glaciers and pinnacles. "But when fog and foul weather harry these dizzy heights the clan comes down into the Hudsonian meadows just below" (1930b: 5).
>
> Homuth noted: "the goat wander widely over the lower slopes of the glaciers, the intervening rock cleavers, and occasionally down into the sub-alpine meadows" (1934: 11).
>
> Seasonal movement is customary for mountain goat, as Brockman reported. "Each winter the Mountain Goat must, of necessity, retreat to lower elevations" (1929a: 2). And again: "Goat, rugged dwellers of the high crags throughout the period when habitation at such places is possible, retreat with the coming of winter to slightly lower elevations and seek out bluffs and cliffs where the winds keep the surface more or less barren of snow—thus exposing whatever scanty vegetation may be found there" (1930b: 5; 1933e: 8).

Schmoe clearly explained why mountain goat hunting was so difficult (1925f: 2–3; 1925g: 237). The animals were wary, and inhabited rugged, barely accessible places among glaciers, rocky crags, precipitous cliffs, and pumice fields, where pursuers needed both experience and mountaineering ability to approach them. Extremely nimble, they were capable of ascending steep angled cliffs and the most slippery ice fields. As a matter of habit, they posted lookouts while feeding, and climbed to higher vantage points when resting. In July and August [when they were hunted on Mount

Rainier, according to my field evidence], they were found as high as 9,000 or 10,000 feet in elevation, which was two or three miles over ice and snow fields beyond the nearest stunted tree growth of the lower slopes. In summer, according to Schmoe's observations, they were never "lower than six thousand feet on the major peak, but occasionally as low as five thousand feet on isolated Mount Wow to the south[west]." Even their winter range was barely 1,000 feet lower down.

Also according to Schmoe, mountain goat occupied the timberline region around the full circumference of Mount Rainier (1925g: 237). However, as already noted, the ethnographic evidence indicates that hunting was secondary to berry gathering as an economic pursuit. Hence, the hunting grounds that were frequented probably were more or less limited to the berrying vicinities, at least during the historic period.

Mountain goat have been specifically reported in the areas listed below. It appears probable that there have been no major alterations in their range since earlier times. Thus, it is suggested that hunting may have occurred in these localities. Hence, temporary camps might have been located at a number of these places. This enumeration proceeds from Longmire in counterclockwise order around Mount Rainier.

(1) Cougar Rock, in the Nisqually valley, about 1-1/2 or 2 miles above Longmire. For ten years prior to 1927 and "perhaps for ages," Schmoe reports, a small band of mountain goat spent the winter on the dome of this rock at 4,000 feet elevation, the lowest he had ever observed mountain goat, even during the severest winters (1925f: 3; 1926g: 3; 1927a: 4). In 1926, Flett had counted five or six here (1926, (9): 2).

In 1928–29 and 1929–30, mountain goat still wintered on Cougar Rock (Brockman, 1929a: 2; 1929d: 8; 1930b: 5; 1935: 28–29). According to Brockman, these "same goats, no doubt, will be found next summer high up among the rocky crags in the vicinity of Van Trump Park" (1929a: 2). From this last statement, it seems unlikely that goats were found at Cougar Rock during the berrying season.

(2) Tatoosh Range (Schmoe, 1926c: 1). A considerable number of mountain goat and many tracks were seen in the Tatoosh Range in late November 1932 (Brockman, 1932e: 4). In early December 1933, a small band was seen on Eagle Peak, at the far western end of the range (Brockman, 1934a: 9; see also Homuth, 1934: 11).

(3) Wapowety Cleaver and the upper portion of Van Trump Park at the Nisqually headwaters. From here, these same goats ranged eastward to Cushman Crest. The park's edges were a normal winter range for bands of these animals, while their summer range here was at and above 5,000 feet. There is evidence for long-standing use by mountain goat. Landes reported that they inhabited this area for years and in large numbers. In August 1924, 14 were seen on Mildred Point alone (Landes, 1924a: 3; 1925c: 2). Schmoe stated, also in 1924, that the Van Trump Park band numbered about 25 (Schmoe, 1924a: 1; 1924d: 3; 1924h: 5; 1925g: 237; 1926g: 3; 1926j: 2; 1926m: 1). In 1934, Homuth observed 40 on the Van Trump Glacier and nearby snowfields and rocky slopes (Homuth, 1934: 11–12; see also Dodge, 1934: 11).

(4) Cushman Crest, to the east of Van Trump Creek, in the upper Nisqually drainage. In the summer of 1857, Lt. Kautz saw numerous mountain goat tracks in the Nisqually Glacier area just east of Cushman Crest (1916: 84–85). In 1923, some 30 or 40 goats made this area their home. In 1924, "everywhere along the upper part of Cushman Crest were noted the dust wallows of these goats." In July 1928, a band of 12 goats was observed in the Cushman Crest area climbing from timberline to the snowfields above 7,000 feet (Schmoe, 1928c: 2–3; see also 1923e: 1; 1926m: 1). Evidently, Landes regarded these animals and those of Van Trump Park as a single group, for he noted that their "range extends from the Kautz glacier [to the west of Van Trump Park and] over the Nisqually glacier [to the east of Cushman Crest]" (Landes, 1924a: 3; 1925c: 2). Schmoe also reported that mountain goat were "quite abundant" at the foot of the Nisqually Glacier (1925g: 52, 61).

(5) Wilson Glacier locality, in the upper Nisqually headwaters (Schmoe, 1926m: 1).

(6) Panorama Point, at the headwaters of the Paradise River (Bonany, 1928: 1). Before the National Park Service extended protection to these animals, 11 goats were known to have been shot on one occasion near the Paradise Glacier. In the early period of white exploration, goats reportedly were commonly seen even in the Paradise Valley (Homuth, 1934: 11–12).

(7) Anvil Rock (9,584 feet), on the Cowlitz Glacier. Despite the high elevation, goats venture into this locality. In 1934, goats were occasionally seen "crossing Muir Glacier below Anvil Rock and above Paradise Valley, evidently passing from the region of the Cowlitz and Whitman Glaciers toward the Nisqually and Van Trump Glaciers" (Homuth, 1934: 11; Schmoe, 1925f: 3; 1927f: 3; Brockman, 1928c: 5).

Hazard Stevens noted in August 1870: "We found many fresh tracks and signs of the mountain-sheep [i.e., goat] upon the snow-fields, and hair and wool rubbed off upon rocks, and places where they had lain at night. The mountain-sheep of Takhoma is much larger than the common goat, and is found only upon the loftiest and most secluded peaks of the Cascade Range" (1916: 124).

Stevens' observations were made above Sluiskin Falls on the Paradise Glacier or the Cowlitz Cleaver, or both. It appears that Stevens did not actually see any mountain goat during his climbing of Mount Rainier. Tufts of hair and wool on rocks and bedding places are characteristically found in mountain goat habitat according to Dalquest (1948: 405–9). Stevens also noted that his guide Sluiskin, who remained behind, hunted these animals through the entire three-day period of his absence; presumably Sluiskin pursued goats above Sluiskin Falls (1916: 124–25).

(8) Stevens Ridge, north of Stevens Creek, a tributary of the Cowlitz (Schmoe, 1925e: 3; 1925f: 3; Brockman, 1932a: 3). Perhaps Brockman was referring to the eastern end of Stevens Ridge when reporting that a "considerable number of Mountain Goat...and many tracks were observed in late November, 1932, on a ridge in the vicinity of the Box Canyon of the Cowlitz" (1932e: 4). Goats also wintered in the Stevens Canyon region, as Brockman noted in February 1932 (1932b: 10).

(9) The Fan; location uncertain, but stated to be in an unfrequented part of the park, probably near Fan Lake at the Muddy Fork of the Cowlitz River headwaters (Dodge, 1934: 11).

(10) Cowlitz Divide, between the upper Muddy Fork of the Cowlitz and the Ohanapecosh rivers. "By actual count, one hundred seventy [goats] were seen in the early [18]90s in the vicinity of the Cowlitz Divide" (Homuth, 1934: 11–12).

(11) Cowlitz Park, at the headwaters of the Muddy Fork of the Cowlitz River. A band of 20 animals was seen here in mid-summer 1927 (Schmoe, 1927e: 1). In August 1931, goat tracks were observed "everywhere" high up in Cowlitz Park (Brockman, 1931d: 2).

(12) Cowlitz Chimneys, between the headwaters of the White and Ohanapecosh rivers. This is one of the finest mountain goat habitats within the national park. In the early 1920s, as many as 40 were seen here in a single herd. In 1926, goats were more frequently observed in this locality than anywhere else in the northern sector of the national park, though goats also occupied many other northern localities (Trolson, 1926: 4. Schmoe, 1924g: 3).

(13) Fryingpan Creek headwaters cliffs, above Summer Land (Schmoe, 1924g: 3), and around Panhandle Gap to the south. Also, a nearby high, isolated peak just north of Summer Land is known as Goat Island Mountain. [Interestingly, charred goat remains were recovered from an archaeological site near Summer Land in 1964 and again in 2001. Associated radiocarbon dates attest to goat hunting in the area more than 1,000 years ago.—Editors]

(14) Yakima Park. In earlier times, a large band of goats was observed here on one occasion (Homuth, 1934: 11).

(15) Winthrop Glacier, at the headwaters of the West Fork of the White River. In July 1896, I.C. Russell camped on the western edge of the glacier "in the highest grove of trees" at an elevation of about 8,000 feet. He noted: "Fresh trail of mountain goats and their but recently abandoned bed showed that this is a favorite resort of those hardy animals" (1916: 170).

(16) Lake James vicinity cliffs, in the Van Horn Creek area of the West Fork of the White River (Schmoe, 1924g: 3).

(17) Sluiskin Mountain (Schmoe, 1924h: 5; 1925g: 237).

(18) Crescent Mountain, on the east side of the Carbon River headwaters. In the early 1880s, Bailey Willis observed that, after leaving

the heavily timbered lower slopes, "at an elevation of 4,000 feet juniper and dwarf pine are dotted over the grassy hillside." Mountain goat—as well as elk and deer—"find here a pleasant pasture" (1916: 147).

(19) Goat Island Rock, at the foot of the Carbon Glacier. On the basis of the toponym, this locality may reasonably be added to this list.

(20) Spray Park, at the headwaters of the North Mowich River (Schmoe, 1924h: 5; 1925g: 237).

(21) Sunset Ridge. In 1929, a band of about 12 goats were observed here (Brockman, 1929g: 4).

(22) Puyallup Cleaver, and the ridges above St. Andrews Park. On July 25, 1930, 22 mountain goat were seen on a single slope in this area (Richards, 1930a: 5–6). In 1934, large numbers of goats were reported between the bridge over the Puyallup River, then under construction, and the hanging snout of the Puyallup Glacier (Homuth, 1934: 11).

(23) Glacier Island, a rocky isolated mass with a few scattered alpine firs. Here, Brockman saw a goat in 1929, and other goat signs were seen below the snout of the South Tahoma Glacier and on the trail leading from Tahoma Creek up to Indian Henrys Hunting Ground (1929g: 3).

(24) Indian Henrys Hunting Ground, between Tahoma and Kautz creeks. The edges of this park were a normal winter range for mountain goat. In the fall and early spring, goats were observed on Mount Ararat. In 1926, 25 to 30 were counted in one band on Mount Ararat by Schmoe; a part of this same band was later seen on Satulick Mountain to the southeast (Schmoe, 1924a: 1; 1924h: 5; 1925g: 237; 1926p: 4–7; 1927b?: 1–2). Mountain goat also were numerous on Pyramid Peak at the northern end of Indian Henrys Hunting Ground (Writer's Program, 1941: 598). According to Meany, mountain goat were hunted by Indian Henry in this area by about 1870. Henry's wife is said to have camped at Squaw Lake, "near

the entrance to Indian Henry's Hunting Ground," while Henry went further up the slopes for game (Meany, 1916: 310, 321).

(25) Satulick Mountain. Several small bands ranged here in wintertime between 5,000 and 5,500 feet in elevation (Schmoe, 1924h: 5; 1925f: 3; 1928a: 4).

(26) Mount Wow, between the South Puyallup and Nisqually rivers. A "favorite haunt" of mountain goat (Homuth, 1934: 11). A band of goats wintered here at about 5,000 feet elevation and also were occasionally found at this altitude in the summer (Schmoe, 1925f: 3). In late June 1928, a band of 20 goats were sighted on this mountain (Schmoe, 1928a: 4); and, in mid-winter 1931, a band of 11 were observed on the top of the peak (Macy, 1931: 4). Mount Wow is sometimes termed Goat Mountain (Meany, 1916: 314; Schmoe, 1925g: 4).

(27) Tumtum Peak, between Tahoma Creek and Kautz Creek (Brockman, 1934d: 11).

In *Washington* by the WPA Writer's Program, two pertinent statements appear in regard to Mount Wow—it is often called "Goat Mountain," and it was a favorite traditional hunting ground for Indian tribes (1941: 586). Also, a "Goat Lake" is located off its northwestern face, and "Goat Creek" flows southwest from the mount into the Nisqually River. The peak lay within upper Nisqually territory, as defined in the present report; hence, it may be assumed that it was primarily the hunters of this group who sought goats on its slopes. My Nisqually informants noted that mountain goat were pursued.

In regard to the mountain's name, "Wow," unquestionably this is a popular rendering of the Sahaptin term (wáu) for 'mountain goat.'[11] It plainly is not a native Nisqually word, despite the mountain's location in Nisqually country. The reason for this Sahaptin designation seems clear when it is recalled that the people occupying the upper Nisqually country were the Sahaptin-speaking Meshal. In short, it seems probable that it was these Nisqually-Meshal (not the more distant Yakama, Kittitas, or Taidnapam) who were responsible for this native toponym.

It seems unlikely that goat hunting was engaged in during the winter season. Nevertheless, it may be useful to list five areas, all in the southern part of the national park, where, in addition to Cougar Rock, goats are known to have passed the winter. According to Brockman (1935: 28–29), these include, from west to east:

(1) Just below Round Pass, at the western end of Emerald Ridge.
(2) East face of Tumtum Mountain, near the Nisqually park entrance.
(3) Between Longmire and the Glacier Bridge, on the Nisqually road.
(4) Lower part of Stevens Canyon.
(5) Box Canyon vicinity on the Muddy Fork of the Cowlitz River.

In 1924, the park's mountain goat population was estimated at 250 animals, and in 1925 and 1927 respectively, at between 200 and 300. In the 1920s, this number was believed to be stable, since goats had few natural enemies and hence were able "to hold their own very well" (Schmoe, 1924d: 3; 1924i: 5; 1925f: 2; 1927e: 1). In the mid-1930s, the number of animals was thought to be increasing (Homuth, 1934: 11). In earlier times, however, they evidently were more numerous. This was the case in the late 19th century, according to Lem Longmire,[12] who spent most of his days from 1885 to the 1930s in the national park region (Homuth, 1934: 11).

Artifacts have been discovered under circumstances that led their finders to interpret them as evidence of mountain goat hunting by Indians. [In the years since Allan Smith completed this report, numerous archaeological hunting sites have been documented in, or near, mountain goat habitat.—Editors]

> In 1922, park naturalist F.W. Schmoe was making his way "along the serrated crest of the Tatoosh Range on the lookout for mountain goat. Within a few feet of the top of Plummer Peak, in the midst of a pumice bed that had no doubt in times past been used as a sunning place by goat," he found an arrow point, "well made…from a flake of volcanic glass not native to the Mount Rainier region" (Schmoe, 1926c: 1–2; also 1925g: 80).
>
> Also, other artifacts identified as "flint arrow heads" were found "in the goat beds above timberline in Van Trump Park" (Schmoe, 1926d: 2; see also 1925g: 80).
>
> According to a park ranger writing in 1930, evidence "of an expedition in search of deer or goat…[has been] found on the upper slopes of Spray Park on the northwest slope of 'The Mountain' in

> the form of a broken arrow head. The arrow was originally a broad hunting head fashioned from pure white quartz with laborious artistry. Only the tip remained of the shaft" (Richards, 1930d: 7).

It is of further interest to note that, according to my informants, mountain goat also were hunted by the Muckleshoot to the north of Mount Rainier on the west side of the White River. And, the four hunted animals clearly referred to by my informants—deer, elk, bear, and mountain goat—are precisely those mentioned by Curtis as the most important of the larger animals pursued by the Yakama in their tribal territory (1911: 6).

Mountain Sheep (*Ovis canadensis*)

According to my informant information, the Muckleshoot also considered mountain sheep fair game, and it was implied that they were pursued in the Mount Rainier region. Whether, in fact, these animals roamed the slopes of Mount Rainier is not wholly certain from the literature. If they once did, they evidently have not been observed in any considerable numbers for many years.

> Dalquest reported that in the past, "mountain sheep inhabited most of the eastern Cascade Mountains.... Their habitat seems...to have included rocky areas from the Upper Sonoran to the Hudsonian life-zones. At the present time they are extinct over most of their range" (1948: 405, 406). Dalquest did not indicate whether the "eastern Cascade Mountains" included Mount Rainier. [It is possible that Dalquest was referring only to the drier east-side Cascade slopes.—Editors]
>
> Schmoe learned from Yakama Indians, who had hunted in what is now the national park, that some 30 or 40 years previous (i.e., ca. 1880s–1890s) "there were a few sheep to be found on the mountain" (1926i: 1). Since Schmoe held that the Indians identified sheep and goats by the same name, he considered it possible that his informants referred to the mountain goat, rather than mountain sheep. Schmoe felt this was so because goats "have always been, and still are, quite abundant on the mountain." Nevertheless, knowing that mountain sheep were native to the Mount Adams locality,[13] he concluded that mountain sheep were present near Mount Rainier also (1926i: 1; 1927e: 1). In fact, a small band was said to have been

seen in 1926, either in the eastern part of the national park or nearby on the eastern slopes of the Cascades; Schmoe's report is somewhat ambiguous on this point (1926o: 2).

One additional documentary note is of interest. "Old Indian Jim" was reported to have killed a sheep about 1890 somewhere on the Cowlitz. Whether or not this occurred inside the national park is unclear (Schmoe, 1926i: 1).

Hoary Marmot (*Marmots caligata cascadensis*)

As opportunity allowed, smaller mammals probably were taken. The marmot (Yakama: wáušiˀtʋn) was hunted by the Yakama, and undoubtedly were sought by other groups as well, within the bounds of the national park. Common in the Mount Rainier area, hoary marmots (whistlers, whistling marmot) are the largest of the American marmots (Dalquest, 1948: 265). According to Schmoe, they weigh about 30 pounds, becoming excessively fat toward the close of the summer season before they hibernate (1925g: 243–44). Dalquest notes that hibernation begins in the early fall: "most adults retire…by the middle of September" (1948: 267).

> Schmoe reports that they are abundant on rockslides or in the nearby meadows from the edge of the heavy forests to "timberline and somewhat above" (1925g: 243–44).
>
> Brockman adds, they are "numerous in the sub-alpine meadows between 5,000 and 6,500 feet in elevation. There in the summer and fall they are often seen about their burrows in the hillsides or in the talus slopes" (1931a: 2). Furthermore, they are "common to the Hudsonian Zone" (1933b: 8; see also 1933e: 8).
>
> In greater detail, Dalquest notes: "This mammal of the higher altitudes rarely goes below the Hudsonian Life-zone. It is most common in the talus slides at the lower edge of the Arctic-Alpine Life-zone…it prefers to live amid loose boulders. The steep talus or 'scab rock' slides in the glacial cirques provide an ideal habitat. The crevices and caves beneath the rocks offer concealment for young and adults" (1948: 266; also 42). [Judging from his habitat description, it is likely that Dalquest was referring to pika (*Ochotoma princes*) rather than hoary marmots.—Editors]

All of the data is in agreement:

(a) The marmot is commonly found on the flanks of Mount Rainier.
(b) Its habitat is at the same general elevation where berrying parties visited.
(c) It is active in the same period when berry gathering occurred.

Thus, the literature confirms the probability that men sought marmots as game, at least occasionally, while the women busied themselves in huckleberry collecting. One published reference reports the hunting of marmot on Mount Rainier.

> In 1870, Hazard Stevens reported that his guide Sluiskin, while camped in the Sluiskin Falls area at the head of the Paradise River, killed and dressed marmot as food. Stevens added without enthusiasm: "Their flesh, like the badger's, is extremely muscular and tough, and has a strong, disagreeable, doggy odor" (1916: 123–24).

My informants did not identify specific places within the national park as favorite marmot hunting localities. In the documentary sources, only one relevant comment was identified. Meany indicated that marmots were particularly plentiful around Marmot Creek, a tributary of Cataract Creek, draining Seattle Park in the northwest part of the national park (Meany, 1916: 313). [In addition to mountain goat, both marmot and mountain beaver (*Aplodontia rufa*) remains have been found in archaeological contexts at Mount Rainier, indicating human use of these animals during the prehistoric past.—Editors]

Grouse (*Bonasa umbellus sabini* and *Dendragapus f. fuliginosus*)

The Yakama informants mentioned that grouse were hunted in the national park area. The literature clearly identifies where grouse are found. What is more, grouse habitat of late summer and early fall was in the same berry patches that attracted Indian gathering parties. Two types of grouse are found in the national park—the Oregon ruffed grouse, which is rare, and the sooty grouse, which is common.

> (a) The Oregon ruffed grouse (*Bonasa umbellus sabini*), also known as native pheasant, bush pheasant, partridge, and drummer, is largely restricted to the lower forests in the southern part of the park.

Oregon ruffed grouse can be observed from the Nisqually entrance to Longmire, and in the Nickle Creek Burn between the Tatoosh Range and the Cowlitz Divide (Kitchin, 1939: 117).[14] They are residents of alder thickets and dark shady places.

(b) The sooty grouse (*Dendragapus f. fuliginosus*), also called blue grouse, wood grouse, and hooter, is referred to by writers in the following four relevant passages:

> (1) Sooty grouse are found throughout the national park from the high alpine meadows down to the thick timber. They abound in the northern sector of the park, and particularly in the locality around Mystic Lake. In summer and fall, they are common in Yakima Park to the northeast. The west side and the slopes of Mount Wow are also favored habitats. But they are most numerous, perhaps, from Reflection Lakes, down through Stevens Canyon, and into the Nickle Creek Burn. Here (as elsewhere in the park), they gather in the fall to feed on huckleberries and other small fruit. Sooty grouse are not migratory birds. Rather, they descend in winter to lower elevations, and many undoubtedly move outside of the national park boundaries at that time (Kitchin, 1939: 116–17).
>
> (2) In Mount Rainier National Park, sooty grouse are found "in meadows between 4,000 and 6,000 feet, strutting about in the huckleberry patches or perched on a gnarled limb of a mountain hemlock" (Brockman, 1928e: 1).
>
> (3) "Blue grouse" or "hooters" are plentiful in the Hudsonian Zone meadows during the summer (Brockman, 1933a: 7).
>
> (4) "Found commonly throughout the national park from the edge of the heavy forests to timberline.... Where hunted the sooty grouse becomes very wild and difficult to approach, but within the national park it appears quite fearless, seldom taking to wing but merely moving a few feet out of harm's way...in the later summer the huckleberries and mountain ash berries supply an abundance of food" (Schmoe, 1925g: 277).

The Oregon ruffed grouse can hardly be the bird to which my informant information referred, at least as a primary game bird. They simply were not found at the higher elevations where native groups were active, according to my evidence. The sooty grouse, on the other hand, seems clearly the variety indicated. As with bears, they are drawn in large numbers to huckleberry patches when the berries ripen.

> According to Kitchin, various birds by the thousands are first attracted to the huckleberry patches and then to the mountain ash areas, where berries persist until the leaves fall and the bushes are bare. Included are sooty grouse, which feast until, with their crops distended, they prefer to avoid flying. Moreover, the fermenting juices of overripe berries can have a decided alcoholic effect on many of the birds (1939: 92).

This evidence (confirmed by Schmoe) affirms that sooty grouse were frequenters of the berry patches in considerable numbers when Indians were gathering the fruit. It suggests that children and active women, as well as men, might have experienced little difficulty in capturing them (1925g: 162). Supporting the above statement regarding the influence of overripe berries on birds, Kitchin reported: "we know from observations that the…coyote gets his fill of…[band-tailed pigeons] during the berry season when their wits are befuddled" (1939: 125). [Bird gastroliths, or gizzard stones, common to galliforme birds such as grouse and ptarmigan, have been found in three sub-alpine archaeological sites at Mount Rainier. The presence of these small, highly polished stones in an archaeological context provides indirect evidence of bird hunting and consumption in the prehistoric past.—Editors]

Other Birds

Although my informants did not specifically identify any additional game birds in the national park area, it is probable that other birds drawn to the huckleberry and mountain ash harvest occasionally were taken, perhaps for their feathers if not as food. This might include robins, flickers, blue birds, and thrushes, as well as the band-tailed pigeon (*Columba f. fasciata*) referred to by Kitchin above, and here again in the following.

> In early fall, band-tailed pigeons gather in large flocks in Sunset Park to gorge on huckleberries. "By the last of August, when the berries of the low-bush huckleberry (*Vaccinium celiciosum* [sic]) are dead ripe,…[pigeons] come by the hundreds to gorge on the

fruit. They soon become doped or 'drunk' by the fermentation of the berry juice; become sleepy and spend hours dozing in a stupefied condition. Much of this area has been burned, the naked trees still standing. These bare trees make ideal roosting sites for the flocking birds. Pigeons, however, are not the only birds that are fond of this over-ripe berry. Robins, thrushes, flickers and even the mountain blue birds over-indulge. When the huckleberry crop is gone the pigeons turn to the fruit of the mountain ash, subsisting on this crop while it lasts. It is then about time to migrate" (Kitchin, 1939: 92, 124, 165–66).

Meat Preparation

According to my informants, meat was cut up, sliced, and dried. Some types were cut into pieces, roasted on sticks thrust in the ground before a fire, and then dried on racks in the same manner as berries.

Bear meat, on the other hand, was cooked by a different process. It was prepared in a pit 3 or 4 feet in diameter. Hot rocks were rolled in to form a sort of floor. Chokecherry or other branches were placed parallel in the pit, and then additional branches were added at right angles, forming a rack arrangement. This then was covered with fir branches and leaves. On this, the meat was placed. Then more branches and leaves were spread on top, and finally covered with earth 3 or 4 inches deep. A stick that had been placed vertically in the middle of the pit when its construction began now was pulled out and 4 or 5 gallons of water were poured down the hole, creating steam from contact with the hot rocks. This method, a combination of roasting and steaming, was termed támes by the Yakama.

The Muckleshoot prepared bear meat in much the same manner. According to informant Louis Starr, however, the Muckleshoot did not pour water into the pit oven. Bears at that time of year were fat from eating berries. In the cooking process, the fat dripped onto the rocks and created steam, making the addition of water unnecessary.[15]

The ethnographic literature furnishes the following relevant data.

Speaking of the Puget Sound groups as a whole, Haeberlin and Gunther describe the process as follows: "Deer and elk meat...was cut in pieces and hung on a frame. Fires were built on three sides and the meat was thoroughly roasted. Then it was hung higher to dry more slowly. When done in this way, the meat would keep a

> long time. Hunters often dried meat in the mountains and cached it in trees, covering it with boughs and mats to keep it dry" (1930: 21).
>
> Marian Smith's description for the Nisqually and Puyallup does not differ significantly. According to her report, however, bear meat was treated in the same manner as deer and elk. No mention is made of cooking bear in pits as described by my informant, though this method was used for seal and porpoise to drain off the fat (1940: 246).

The Yakama transported dried meat and berries back to the winter villages in cedar bark sacks. The Coast groups, on the other hand, used large and small, hard, coiled, cedar-root baskets covered with leaves (the baskets darkened over the years from repeated use for holding huckleberries and blueberries). These containers were hung from saddles on the sides of pack animals. My data differs here somewhat from the following reports for the Yakama and the Puyallup-Nisqually.

> Curtis states that the Yakama used flat wallets in large sizes, woven from fiber obtained from native hemp, for packing on horses (1911: 5).
>
> According to Marian Smith, the Nisqually and Puyallup wrapped dried meat in deer or elk skin. These packages were transported by being hung on the sides of pack horses (1940: 246).

Unquestionably, this meat was of economic importance. However, the statements of all my male and female tribal informants clearly indicate that the principal economic attraction of the national park, and the chief reason for the late summer visits to the area, was to acquire a berry supply.

Fishing

My informants made no mention of fishing as an economic activity in the national park. This clearly seems to be due to the limited fish resources in the area.

> According to Schmoe, "only three [indigenous] species occur commonly in the streams of the park. These are the Rainbow [*Salmo shasta*], the Cutthroat [*Salmo clarkii*] and the Dolly Varden

> [*Salvelinus malma*]. A fourth species, the Steelhead is known to occur in the rivers flowing from the mountain but outside the national park. It is not unlikely that they sometimes occur in the upper streams but they are not common.... All of the numerous lakes and many of the smaller streams of the region are cut off from the rivers by waterfalls which are too high to be passed by the fish as they ascend the streams to their spawning ground, and consequently they contained no native trout" (1925b: 3).
>
> In another publication, Schmoe adds the Silver Trout (*Oncorhynchus nerka kenerlyi*) to the list of native fishes. He reported that it is not abundant in the park. (1925g: 329–30, 339).

This data suggests that any archaeological research undertaken along river and lake shores for fishing sites probably would have negligible results.

Collecting of Technological Plants

Although my informants did not provide data in this regard, it appears probable that the Mount Rainier area provided at least some plant materials of technological importance. Such is the case with bear grass (*Xerophyllum tenax*), also known as mountain lily, pine lily, elk-grass, turkey plume, bears-paw, squaw-grass, and Indian basket grass. It grows from a low elevation of about 2,750 feet to above timberline, and throughout all of the life zones except the Arctic-Alpine (Flett, 1916: 17–18; Piper, 1916: 280; Schmoe, 1924c: 2; 1925g: 141; 1926h: 4; Brockman, 1947: 58; 1933c: 7).

Bear grass is common and sometimes particularly prominent in the upper Canadian and lower Hudsonian zones. It grows especially well in open sunny locations and where the trees are small and generally in rather dry, volcanic ash soil. According to Schmoe, "It reaches its finest growth in burns and meadows between 4,000 and 6,000 feet in elevation" (1925g: 141). This was the altitudinal zone most frequented by traditional berrying parties. The literature identifies several localities in Mount Rainier National Park where it is found:

> (1) According to Flett, bear grass occurs "in several of the meadows" in the Hudsonian Zone. "In the upper part of Paradise Valley, on the ridge west of Sluiskin Falls, there is a large field of it near timber line" (1916: 43).

(2) Conditions were particularly well suited for its growth in the "silver forest" locality of the Paradise Valley (Schmoe, 1924c: 2; Brockman, 1929e: 5; 1931c: 4; 1933c: 7; 1934g: 7).

(3) At the western end of the Tatoosh Range near the top of Eagle Peak, "the Indian Basket-grass is found...in larger quantities than in most regions of the national park" (Schmoe, 1924e: 3).

(4) In 1927–28, it thrived in great profusion in the open, burned-over land along the top of Rampart Ridge (Landes, 1929: 5).

(5) In August 1930, it was abundant in an old ridge-top burn at the southern end of Indian Henrys Hunting Ground (Richards, 1930a: 2).

The utilization of this plant by Northwest Indians is well known.

When speaking of Puget Sound basket-making in general, Haeberlin and Gunther stated: "The material for white imbrication was bear grass or Indian grass (*Xerophyllum tenax*)..., which grows in the Cascades and around Mount Rainier about 500 to 1,500 feet below the snow line during the summer. This was also used as the overlay strip in twined baskets.... [This material was] dried and stored until used" (1930: 33).

Flett noted that "Indians use it in making their baskets" (1916: 17–18).

According to Schmoe, the "grass or leaf was, and still is, used by the local Indians in making some very wonderful baskets; baskets that will hold water and are used in cooking and so durable that I have seen specimens that were still in use after being handed down for three generations. They would still hold water and were made from nothing more than the leaf of the squaw grass" (1924c: 2).

Collecting of Medicinal Flora

Mount Rainier's meadows and forests also were a source of medicinal flora not available in the tribal territories ordinarily occupied throughout most of the year. These plants, of course, were not acquired in the same bulk as dried berries and meat. However, these substances were considered as significant products of the national park area.

It proved impossible for me to secure much specific information as to the precise plants gathered and the ailments for which they were specified. However, two of my informants said the Yakama sought the áiyʊn root, a remedy for colds, cough, and croup. [This plant possibly is Gray's lovage (*Ligustichum grayi*).—Editors] It grows only in mountain berry fields, and its odor carries a long way. As much as 20 pounds (a 3- or 4-year supply) was dug up at one time. When thoroughly dried, the root was scraped with a knife. The scrapings then were mixed with Bull Durham rolling tobacco and inhaled so as to draw the healing smoke deep into the lungs.

While áiyvn was the only remedy mentioned by my informants, there is no doubt that Indian people gathered an array of medicinal plants from the Mount Rainier area.

Guardian Spirit Quests

Though none of my informants mentioned the matter, the literature suggests that the national park area was visited during guardian spirit quests. This is entirely consistent with the ethnographic knowledge that Northwest Indians, usually individually, visited high and relatively unfrequented mountainous regions for spiritual contacts.

In the Haeberlin myth-narrative extracted in chapter 3, one of the two legendary characters is reported to have visited the "head of the Cowlitz River" to secure a guardian spirit (1924: 417–18). This locale in the eastern portion of Mount Rainier National Park was in traditional Taidnapam country.

In a Puyallup narrative of an actual occurrence—reported by Ballard in two versions—a man who apparently was a Puyallup from near Orting is described during his search for guardian spirit power. Using elkhorn wedges or copper-tipped arrows (depending upon the version accepted) to assist his ascent over the ice and snow, he climbed to the summit of Mount Rainier, where he stayed one night and experienced his desired vision (1929: 142–44).

Conclusion

The data seems to point to a main conclusion—any archaeological sites discovered in Mount Rainier National Park most likely will represent camps for gathering and hunting. Furthermore, it appears that any recovered stray or isolated artifacts also probably will have been associated with these economic pursuits. Camp locations should be found near important huckleberry fields between 3,000 and 5,500 feet in elevation. Random artifactual evidence from hunting activities should occur at these elevations and still higher, to 6,500 or even 7,000 feet, where hunters ascended the slopes pursuing game. In addition to gathering-hunting camps, two other types of sites might occur—(a) guardian spirit quest sites, though too little data currently is available to intimate their artifact content and likely locations; and (b) temporary camp sites along trails (these will be discussed in chapter 6).

[In the four decades since Allan Smith completed this study, more than 90 prehistoric archaeological sites have been documented at Mount Rainier. True to Smith's prediction, the majority of these are located in the patchy sub-alpine meadow and tree associations above 5,000 feet (Smith's Hudsonian Zone). Most sites appear to have been used as short-term hunting camps. Interestingly, however, the largest and most complex sites (in terms of the number and range of artifacts recovered) tend to be located somewhat lower at the forest margins. These larger sites may have functioned as base-camps at which mixed age and gender groups resided and from which small, task-specific groups accessed higher-elevation resource areas. The forested, base-camp settings would have provided some degree of shelter from the mountain's unpredictable weather, and, perhaps, access to a wider variety of resource procurement places.—Editors]

On the basis of this extended discussion of aboriginal utilization of Mount Rainier's resources, it might be concluded that this use was extensive and of major importance to these groups. The matter may be brought into further perspective by noting three general points.

> (a) It should not be assumed that the "entire" population of a tribal group actually ventured to Mount Rainier at one time. Throughout Washington's Cascades, there are numerous peaks, creeks, lakes, gaps, and prairies named after "Huckleberry," "Goat," and "Bear," indicating that these and other resources were widespread throughout this vast range and accessed by numerous tribes and bands that claimed these high-elevation territories. It is true that Mount Rainier's berries were said by my informants to be especially fine, but normally only the tribal villages most conveniently situated for access probably visited the Mount Rainier area.
>
> This is made clear in the case of the Yakama villages. Some bands evidently rarely, if ever, berried at Mount Rainier in earlier times.

Instead, it was more convenient for them to obtain their supply near Mount Adams (Yakama: pá·Du). Some of them, too, hunted mountain goat on Mount St. Helens. Such was the case with groups residing on Toppenish and Simcoe creeks. Seemingly, on the other hand, the population along the Naches and Tieton (Yakama: taíton)[16] rivers mostly frequented Mount Rainier and its environs. Furthermore, it appears improbable that the "entire" able-bodied population of a village would visit the mountain in a single season, though no precise data about this available.

(b) It is possible that the tribal sub-units frequenting the park area did not secure a major part of their annual game kill here. At least during the historic period, however, a major part of the huckleberry harvest probably was obtained at Mount Rainier. Even the berry harvest may have varied from year to year depending on the fluctuations in abundance or shortage of berries in different localities, both within and outside of the park. Other factors may have been involved as well, but the information currently at hand is insufficient to permit a sound assessment of this aspect.

(c) It is noteworthy that traditional tribal populations were modest in size. In 1855, territorial governor Isaac I. Stevens estimated that the Yakama population was 1,200 (Curtis, 1911: 159). The Yakama claimed a vast territory, with only a portion of the tribe, of course, situated in the northwestern stream valleys adjacent to the Mount Rainier area. Among the Puget Sound groups, Marian Smith noted that the villages averaged from about 20 to 50 residents. "It is probable that no village exceeded seventy-five members and that most were not nearly so large" (1940: 37). In the context of the present study, it should be noted that two upper Nisqually villages (nos. 25 and 26 in Fig. 3.6; the latter being the "Meshal" settlement), and perhaps three upper Puyallup villages (nos. 9–11 in Fig. 3.6), were in the most advantageous geographical position to visit the national park area. Estimating an average population of 50 for each settlement, we see that the total Nisqually and Puyallup population in geographical proximity to the national park could hardly have exceeded 250 persons—men, women, and children. Apparently the Taidnapam and possibly the Muckleshoot were more numerous in the Mount Rainier vicinity, but neither could have been very populous groups during the historic and proto-historic periods.

[In the mid-1960s when this ethnography was written, few anthropologists and historians fully recognized the devastating population reducing effects of introduced Old World diseases (e.g., influenza, smallpox, whooping cough, and malaria) on Indian people. It is likely that, prior to the advent of these diseases (i.e., before the latter 1700s), the Native American population density in the Mount Rainier vicinity and across the region generally was far higher than what is reflected in the above estimates. It is now believed that the Mount Rainier area was integrated into the network of vibrant and complex societies living on both sides of the Cascades. The observations of early immigrants and ethnographers, while providing useful information about Indian life in the 1800s, nonetheless might not reflect a more complex past cultural and population reality.—Editors]

Endnotes

1. Compare with Teit's statement regarding the Wenatchi in their ecologically similar country to the north of the Yakama: "Much of the summer and fall season was spent on the higher grounds, hunting, root-digging, and berrying" (1928: 114).
2. In an essentially identical statement elsewhere, Schmoe substituted "high mountains" for "high valleys" (1925g: 80).
3. According to Curtis, the Yakama word is á-tit [átit] (1911: 174).
4. Plummer records four huckleberry types, but without their biotic associations: *Vaccinium parvifolium*; *V. myrtilloides*, "myrtle-leaved huckleberry"; *V. myrtillus* var. *microcephyllum* [sic], "small red huckleberry"; and *V. ovatum*, for which he gives "black huckleberry" as the popular designation (1900: 131–32). Piper identifies *V. myrtillus microphyllum* as *V. scoparium* (1916: 268). Flett commented that "red, black, and blue huckleberries are also common…[in the floral zone between 2,000' and 2,800'], especially in openings through the forest" (1916: 7). This altitudinal range corresponds to Jones's Humid-Transitional Zone.
5. The Frank family informants told me that cattails grew in two sexes—the males had a heavy brown cylindrical spike; the females did not. They professed to be unfamiliar with the term "tule." According to Wayne Suttles (per. comm.), Puget Sound Indians regarded the broad leaves of the cattail as the female plant, and the round stem with a brown spike as the male.
6. Salmonberries [*Rubus spectabilis*], in both its yellow and garnet-red varieties, grow profusely along the streams and the borders of swamps at the national park's lower elevations and up to 5,000 feet or more. These edible berries ripen from early June to late August, depending on elevation. Schmoe, however, did not report that the Indians actually gathered them. Traditionally, Indians visited the national park before the close of the salmonberry season; however, my informants did not list them among the food resources collected in the national park.

Also according to Schmoe, the "young fleshy shoots of the salmonberry are sweet and were…used by the Indians as food" (1926k: 1). It would appear, though, that the trips to the national park were too late in the season for acquiring the shoots when still tender. Presumably, Schmoe's observation was based upon knowledge of the food gathering habits of the Indians at other locations than Mount Rainier.

According to Piper, *Cirsium edule*, a thistle, was plentiful up to timberline on the ridges of Moraine Park and also occurred in the open woods near timberline in Cowlitz Canyon (1916: 259). It grows abundantly at sea level and the roots traditionally were a favorite food. There appears to be no specific indication, however, that visitors to the national park secured them.

Other edible plants known to have be collected elsewhere doubtlessly could be identified among the national park's extensive flora, but there is a lack of information that they were actually obtained in the park limits.

7. Compare Yakama: yá-mash̓ [yámaš], 'black-tail deer' (Curtis, 1911: 173), and Nisqually: ske′gwúts [skégwəc], 'deer' (Curtis, 1913: 184).
8. Cf. Yakama: wi-ya-pŭ-nít [wiyapenít] (Curtis, 1911: 173); Nisqually: tsŭqsh̓ [cəqws] (Curtis, 1913: 184).
9. Cf. Yakama: a-na-húi [anahúí] (Curtis, 1911: 173); Nisqually: schŭ́t-h̓ud [sčátxə́pd] (Curtis, 1913: 184).
10. Cf. Yakama: wô[wau] (Curtis, 1911: 173); Nisqually: sh̓wé-tle [sx^{w}eƛe] (Curtis, 1913: 184).
11. Homuth noted that Mount Wow's name "is derived from the Indian word for goat" (1934: 11), and Matthes speaks of "Mount Wow (Goat Mountain)" (1916: 203).
12. Lindsey (1933) consistently identified him as "Len"; while Homuth used "Lem."
13. Dalquest recorded that the mountain sheep specimen *Ovis canadensis californiana* was identified in 1926 from near Mount Adams. This type of mountain sheep presumably would have been the same for Mount Rainier, if sheep existed there (1948: 406).
14. According to Schmoe, though wholly a bird of the forest, Oregon ruffed grouse occasionally venture as high as the alpine meadows (1925g: 278).
15. Haeberlin and Gunther mention that this pit steaming method was typical for the Puget Sound peoples as a whole (1930: 23).
16. Large quantities of hazelnuts were a resource along the Tieton River. [Charred hazelnut tissue has been found in a circa 1,000-year-old archaeological site in a rockshelter near Mount Rainier's Fryingpan Creek. Since hazelnut does not grow at this altitude (4,900 feet), the nuts must have been brought from lower elevation habitats, such as the Tieton River valley.—Editors]

6

Trails, Travel, and Trade

Clearly, a number of traditional local access routes converged spoke-fashion toward Mount Rainier, terminating on various mountain flanks. Also, major east-west trails between the Coast and the Plateau regions passed through the Cascade Range near or in Mount Rainer National Park (see the List of Passes in chapter 1). The most significant in terms of proximity to Mount Rainier, listed from north to south, were Naches, Chinook, Carlton, Cowlitz, and White passes (see Fig. 1.1). These passes range from 4,100 to 5,440 feet in elevation, altitudes that were not of any real consequence for Indian parties traveling in decent weather.

My informants provided few detailed facts about the trails in the national park vicinity. However, the contention was general among them that the known passes used today were those followed in traditional times. On the other hand, Nisqually informant Billy Frank contended that his father was acquainted with an important pass through the Cascade Range that remained unknown to whites.

Unfortunately, time and logistical limitations during the 1963 field period made it impractical for my informants to actually visit the national park area and attempt to make identifications directly. At any rate, the known information from informants and the literature regarding trails and routes in the national park area is presented here.

Passes

Chinook Pass (5,440 feet)

The trail through Chinook Pass is shown on the earliest topographic maps of Mount Rainier printed in 1915. This is the sole pass that crosses the Cascade Divide directly into Mount Rainier National Park (see Fig. 1.1). Chinook Pass sits at the mid-point on the national park's eastern boundary. It links the Rainier Fork of the American River on the east, to a lower divide within the national park (Cayuse Pass) that separates the White River headwaters to the north from the Ohanapecosh headwaters at the south. According to the tribal territorial definitions identified for the present study, Chinook Pass was in Yakama territory (see Fig. 3.4).

Specific information exists to confirm the traditional use of this pass, significantly coming from my Yakama informants. They noted that their forebears traveled via both Chinook and Naches passes (see *Naches Pass* below). According to Alec Saluskin, who visited the Mount Rainier berry fields once when he was a youth, the trails used by the Yakama followed almost exactly the present-day routes through both of these mountain gaps.

Naches Pass (4,988 feet)

Naches Pass is situated northeast of the national park (see Fig. 1.1). Well used by the Yakama, this defile likewise was known to Puget Sound groups. Haeberlin and Gunther reported that members of the Nisqually tribe "often traveled east of the Mountains" through Naches Pass, and likewise through Cowlitz Pass (1930: 9) (see *Cowlitz Pass* below).

A main route via Naches Pass between the Coast and the Plateau ran along the White and Naches river systems to the north of Mount Rainier National Park. This was confirmed by my Muckleshoot informant, Louis Starr, who reported that practically all of the Muckleshoot could talk Yakama, but not the reverse. He said that "the Muckleshoot went to the Yakama country to get things they could not obtain in their own territory, for example roots. And similarly the Yakama came over to the Muckleshoot country to catch and dry fish." The Muckleshoot's trail, he reported, went east along the White River and its tributary, the Greenwater River, and then crossed Naches Pass to the Naches River.

> A variation in the line of march to Naches Pass was followed by Lt. Robert Johnson and his exploring party in an eastward crossing of the Cascades in May 1841 (Wilkes 1916: 18). If Edmond Meany's apparently accurate topographic identifications are accepted, this trail led eastward up the Puyallup (identified by Johnson as the "Puyallup"), the Carbon (Johnson: "Upthascap"), and South Prairie Creek; then, overland to the White River (Johnson: "Smalocho") and up it to the Greenwater River to Naches Pass. On the eastern slope of the Cascade Range, the trail ran down the Little Naches River (Johnson: "Spipen") (1916: 13–33). This line of travel is just north of the national park.

Carlton Pass (4,100 feet)

This pass is the first significant break in the Cascade Divide south of Chinook Pass (see Fig. 1.1). Carlton Pass links the Bumping River on the east with Carlton Creek to the west, an Ohanapecosh tributary (Carlton Creek flows into the north side of Summit Creek 2 miles from the Ohanapecosh). The national park boundary follows a ridgetop to the north, mostly within a mile, along the 9-mile-course of Carlton Creek. Carlton Pass, if used, would have provided a link between Yakama and Taidnapam territories.

Though a low defile, neither my informants nor the documentary sources confirmed aboriginal use. However, the U.S.G.S. quadrangle map for this locality shows a modern trail over Carlton Pass. After reaching the Ohanapecosh River, this route, if used, would have eventually connected up with the Cowlitz/Nisqually river trails.

Cowlitz Pass (5,191 feet)

Also called Packwood Pass, it lies on the Cascade Divide about six miles southeast of the national park's southeastern corner, and about five miles southeast of Carlton Pass (see Fig. 1.1). While not mentioned by my informants, the literature demonstrated aboriginal travel through Cowlitz Pass.

> Haeberlin and Gunther reported that the Nisqually "often traveled east of the Mountains using Cowlitz" pass (1930: 9).
>
> The Yakama, as well, knew of Cowlitz Pass and used it. Haeberlin and Gunther noted: "Just east of the Muckleshoot and the Nisqually lived the Klikitat, whose lands extended south to the Columbia River and eastward to the mountains. The Klikitat in family groups crossed the mountains once a year in July or August, using Cowlitz Pass. There is a stream near the waterworks in Tacoma called Swā′dabc meaning 'Plains People,' because the Klikitat used to travel along its banks down to the Sound" (1930: 9–10).
>
> Plainly, these authors used the term "Klikitat" for all of the Sahaptin-speaking peoples immediately to the east of the Cascades. Since Cowlitz Pass leads eastward to the upper Tieton River, and because the Klikitat country proper was well to the south of this area, it may certainly be presumed that the Yakama were the Sahaptin group involved. Hence, the Haeberlin-Gunther statement more precisely attests to contacts between the Muckleshoot-Nisqually and the Yakama.

No published information is available to indicate the precise route of the Cowlitz Pass trail on the western slopes of the Cascade Divide. However, my Nisqually informant, Billy Frank, provided the following possibly relevant data. Frank stated that Indian Henry (Satulick, the Meshal Nisqually of Indian Henrys Hunting Ground note) often used a trail that bore his name. In proceeding eastward, the trail forded the Nisqually River (probably at or very close to Bear Prairie Point) about a mile below Longmire Hot Springs. Typically, the crossing on horseback had to be made about 4 p.m., when the stream was lower and not as swift as at other times in the day. The trail then led to the southeast through Bear Prairie (and certainly down Skate Creek). Billy Frank said this was the old horse trail from Nisqually country to the Yakama lands.

From here, it is necessary to join the southeast end of the Skate Creek Trail (where it reaches the Cowlitz valley) with the western entrance of Cowlitz Pass (which, as already noted, is documented to have been an important east-west connection). A route probably ascended the Cowlitz valley along the Ohanapecosh River to the mouth of Summit Creek, and then continued up the latter past the mouth of Carlton Creek and on to the headwaters of Summit Creek and to Cowlitz Pass. This is a distance of about 18 miles. While my field results did not indicate such a route directly, it does coincide with the known facts and is plausible when studying the topography.

Judging from modern-day maps, an alternative trail also might have led directly eastward from the Skate Creek trail terminus in the Cowlitz valley. A route could have gone east up into the mountains, along the north side of Packwood Lake to Lost Lake, crossed over Coal Creek Mountain, continued east across the Clear Fork Cowlitz River, and then northeast along the Cascade Divide to Cowlitz Pass. Though twisting and turning, the distance in this case is about 22 miles. Again, it must be stated that there is no available evidence confirming that this route was used in traditional times. Despite this conjecture about west side access routes, it is certain that Indian groups used Cowlitz Pass and accessed it by some means, with the most plausible routes being those described above.

Passes North of Naches Pass: Yakima, Snoqualmie, and Others

Although well north of Mount Rainier National Park, several passes through the Cascades clearly were used as thoroughfares between the Plateau and Coastal areas (see the List of Passes in chapter 1). The following data attests to travel through two of these—Yakima and Snoqualmie passes. While somewhat peripheral, both appear to be relevant to the present study.

> In regard to the Wenatchi, Teit observed: "Trading parties of Wenatchi...went toward the coast by way of the Yakima, Snoqualmie, and other passes through the Cascades, where they traded with the Snuqualmi, Snohomish, Nisqually, Puyallup, and Cowlitz.... [T]he first horse seen by the Coast tribes...was brought over by the Wenatchi. A great impetus was given to trading by the introduction of the horse" (1928: 121).

This is highly suggestive. Taken in conjunction with Teit's statement that "other passes" than Yakima and Snoqualmie likewise were used, and that trading was carried on with the Puyallup, Nisqually, and Cowlitz, this information implies that on trading expeditions to the west the Wenatchi probably also used passes to the south of Yakima Pass, and toward the Mount Rainier area.

Also, if evidence in a Puyallup tale is relevant, the use of Yakima Pass or Snoqualmie Pass, or both, confirmed contacts between the Puyallup and Yakama:

> Ballard recorded the following: Two presumably Puyallup mythological personages set out for Plateau country to play slahal (a stick game) with the Yakama. While en route, they camp at Lake Keechelus before reaching the Yakamas. Lake Keechelus, of course, is just east of Snoqualmie and Yakima passes on the upper Yakima River, and between the territories of the Kittitas and the Snoqualmi. This is well north of Puyallup country and somewhat north of Yakama territory; it is a strange route for these travelers to be following. Perhaps the Kittitas and not the Yakama were involved. But at any rate, the tale does suggest, despite the mythological context of the narrative, that direct contact over mountain passes between the Puyallup and Yakama did exist (1929: 135–36).

Passes South of Cowlitz Pass: White and Tieton

White Pass and Tieton Pass are situated south of Cowlitz Pass, respectively about four and ten miles away. As with the Carlton and Cowlitz passes to the north, these two defiles, if used, likewise would have linked the Yakama and Taidnapam. The Taidnapam and Yakama, both Sahaptin-speaking, were linguistically so similar that the two speech forms are no more than minor dialect variants of a common language. These people also were bonded by frequent intermarriage. These linguistic and social connections suggest the possibility that both groups used White Pass and Tieton Pass, in addition to Cowlitz Pass.

Cayuse Pass (4,700 feet)

Cayuse Pass is located entirely within the national park, only about two miles west of Naches Pass (see Fig. 1.1). Uniquely situated on a north-south axis, it is a natural connector between the headwaters of the White River system at the north, to the Ohanapecosh-Cowlitz system in the south. Its use in aboriginal times is strongly suggested by the Coastal myth published by Haeberlin (1924: 417–18). The route followed by Kapoonis, a key legendary figure in the story, from the White River over to the upper reaches of the Cowlitz, would have been through this pass.

Mountain Access Routes

In addition to the major Cascades trails and mountain passes used by Plateau and Coastal groups as described above, other shorter trails accessed the widespread berry fields and hunting areas in the Cascade Range. Just north of the national park, for example, parties could have easily turned off the Naches Pass trail and continued southeast up the White River toward the northeastern part of the park. Then by choosing, for example, either the West Fork White River or Huckleberry Creek, or perhaps the nearby ridges, they could have moved onto the northern flanks of Mount Rainier to such places, among others, as White River, Bear, Huckleberry, Green, or Grand parks (see Fig. 1.1). Topographically, this kind of access appears entirely feasible.

No doubt a network of routes led up to the higher slopes around much of Mount Rainier and to other adjacent mountainous ridges. According to my Nisqually informant data, for example, the Nisqually frequented an important berry ground on the Skate Creek trail just south of the national park. They would proceed about half way up Bear Prairie, and then onto the hillside to the berry gathering area.

Unfortunately, these shorter, exploitative routes, largely lateral to the main through-mountain trails, have not been identified in detail. However, suggestions as to the locations of some have appeared elsewhere in the present study. For example:

> (a) A side-trail off the main Nisqually River-Cowlitz Pass trail led up into Indian Henrys Hunting Ground in Nisqually-Meshal territory.
>
> (b) A route from the Taidnapam country extended up to the Lookout Mountain locality, and then along the Tatoosh Range to the Reflection Lakes and Paradise Glacier areas.
>
> (c) A possible track via the Carbon River and up its Tolmie Creek tributary would have led to Mowich Lake, Mist Park, and Spray Park in Puyallup territory.
>
> (d) A deviation from Carlton Pass, west down Laughingwater Creek, across the Ohanapecosh River, and up Olallie Creek to Cowlitz Divide may have been the route that brought Yakama hunters to the southeastern flank of Mount Rainier in 1886 as reported by Brockman and Haines (1934i: 5; 1962: 81–82).

Once at the base of Mount Rainier, travelers often chose access routes that followed the ridgelines, rather than attempting the more difficult, twisting, and often precipitous creek bottoms.

> Early forest surveyor Fred G. Plummer emphasized this point: "Most of the trails shown upon the map are hardly deserving of the name, but indicate blazed lines where better progress can be made than by taking a course through the timber and brush. The Indian's policy was to go only where his pony could take him…; therefore, his lines of travel were along the sparsely timbered ridges, where feed was generally plenty, where game abounded, or where huckleberries grew" (1900: 89).
>
> A few years later, G.F. Allen observed: "Every summer parties of hunters and berry pickers from the sagebrush plains crossed the Cascades with their horses. They followed the high divides and open summits of the secondary ridges until they came around to the open parks about Mount Rainier where they turned their horses out to graze and made their summer camp. (1916: 5–6).

Traveling and Trading

Camp Sites

It is probable, of course, that certain convenient camping localities were recognized and continually used, both along the major east-west trails and on the side routes up to the berry and hunting grounds. Sluiskin, for example, frequently occupied one particular campsite along the ridgeline route northeast of Bear Prairie. However, my informants could provide no data about this, and the literature, too, seems mostly silent on this matter. [In recent years, a series of archaeological sites have been documented along ridgelines and other plausible travel routes. Four sites have been identified along what is locally referred to as the Yakama trail between Chinook Pass and Sunrise Ridge (a.k.a. Yakima Park) on the northeastern flank of Mount Rainier. While ancient trails, or more appropriately routes, are difficult to identify unambiguously, it is likely that many of these sites were camping localities as anticipated by Allan Smith.—Editors]

Traveling on Mountain Access Routes

It can be assumed that the mountain access trails were primarily used by those tribes in whose territory that they lay (see Fig. 3.4). The documented route up to Indian Henrys Hunting Ground in Nisqually territory is a case in point. Also, Hazard Stevens' account of Sluiskin's route to the Paradise area as described in chapter 3 hints at the importance of respecting territorial integrity in the historic period.

Traveling on Major East-West Trails

The case with the east-west trails, on the other hand, was rather different, in that there usually was multi-tribal use of these routes. In universal accord, my informants stated that the Cascade pass trails were traveled more often by the Yakama visiting Coastal groups, than by Coastal tribes journeying to the Plateau. There were various compelling reasons for cross-Cascades travel. Those believed to be the most important are discussed here.

Trade

The aboriginal products of the Coast and Plateau peoples, particularly their food stuffs, were in many respects sharply different. Thus, there was a natural tendency among either group to desire the goods and items produced by the other.

Plateau Groups in Coastal Territory

Nisqually trade with the Sahaptins is described by Haeberlin and Gunther. In their account, however, the authors use the term "Klikitat" in reference to the Sahaptins. Nevertheless, the known facts—including the authors' statement that when crossing the Cascades the "Klikitat used...Cowlitz" Pass (actually in Yakama country)—suggests that the Sahaptins being described actually might more commonly be the Yakama (1930: 11–12).

> According to Haeberlin and Gunther, the bartering took place in Nisqually territory: "The Nisqually traded largely with the Klikitat, using shell money for payment. Shell money was highly prized by the Indians east of the mountains and the coast tribes used it more in trading with them than among themselves. The shell money which the Klikitat obtained from the Nisqually they in turn passed on to the Indians of Idaho and Montana. When the Klikitat came to the coast in summer they bought clams, herring, smelts and berries. In return they gave the Nisqually dried Columbia salmon, which is highly prized by the coast people. They also brought dressed buckskins and clothing made of skins. The Nisqually never bought baskets from the Klikitat because they made better ones themselves, but the Klikitat bought coiled baskets from the Nisqually" (1930: 32).
>
> This last aspect of the trade is hardly surprising if, as Haeberlin and Gunther contend, the Nisqually in fact taught the Klikitat the technique of weaving coiled baskets. However, the Nisqually often "bought pipes from the Klickitat." These were fashioned out of a black stone.
>
> Haeberlin and Gunther also described the shell money mentioned above. One type was a white clamshell disc, about 1 cm in diameter and perforated; these were from Snohomish country. Solax beads, tubular or round, were acquired by Puget Sound groups from tribes to the north. Another type was fashioned from a very large clamshell, also originally traded from the north (1930: 29).
>
> Marian Smith reported that the inland Nisqually and Puyallup obtained the edible root of an unidentified plant "from the Sahaptin-speaking peoples.... It grows only high in the mountains.... These

> root are…called pia'xé." In addition, the Nisqually also obtained some kind of dried root cake from the Yakama (1940: 249–50).

Even though the Snohomish occupied territory well to the north of the Puyallup, the following data is of interest concerning Plateau-Coast trade relations.

> Haeberlin and Gunther report that the Snohomish "bought pipes, made of a soft stone not found in Snohomish country, from the Yakima. They paid for…[them] with shell money." Furthermore: "In summer the Indians east of the mountains came to the coast to trade and get sea food for winter use. They used three passes to cross the mountains: the Cowlitz, the Snoqualmie and the Naches. The Klikitat [i.e., Yakama] used the Cowlitz, and the Wenatchee came through Snoqualmie" (1930: 10–11).

Teit's comments about the Wenatchi are also of comparative value, suggesting the kinds of products transported and traded by the Plateau groups. Teit also draws attention to the importance of the horse in stimulating significant long distance trade across the Cascades. Greater access to horses may help explain why most trade was directed from the Columbia Plateau toward the Coast rather than the reverse.

> In regard to the Wenatchi contacts with the Nisqually, Puyallup, and Cowlitz: "A great impetus was given to trading by the introduction of the horse. Root-cakes, dried berries, buffalo robes, and many other heavy or bulky packs, which in former days it did not pay to carry, were now transported across the mountains. Before the introduction of the horse, the trading with Coast tribes was chiefly in light and valuable articles. Pipes, tobacco, ornaments of certain kinds, Indian-hemp, dressed skins, bows, and some other things, were sold to the Coast tribes, the chief articles received in return being shells of various kinds. Some horses were also sold to the Coast people" (1928: 121).
>
> In light of Teit's mention of pipes and tobacco, Curtis noted that smoking was not common among the Puget Sound Salish, however, they obtained native tobacco, in part, at points reached by trails across the Cascades (1913: 59). Unfortunately, neither the specific trading localities, trails, or groups involved are mentioned by Curtis.

Teit stated that important trading centers were at "the middle Nisqually" and "the upper Puyallup" (1928: 122). It seems quite probable that the Yakama participated at these locations, at least to some degree and in some seasons.

Coastal Groups in the Plateau

The above refers to Plateau people visiting the Coastal groups west of the Cascades for trading purposes. A reference in the literature also indicates at least occasional visits by Puget Sound groups to the country east of the mountains for the sake of trade. Curtis reported that Puget Sound parties with shells and deerskins came to trade with the Yakama on the lower and middle reaches of the Yakima River (1911: 14).

Resource Utilization

In addition to trading with Coastal groups, the Yakama crossed the Cascades to secure natural resources for themselves. Extensive data on berrying and hunting activities in the national park has been presented in chapter 5. The Yakama, of course, shared the food resources of their friendly Coastal neighbors in other places as well. For example, my Yakama informants noted that their people went over the mountains to the Cowlitz River in Taidnapam country to catch the king (red) salmon, which spawned there. And, according to my Muckleshoot informant, the Yakama also journeyed through Naches Pass to Muckleshoot lands to catch and dry fish.

At least on occasion, Coastal groups crossed the Cascades to secure east side resources not present in western Washington. My Muckleshoot informant stated that the Muckleshoot traveled through Naches Pass to Yakama country to obtain food resources (e.g., roots).

Marriage and Affinial Activities

Although my informants did not address the matter, it is clear that some movement over the Cascade trails was occasioned by a desire to obtain spouses and to maintain contact with intermarried relatives. In regard to marriage formalities and post-nuptial relationships, groups must have exchanged material items east and west via the mountain passes. In these instances, of course, the impetus for exchange was quite different from that arising from simply trading.

> For example, Marian Smith reported that among the Puyallup and Nisqually an exchange of property was called for between the respective sets of parents and relatives in an intertribal marriage. This required a series of visits—the first being in the direction of the village of residence of the newly married couple, and subsequent visits in the reverse direction (1940: 166).

In the present study, much evidence already has been presented about intermarriages between Puget Sound and Sahaptin groups. My Yakama and Taidnapam informants agree with Jacobs' observation (1937) that Yakamas gradually were moving westward, over the Cascade Divide, into the upper Cowlitz River valley to establish residence. The closest of relationships was maintained between the Taidnapam (traditional occupants of the upper Cowlitz area) and the Yakama.

The Meshal, also a Sahaptin-speaking group, support the same view. Moreover, my Nisqually-Puyallup and Muckleshoot informants reported substantial numbers of Yakama intermarriages in the upriver villages of their respective tribes. Such intermarrying was mostly the result of Coast men securing Yakama wives and establishing virilocal residences. The same was the case, of course, to an even greater extent with the Taidnapam. On the other hand, some few Nisqually-Puyallup and Muckleshoot women were married to Yakama men and maintained residence with their husbands' groups. Hence it is logical that travel between the Coastal and Yakama relatives also occurred.

> In a similar vein, Haeberlin and Gunther noted: "Many Nisqually spoke Klikitat and there were frequent intermarriages between the two tribes" (1930: 11). Because these authors evidently employed "Klikitat" as a general designation for all Sahaptins in the eastern Cascades, it is probable that at least some Yakama were involved. They added, interestingly enough, that before white contact, the Nisqually did not permit the marriage of their own people within their own tribe, a rule especially enforced for the upper classes. Ideally, marriage was only allowed with outside tribal people (Haeberlin and Gunther, 1930: 50).

The distance over the mountains between the intermarrying groups was great. Presumably, however, at least a minimum of exchange visits was required and at least some transfer of goods was necessary. Unfortunately, no informant data was secured about the exact kinds of items that passed hands under such circumstances, and I know of no information in the documentary sources bearing on the question. It may be assumed, however, that at least some of the same regional products involved in normal intergroup trading activities also changed hands in the ceremonial obligations of intermarriage.

Gambling

From the literature, it likewise is clear that personally owned goods and objects were brought over the mountain passes to serve as betting items in intertribal stick (bone) games. Sometimes, it appears that parties actually crossed the Cascades with the specific purpose of participating in gambling events. In a previously cited story in this chapter, two legendary Puyallup mythic personages camped at Lake Keechelus while on their way to play the stick game with the Yakama (Ballard, 1929: 135–36). The myth seems to reflect a basic pattern of intertribal contact.

> Presumably, Marian Smith refers to this same myth when she noted "a mythologically described game between the Sahaptin-speaking peoples east of the mountains and the Salish-speaking residents of Puget Sound." She added the important point that these contacts were real and that the games continued into the historical period (1940: 209).
>
> Moreover, Smith reported that in about 1868, the Puyallup and Yakama had a stick game in which the Yakama lost everything they bet, including many of their horses and mules (1940: 217).

It may be presumed, of course, that gambling sometimes was a secondary aim of traveling. It is nonetheless true that gaming also spontaneously arose as a pastime of mutual interest as groups were meeting for trading or other social reasons.

Warfare and Raiding

Finally, the Cascades passes and the major east-west trails through the peripheries of the national park area apparently were taken occasionally by war parties, despite the normally peaceable relations that supposedly prevailed between the Coastal and Plateau tribes. No data on this point were secured from my informants. However, Teit reported: "Occasionally war-parties of the eastern Columbia [Mid-Columbia Salish] crossed the Cascades, and attacked and plundered some of the Coast tribes" (1928: 123). Since Teit's evidence placed some Plateau Salish formerly in the country eventually occupied by the Yakama, it may be presumed that plundering parties, at least on occasion, once made their way through the Cascade passes on the western borders of what later became Yakama territory.

7

Summary and Conclusion

The primary objectives of this study have been to determine by ethnographic and related techniques the extent to which the resources of the forests, ridges, alpine parks, and rocky crags of Mount Rainier National Park were known and utilized by aboriginal groups. Then, by an analysis of this data, to estimate the archaeological potential in the national park area, and to provide serviceable information to assist in the interpretation of the archaeological field results.

Ethnographic data was secured from informants representing the Yakama, Taidnapam, Nisqually, and Muckleshoot tribal groups. Though a fuller informant inquiry over a longer period of time would have been desirable, I believe that the findings presented here are valid and significant. The informant data has been supplemented by a review of the relevant historical, ethnohistorical, and ethnographic accounts. In addition, information from the natural sciences also has been consulted.

The results of this study lead to a number of conclusions regarding traditional use of the Mount Rainier locality. During the proto-historic and early-historic periods, the Yakama, Taidnapam, Nisqually (including the Meshal), Puyallup, and Muckleshoot—here termed as "tribes" for convenience—all claimed portions of the Mount Rainier area. Owing, however, to intertribal marriages, the absence of marked cultural and linguistic differences (for some elements), and weak tribal political structures, the population units comprising these social groups were not sharply distinct. Even so, tribal limits apparently were recognized. In general, tribal borders in the national park are thought to have followed mountain crest-lines essentially as shown in Figure 3.4.

Mount Rainier's eastern flanks are of special interest. According to the aboriginal drainage ownership principle, it would seem that the Taidnapam held claim to the Ohanapecosh-Cowlitz headwaters, while the Muckleshoot claimed the sources of the White River. But the facts regarding traditional use present another picture (see Fig. 3.4). Contrary to statements in the published ethnographic literature, the more northern Yakama (i.e., particularly those from the Tieton, Naches, and Cowiche valleys) berried and hunted on the eastern slopes of Mount Rainier. Perhaps, the Yakama and the linguistically and culturally related Taidnapam jointly made use of the Ohanapecosh headwaters. I presume, however, that the Yakama made greater use of this locality than the Taidnapam, for the latter held sole claim to other high mountain areas nearer to their Cowlitz River villages.

Thus, it was on Mount Rainier's eastern flanks that the northern Yakama found the most readily accessible high mountain resources for exploitation. These Yakama also probably hunted and berried north of the Ohanapecosh-White River divide, in territory theoretically claimed by the Muckleshoot. There is no explicit evidence for this, but it is suggested by the fact that Yakama parties ascending the American River and entering the park area via Chinook Pass would have been directly on the divide between the Ohanapecosh and White River watersheds. Furthermore, the Muckleshoot may have only rarely visited the uppermost White River headwaters. There are two reasons that support this: (1) the nearest known Muckleshoot settlement appears to have stood far downstream, and (2) the Muckleshoot were known to have used the more accessible West Fork White River country, which has its sources on the northern face of the mountain. Hence, the uppermost White River area might have been left open to Yakama exploitation, a probability indicated in figures 1.3 and 3.4, while the Muckleshoot focused on the West Fork and Huckleberry Creek localities further north and west.

In a somewhat earlier period, prior to the coming of the Yakama, the Kittitas evidently had claimed the eastern part of the national park area, as indicated by the native toponymy for Mount Rainier (see chapter 2). This suggests, of course, that the Kittitas once occupied the Cascades foothills east of Mount Rainier, which became Yakama territory in more recent times. At an even earlier period before the supposed arrival of the Kittitas, the eastern park area may have been claimed wholly by Salishan people. This might be concluded from the fact that Sahaptin groups, including the Yakama, referred to the peak by a reportedly Salishan term.

The linguistic evidence implies that Sahaptins had extended their range into the Yakima watershed—at first, the Kittitas forced the Salishans out, and then the Yakama in turn pressed the Kittitas to the north (see Fig. 3.2). This sequence of events also is supported, to some degree, by tradition. This suggests that archaeological finds on the eastern and southeastern flanks of Mount Rainier can probably be attributed to the historic Taidnapam and Yakama only if the sites are of relatively recent date.

In the proto-historic and historic periods, tribal boundaries in the park, at least theoretically, may have indeed been rather sharp and distinct. Nevertheless, in practice, group boundaries within the national park were by no means inviolate to members of neighboring tribes. Where kinship and friendship bonds existed, there evidently was much movement across tribal borders. Since trading, social, and marriage connections were widespread, tribal interaction was common. Given such fluid boundaries, we should expect to see significant amounts of intrusive material culture items at a number of archaeological sites.

No permanent settlements—in the sense of winter villages or long term summer encampments—were established within the national park area. The locations of the nearest known permanent village sites are indicated in Figure 7.1.

Figure 7.1. Locations of the nearest known villages to Mount Rainier National Park.

Tribe	*Village Locations*	*Approximate Distance by Trail to the National Park*
Yakama	Bumping Lake on the Bumping River Rimrock on the Tieton River	8 miles 20 miles
Taidnapam	Junction of the Muddy and Clear Forks of Cowlitz River	5-1/2 miles
Nisqually	Elbe Eatonville	13-1/2 miles 17 miles
Puyallup	Junction of Voight Creek and the Carbon River Junction of the Puyallup and Carbon Rivers	17-1/2 miles 23 miles
Muckleshoot	?	?

Except for the Muckleshoot (for which the evidence appears to be incomplete), all of the tribal groups maintained traditional villages within 20 miles of the national park boundaries. The nearest Taidnapam and Yakama occupation sites, in particular, were only 5-1/2 and 8 miles away respectively. This raises the possibility that the latter two groups may have utilized the economic resources in the national park to a greater degree than other tribal claimants. Possibly, the archaeological evidence may be richer in their areas than elsewhere.

Economic utilization by all of the tribes was highly seasonal in character, with most use concentrated in the late summer and early autumn. Dominant uses focused on collecting plant foods, hunting, and gathering medicinal roots and possibly other plant materials for technological purposes. For the most part, small parties conducted these activities.

Three species of huckleberries (blueberries)—*Vaccinium membranaceum*, *V. ovalifolium*, and *V. deliciosum*—seem to have been most favored, and were gathered in burned-over areas in the lower sub-alpine meadows of the Hudsonian Zone (see Fig. 7.2). Apparently, the intentional firing of vegetation was an aboriginal practice to improve berry yields by maintaining meadows and suppressing the regrowth of trees. Possibly, some of the old burns that might yet be obvious [in 1964—Editors] at forested middle elevations give testimony to this practice, and may have been the general locations of camping and huckleberry harvesting sites. A few specific localities frequented by gathering parties are known for the Nisqually, Puyallup, and Taidnapam (see the Berries section in chapter 5). Some evidence of temporary campsites must exist at least in these sectors of the national park.

Huckleberries clearly were the most important plant resource gathered around Mount Rainier—certainly it was the only crop collected in large quantities. However, the possibility exists that *Claytonia* roots also were dug up as food, and white-bark pine nuts might have been gathered. These latter resources, as with two of the three species of huckleberries, are found in the Hudsonian Zone (see Fig. 7.2).

Hunting was a secondary activity from the Indian viewpoint, carried out by men while women were engaged in securing a berry supply. Hunting activities focused primarily on mountain goat, deer, elk, and bear, though the pursuit of smaller animals was not wholly neglected—e.g., hoary marmots, mountain beaver, and sooty grouse. Elevations where these animals occur in the greatest numbers in late summer are indicated in Figure 7.2. With remarkable consistency they are in the sub-alpine Hudsonian Zone.

Mountain goat and deer are known to be plentiful in certain localities within the national park (see Hunting in chapter 5). Bear seem to have been more uniformly scattered through the forests. However, like the sooty grouse, bear congregated in the berry grounds in late summer, at precisely the time when Indian parties were gathering huckleberries. Hence the hunting of bear and grouse—to a greater degree than for deer, elk, and mountain goat—might have occurred in the immediate vicinity of the women's berrying parties. It is possible that, periodically, mountain sheep were present in the national park area, and, if so, were hunted. The evidence indicates, however, that at least in relatively recent times, mountain sheep could not have been secured in appreciable numbers.

Figure 7.2. Late summer resources and altitude ranges. Bear are shown at late summer in the same altitudes as the main huckleberry grounds. As with several other large mammals, their range in the national park varies depending on the season.

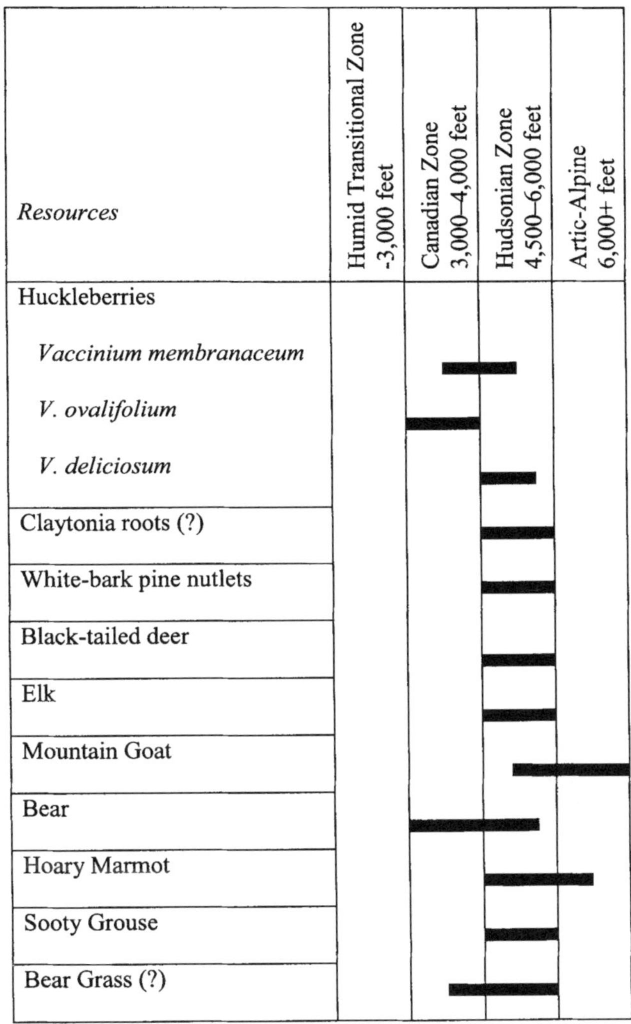

My informant inquiry failed to reveal specific locations within the national park where parties camped while engaged in gathering-hunting pursuits. In the literature, there is only one specific reference to such a site—a Meshal-Nisqually camp at Squaw Lake east of Indian Henrys Hunting Ground.

Here, Indian Henry went up into Indian Henrys Hunting Ground seeking game while his wife remained at the lake campsite, presumably following other economic pursuits. [More than 90 archaeological sites related to pre-contact hunting and gathering activities have been documented in Mount Rainier National Park since Allan Smith wrote these words. Sites have been recorded on all sides of the mountain, predominantly in the sub-alpine (or Hudsonian) zone above 5,000 feet. These sites attest to thousands of years of Native American use of this mountain landscape. Undoubtedly, more sites will be found as archaeological research continues.—Editors]

As already mentioned, the small parties exploiting the national park's natural resources included both women and men, the former engaged in berrying and the latter perhaps mainly in hunting. It seems probable that temporary campsites would have been established at the berry grounds rather than in hunting areas. Historically, berrying was regarded as the chief reason for visiting the slopes of Mount Rainier. Despite some annual variation in their abundance, a productive berry harvest was almost certain. Moreover, the berries, it must be supposed, were gathered in a relatively small locality for at least several days at a time, if not for the entire short season. The berries had to be picked, carried to drying racks, tended during the drying process, and then packed. Hence, this was a relatively sedentary activity.

Hunting, in contrast, was more uncertain. Its locus, it may be presumed, varied not only from day to day but required much wider movement over the mountain flanks, except for the hunting of bear and grouse that were attracted to the berry patches. These facts indicate that it would have been most practical for the camps to be located at the berrying areas, where the women could carry on their important food-gathering responsibilities, while the men ranged about in the general vicinity.

A review of the data presented in Figure 7.2 demonstrates that the berrying grounds were, on the whole, perhaps slightly below the elevations where much of the hunting was conducted. This at least suggests the possibility that higher berrying grounds might have been favored, since this would have put the camps closer to the hunting areas. Such evidence as is relevant to this point seems to support this speculation. In regard to archaeological surveys, it would appear logical to investigate burns, alpine parks, and huckleberry grounds in the upper elevations of the forested Canadian Zone and the lower levels of the sub-alpine Hudsonian Zone.

[There is no doubt that huckleberry collecting was the dominant economic activity in the early historic and late pre-contact period known to Allan Smith's informants. Smith does an excellent job in directing our attention to this fact, and to the areas and general conditions under which this collecting and the ancillary hunting activities took place (and to their archaeological implications). Important as it was, however, huckleberry collection was not the sole reason for visiting Mount Rainier. Yakama hunting parties, for example, were found encamped with horses well above berry grounds on Sunrise Ridge in 1915 and 1917. With the archaeological record virtually unknown, Smith's necessary reliance on informant and historical accounts collected over a short period of time may have led him to underestimate the importance of hunting and the gathering of medicinal and other useful plants. We now know that Indian people used Mount Rainier for thousands of years before horses were available to bring people into, and to transport bulky and heavy loads away from, the mountain. Under these conditions, and with some exceptions, on-the-spot consumption of gathered plants and hunted animals might have assumed greater importance in earlier times. The growing number of archaeological sites in high sub-alpine and alpine contexts–as well as nearby plausibly productive berry grounds—suggests that people employed mixed strategies that integrated a wide variety of available resources into a sustainable subsistence system. This is not to lessen the importance of huckleberries, but only to indicate that they were part of a wider range of resources and objectives that attracted Indian groups to Mount Rainier for millennia.—Editors]

At least one plant of technological value—bear grass, a material employed in basket weaving—may well have been gathered while the berrying-hunting parties were active. In addition, at least one medicinal root—a′iyʋn—was said by my Yakama informants to have been secured on the slopes of Mount Rainier.

Apparently, no fishing was conducted in the park, and, indeed, the area's aquatic resources are negligible due to downstream barriers to passage of significant numbers of salmon—the region's most important fish resource.

The national park area was visited for guardian spirit quests, though presumably with infrequency. Nevertheless, rock cairns at prominent elevations and other occasional evidences of vision quest or other spiritual sites may occur within the national park.

Though parties from as many as five historic tribes may have entered the area annually, the number of visitors in any year probably was not numerous. Available information suggests that individual gathering-hunting parties normally were small. Moreover, the overall population of the Coastal and Plateau tribal groups in the national park region was not large in the

1800s, and there were other mountain resource areas outside of the national park's limits where similar gathering-hunting activities occurred.

So far as is known, few artifacts have been found within the confines of the national park. A single projectile point was reported from the topmost peak in the Tatoosh Range (in Taidnapam country), a number of points were recovered above timberline in Van Trump Park (Meshal-Nisqually territory), and a point was found on the upper slopes of Spray Park (Puyallup area). Interestingly enough, all three finds are in mountain goat country. Other finds, however, should be expected. [As indicated earlier, the number of documented archaeological finds has increased dramatically since Allan Smith made these observations.—Editors]

East-west Cascade trails were widely used in vicinities adjacent to Mount Rainier National Park. Two of these routes appear to have actually passed within the national park's limits—the Nisqually River portion of the Nisqually-Skate Creek trail along the park's southwest boundary, and the Chinook Pass-American River trail on the park's eastern side. A single north-south route, via Cayuse Pass on the east side of the mountain, also is located within the park boundaries. Though Coastal groups traveled on these routes, Yakama use probably was more frequent. No data was secured in the field or literature research to specify any specially favored camping sites along these trails, though they certainly must have existed. [Several have now been identified.—Editors]

Access trails led off from the major Cascades east-west routes and up onto the higher slopes around Mount Rainier. Apparently, these generally followed ridgelines and mountain crests, rather than stream valleys, up to the flanks of the peak. These access trails remain unknown for the most part, though the presumption is strong that many of the national park's modern-day hiking trails, especially those that pre-date the park's inception, follow along traditional Indian access routes. A few traditional routes, however, are known. One is the route from Yakama country that entered the national park through Chinook Pass. Others extended from the Nisqually River up into Indian Henrys Hunting Ground, from the Cowlitz River country via the Tatoosh Range to Mazama Ridge and also along the Cowlitz Divide, and up Tolmie Creek into nearby alpine parks on the northwest side of Mount Rainier. Small parties in the late summer traveled along these and similar routes on their berrying and hunting expeditions. No specific and convenient camping places along these lateral trails were identified in the present study, though such sites undoubtedly were frequently used. [Again, some have since been found.—Editors]

It appears that any evidence of structures will be limited to places occupied or utilized at the small temporary summer camps in the hunting-gathering areas or along the trails. These may have included mat-covered tipis or rectangular structures; mat-, skin-, or brush-covered lean-tos with outside fire pits; berry-drying mounds with fires pits before them (Yakama); berry-drying racks with small fire pits beneath (in the other tribal sectors of the national park); meat-drying racks with fire pits below; and meat-steaming (bear) pits with diagnostic fire-exposed rocks.

Evidences of other aspects of material culture might be recovered in the national park, but only in special situations where favorable conditions exist for preservation. These objects may be divided into two categories: (1) possessions which the berrying-hunting parties brought with them, e.g., weapons, baskets, packing bags, and items of everyday living, and (2) objects carried by east and west travelers through the national park. The latter would include things required in the daily routine of traveling, as well as trade, gift, and gambling articles, such as dried foods (e.g., berries, roots), shell money, adornment accessories, baskets, stone pipes, and spiritual objects.

With the study's primary purpose now summarized, we may turn briefly to two final points.

> (a) A secondary objective was to test the notion that a thorough forehand ethnographic and ethnohistorical study can substantially and significantly aid archaeological surveyors in an area that previously has been little known to investigators. The present study has revealed much information in this regard for the Mount Rainier area. Though the acquired information sometimes has been fragmentary, nevertheless it is surprisingly revealing when pieced together into a total picture. I believe that the results of this study demonstrate the feasibility of undertaking such a thorough analysis as a preliminary step to archaeological field research.
>
> (b) Another incidental objective was to examine the notion that Pacific Northwest tribal groups exploited even the most remote and rugged localities for economic and other purposes. The data presented in the present study clearly supports this idea, with interesting theoretical implications for cultural ecology. The data also indicates that use of such rugged terrain was not limited strictly to economically productive activities. Mount Rainier at least occasionally was

visited for spiritual purposes. It also served, by its trails, to link regions of more concentrated populations.

In closing, I wish to thank the National Park Service and especially my Indian informants for making this study possible. It is my hope that the present ethnographic study will be of some value in assisting archaeologists, anthropologists, and other individuals genuinely interested in understanding the importance of Mount Rainier to Native American people living in its vicinity. To the extent that it has succeeded in doing so attests to the insights of my informants, and to the value of historical records. Its shortcomings are my own. I believe that it is important to recognize that Mount Rainier—known, in essence, as "The Mountain" by the Sahaptin and Salishan speaking peoples of the region—has played a significant role in the lives of Indian people for a very long time. I can only hope that it will continue to do so for a long time to come.

References

Abbreviations—

BAE – Bureau of American Ethnology
MRNN – Mount Rainier Nature Notes
UWPA – University of Washington Publications in Anthropology

* * *

Allen, G.F.
1916 *Forests of Mount Rainier National Park.* U.S. Department of the Interior.

Anderson, Robert
1929 Round the Mountain, *MRNN* 7 (12): 2–4.

Ballard, Arthur C.
1929 Mythology of Southern Puget Sound, *UWPA* 3 (2): 31–150.

Bonany, Douglas
1928 Ancient History, *MRNN* 6 (3): 1.

Brockman, C. Frank
1928a Trees of Mount Rainier National Park, *MRNN* 6 (6): 3.
1928b We Go Huckle "Bearying," *MRNN* 6 (6): 4.
1928c The First Snowfall of the Season at Paradise Valley, *MRNN* 6 (6): 5.
1928d Mazama Ridge and Its Animal Tracks, *MRNN* 6 (7): 4.
1928e The Sooty Grouse, *MRNN* 6 (8): 1.
1928f Brownie and Her Three Cubs Again, *MRNN* 6 (8): 4.
1929a Mountain Goat on Cougar Rock, *MRNN* 7 (2): 2.
1929b Squilchow and Enumclaw, *MRNN* 7 (2): 2.
1929c A Tragedy of the Wilds, *MRNN* 7 (4): 4.
1929d A Fortunate Close Up of a Mountain Goat, *MRNN* 7 (5): 8.
1929e Notes on Indian Basket Grass, *MRNN* 7 (8): 5.
1929f Just Between Us, *MRNN* 7 (12): 5.
1929g A Trip to Indian Henry's, *MRNN* 7 (13): 3–4.
1930a Stevens and Van Trump, *MRNN* 8 (3): 4.
1930b What Do They Eat? *MRNN* 8 (3): 5–6.
1930c Just Here and There, *MRNN* 8 (5): 6.
1930d Just Here and There, *MRNN* 8 (7): 6.
1930e Just Here and There, *MRNN* 8 (8): 6.
1930f Gay Days on "The Mountain," *MRNN* 8 (9[10]): 2–3.
1930g Flowers as Summer Fades, *MRNN* 8 (10[11]): 3–4.
1931a An Old Fashioned Weatherman, *MRNN* 8[9] (2): 2.
1931b An Indian Legend Concerning "The Mountain," *MRNN* 8[9] (3): 2.
1931c Flowers of the Season, *MRNN* 9 (5): 4–5.
1931d On the Trail, *MRNN* 9 (9): 2–3.
1932a On Winter Trails, *MRNN* 10 (2): 2–3.
1932b Just Here and There, *MRNN* 10 (6): 9–10.
1932c The Fruit of Some Common Plants, *MRNN* 10 (11): 2–3.
1932d Down the East Boundary, *MRNN* 10 (11): 7–8.
1932e Brief Items of Interest, *MRNN* 10 (12): 4.

1933a Just Here and There, *MRNN* 11 (1): 7–8.
1933b Just Here and There, *MRNN* 11 (3): 8.
1933c Flowers of Midsummer, *MRNN* 11 (6): 6–7.
1933d Milestones in the Historical Development of Mount Rainier National Park, *MRNN* 11 (7): 7–9.
1933e Preparations for Winters, *MRNN* 11 (9): 7–8.
1934a Just Here and There, *MRNN* 12 (1): 9–10.
1934b Just Here and There, *MRNN* 12 (3): 9.
1934c Highlights of History in Mount Rainier National Park, *MRNN* 12 (4): 3–4.
1934d Just Here and There, *MRNN* 12 (4): 10–11.
1934e Highlights of History in Mount Rainier National Park, *MRNN* 12 (5): 3–4.
1934f Just Here and There, *MRNN* 12 (5): 10–11.
1934g Early Arrivals among Our Flowers, *MRNN* 12 (6): 6–7.
1934h August's Flowers, *MRNN* 12 (8): 8–10.
1934i Noted Ascents of Mount Rainier, *MRNN* 12 (9): 5–6.
1935 Just Here and There, *MRNN* 13 (2): 28–29.
1947 *Flora of Mount Rainier National Park.* National Park Service, Washington, D.C.

Coleman, Edward [Edmund] T.
1869 Mountaineering in the Pacific Northwest, *Harper's New Monthly Magazine* 39 (234 [November 1869]): 793–817.

Curtis, Edward S.
1911 *The North American Indian*, vol. 7. Cambridge, Mass.
1913 *The North American Indian*, vol. 9. Cambridge, Mass.

Dalquest, Walter W.
1948 *Mammals of Washington.* University of Kansas, Museum of Natural History, 2.

Davis, John M.
1931 Park Winter Conditions, *MRNN* 8[9] (1): 7.

Dodge, Natt
1934 Just Here and There, *MRNN* 12 (11): 11.

Eells, M.
1887a The Indians of Puget Sound, *American Antiquarian* 9 (1): 1–9.
1887b Decrease of Population among the Indians of Puget Sound, *American Antiquarian* 9 (5): 271–76.

Flett, J.B.
1916 *Features of the Flora of Mount Rainier National Park.* U.S. Department of the Interior.
1926 Three Little Known Characteristics of the Mountain Goat, *MRNN* 4 (8): 2–3; 4 (9): 2–3.

Fogg, P.M.
1925 Blueberries Are Ripe, *MRNN* 3 (8): 1.

Haeberlin, Hermann K.
1934 Mythology of Puget Sound, *Journal of American Folk-Lore* 37: 371–438.

________, and Erna Gunther
1930 The Indians of Puget Sound, *UWPA* 4 (1): 1–84.

Haines, Aubrey L.
1962 *Mountain Fever: Historic Conquests of Rainier*. Oregon Historical Society.

Hale, Horatio
1846 *Ethnography and Philology*. Volume 6 of Charles Wilkes, *United States Exploring Expedition during the Years 1838, 1839, 1840, 1841, 1842*. Philadelphia.

Hodge, F.W.
1910 Handbook of American Indians North of Mexico, *BAE Bulletin* 30, pt. 2.

Homuth, Earl
1934 Notes on Mountain Goat, *MRNN* 12 (8): 11–12.

Hoverson, Julius
1936 Huckleberries, *MRNN* 14 (2): 82–86.

Hulse, Frederick S.
1957 Linguistic Barriers to Gene-Flow: The Blood-Groups of the Yakima, Okanogan and Swinomish Indians, *American Journal of Physical Anthropology* 15 (2): 235–46.

Jacobs, Melville
1931 A Sketch of Northern Sahaptin Grammar, *UWPA* 4 (2): 85–292.
1937 Historic Perspectives in Indian Languages of Oregon and Washington, *Pacific Northwest Quarterly* 28: 55–74.

Jones, George Neville
1938 *The Flowering Plants and Ferns of Mount Rainier*. University of Washington Publications in Biology 7.

Jones, S.B.
1927 Stevens Ridge Notes, *MRNN* 5 (9): 3.

Kautz, August V.
1916 First Attempted Ascent, 1857. In Meany, 1916: 73–93; reprinted from *Overland Monthly*, May 1875.

Kitchin, E.A.
1939 Birds of Mount Rainier National Park, *MRNN* 17 (3–4): 85–207.

Landes, Charles
1924a Black Fox on Cushman Crest, *MRNN* 2 (10): 3–4.
1924b The Kautz Creek Trail to Indian Henrys, *MRNN* 2 (9): 3 [August 13, 1924].
1925a Huckleberry Time, *MRNN* 3 (8): 1.
1925b Deer in the Mountain Meadows, *MRNN* 3 (8): 2.
1925c Animal Habits, *MRNN* 3 (10): 1–2.
1929 Notes on Indian Basket Grass, *MRNN* 7 (8): 5.
1934 The Flora of Rainier's North and South Flanks, *MRNN* 12 (10): 3–6.
1935 Distribution of Plants on Mount Rainier, *MRNN* 13 (3): 41–45.

Lindsey, Alton A.
1933 An "Old-Timer" Recalls Some Interesting Happenings of the Past, *MRNN* 11 (7): 4–6.

Macy, Preston P.
1931 Obstinacy or Fear, *MRNN* 8[9] (2): 4.

Matthes, F.E.
n.d. The Mount Rainier National Park. On reverse of U.S.G.S., Mount Rainier National Park Quadrangle, 1955.
1916 Glaciers of Mount Rainier. In Meany, 1916: 201–40; reprinted from Mount Rainier and its Glaciers, U.S. Department of the Interior, 1914.

McCullough, Dale R.
1964 Relationship of Weather to Migratory Movements of Black-Tailed Deer, *Ecology* 45 (2): 249–56.

Meany, Edmond S. (editor)
1916 *Mount Rainier: A Record of Exploration.* MacMillan: New York.

Piper, Charles V.
1916 The Flora of Mount Rainier. In Meany, 1916: 254–86; reprinted from *The Mazama* 2 (2) (April 1901) and 2 (4) (December 1905).

Plummer, Fred G.
1900 Mount Rainier Forest Reserve, Washington. In *21st Annual Report of the Survey, 1899–1900*, pt. 5, *Forest Reserves*, 81–143.

Ray, Verne F.
1936 Native Villages and Groupings of the Columbia Basin, *Pacific Northwest Quarterly* 27: 99–152.

Richards, L.G.
1930a Alone, *MRNN* 8 (9): 2–3.
1930b Cliff Dwellers, *MRNN* 8[9] (9): 5–6.
1930c Just Here and There, *MRNN* 8 (8): 6.
1930d Just Here and There, MRNN 8 (11): 7.

Russell, I.C.
1916 Exploring the Mountain and Its Glaciers, 1896. In Meany, 1916: 159–82; reprinted in condensed form from *18th Annual Report of the U.S. Geological Survey for 1896–1897*.

Schaeffer, Claude
1958 (Map) Indian Tribes and Languages of the Old Oregon Country. Oregon Historical Society.

Scheffer, Victor
1933 Commutation, *MRNN* 11 (9): 6.

Schmoe, F.W.
1923a Nature Bulletin for Paradise Valley, *MRNN* 1 (1): 1.
1923b Blueberries Ripe, *MRNN* 1 (5): 1.
1923c Red Berries Conspicuous, *MRNN* 1 (5): 1.
1924a Mount Rainier National Park Notes, *MRNN* 2 (1): 1–4.
1924b The Silver Forest, *MRNN* 2 (4): 1–2.
1924c Squaw Grass, *MRNN* 2 (4): 2.

1924d White Rocky Mountain Goat, *MRNN* 2 (5): 3.
1924e The Eagle Peak Trail, *MRNN* 2 (7): 2–3.
1924f List of Mammals Occurring in Mount Rainier National Park, *MRNN* 2 (12): 3.
1924g Animal Life, *MRNN* 2 (13): 1–4.
1924h Animal Trails, *MRNN* 2 (13): 5.
1924i Game Census, *MRNN* 2 (13): 5.
1924j Elk, *MRNN* 2 (14): 3.
1925a Bears Dens, *MRNN* 2 (20): 2–4.
1925b Fishes of the Park, *MRNN* 3 (1): 2–3.
1925bb Vital Statistics, *MRNN* 3 (2): 1.
1925bbb Wild Animal Life of the Park, *MRNN* 3 (4): 2–3.
1925c Sub-Alpine Trees, *MRNN* 3 (8): 3.
1925d Bears Welcome Huckleberry Time, *MRNN* 3 (10): 2–3.
1925e Goats Great Climbers, *MRNN* 3 (10): 3.
1925f The Range of the White Mountain Goat, *MRNN* 3 (13): 2–3.
1925g *Our Greatest Mountain: A Handbook for Mount Rainier National Park.* Putnam: New York.
1926a Columbia Black-Tailed Deer, *MRNN* 3 (14): 3.
1926b The Noble Fir, *MRNN* 3 (15): 1.
1926c Indians of Rainier, *MRNN* 3 (15): 1–2.
1926d Indians Never Lived Permanently in Park, *MRNN* 3 (15): 2.
1926e Two Distinct Types of People, *MRNN* 3 (15): 2–3.
1926f Indians Still Visit Park, *MRNN* 3 (15): 3.
1926g Deer, Bear and Goat, *MRNN* 3 (19): 3.
1926h Flower Notes, *MRNN* 3 (19): 4.
1926i Big-Horn or Mountain Sheep, *MRNN* 4 (3): 1.
1926j Wild Life Notes, *MRNN* h (3): 2.
1926k The Salmonberry (*Rubus Spectabilis*), *MRNN* 4 (4): 1.
1926l Signs of the Season, *MRNN* 4 (6): 2.
1926m A Page from a Notebook, *MRNN* 4 (9): 1–2.
1926n Bears Laying Supply of Huckleberries, *MRNN* 4 (11): 2.
1926o Big-Horn Sheep, *MRNN* 4 (13): 2.
1926p Friendly Rocks, *MRNN* 4 (13): 4–7.
1927a Billy of Cougar Rock, *MRNN* 4 (15): 4.
1927b? Who Said Goats are Dumb? *MRNN* 4 (16?): 1–2.
1927c Our Hall of Fame, *MRNN* 4 (18): 1–3.
1927d Every Day Is Bath Day, *MRNN* 5 (5): 1.
1927e Goats and Sheep, *MRNN* 5 (6): 1.
1927f The Wild Life "Ceiling," *MRNN* 5 (9): 2–3.
1928a Nursery Notes, *MRNN* 6 (1): 3–4.
1928b Along the Trail, *MRNN* 6 (2): 3–4.
1928c Goats Back Again, *MRNN* 6 (3): 2–3.

Sedergreen, Oscar A.
1933A "Snag" at Eve, *MRNN* 11 (2): 9–10.

Sluiskin
1916 Indian Warning Against Demons. In Meany, 1916: 132–34.

Smith, Marian W.
1940 *The Puyallup-Nisqually.* Columbia University Contributions to Anthropology 32.
1941 The Coast Salish of Puget Sound, *American Anthropologist* 43: 197–211.
1947 (editor) *Indians of the Urban Northwest.* Columbia University Press.

Spier, Leslie
1936 *Tribal Distribution in Washington*, General Series in Anthropology 3.

Stevens, Hazard
1916 First Successful Ascent, 1870. In Meany, 1916: 94–131; reprinted from *Atlantic Monthly*, November 1876.

Swanton, John R.
1952 The Indian Tribes of North America, BAE Bulletin 145.

Teit, J.
1928 Middle Columbia Salish, UWPA 2 (4): 83–128.

Tolmie, William Fraser
1916 First Approach to the Mountain, 1833. In Meany, 1916: 6–12.

Trolson, Roy
1926 Animals in the Northern Section of the Park, *MRNN* 4 (8): 4.

U.S. Geological Survey (Quadrangle Maps)
1901 *Snoqualmie Pass.*
1902 *Mount Aix.*
1924 *Mount Rainier.*
1942 *Lake Tapps.*
1955 *Mount Rainier National Park.*
1956 *Enumclaw.*
1956 *Greenwater.*
1956 *Kapowsin.*
1956 *Mineral.*

U.S. Government
1953 *Report with Respect to the House Resolution Authorizing the Committee on Interior and Insular Affairs to Conduct an Investigation of the Bureau of Indian Affairs*. Union Calendar No. 790; 82d Congress, 2d Session: House Report No. 2503.

Warren, F.A.
1926 Red Berries, *MRNN* 4 (8): 1–2.

Wilkes, Charles (Meany cited the author as Lt. Robert E. Johnson.)
1916 First Recorded Trip through Naches Pass, 1841. In Meany, 1916: 13–33; reprinted from *The United States Exploring Expedition*, 1845, vol. 4: 418–29, 468–70.

Willis, Bailey
1916 Explorations on the Northern Slopes, 1881–1883. In Meany, 1916: 142–49; reprinted with revisions from *The Northwest* 1 (2) (April 1883).

Winthrop, Theodore
1916 Tacoma and the Indian Legend of Hamitchou. In Meany, 1916: 34–72; reprinted from *The Canoe and the Saddle* (New York, 1862: 43–45, 123–176).

Writers' Program, Work Projects Administration
1941 *Washington: A Guide to the Evergreen State.*